THE VMWARE WORKSTATION 5 HANDBOOK

THE VMware WORKSTATION 5 HANDBOOK

STEVEN S. WARREN

CHARLES RIVER MEDIA, INC.
Hingham, Massachusetts

Acquisitions Editor: James Walsh
Cover Design: Tyler Creative

VMware product screen shots reprinted with permission from VMware, Incorporated.

CHARLES RIVER MEDIA, INC.
10 Downer Avenue
Hingham, Massachusetts 02043
781-740-0400
781-740-8816 (FAX)
info@charlesriver.com
www.charlesriver.com

This book is printed on acid-free paper.

Steven S. Warren. *The VMware Workstation 5 Handbook.*
ISBN: 1-58450-393-9

All brand names and product names mentioned in this book are trademarks or service marks of their respective companies. Any omission or misuse (of any kind) of service marks or trademarks should not be regarded as intent to infringe on the property of others. The publisher recognizes and respects all marks used by companies, manufacturers, and developers as a means to distinguish their products.

Library of Congress Cataloging-in-Publication Data
Warren, Steven S.
  The VMware workstation 5 handbook / Steven S. Warren.
     p. cm.
  Includes index.
  ISBN 1-58450-393-9 (pbk. with cd-rom : alk. paper)
  1. VMware. 2. Operating systems (Computers) 3. Virtual computer systems. I. Title.
  QA76.76.O63W3665 2005
  005.4'3--dc22
                         2005010053
Printed in the United States of America
05 7 6 5 4 3 2

CHARLES RIVER MEDIA titles are available for site license or bulk purchase by institutions, user groups, corporations, etc. For additional information, please contact the Special Sales Department at 781-740-0400.

Danna, forever

Contents

Acknowledgments   xvii

1   Introduction   1

    What's Inside?   2

    What Is VMware Workstation?   2

       History of VMware   3

    What's New in Version 5?   3

       Multiple Snapshots   4

       Linked and Full Clones   5

       Linux User Interface   5

       Enhanced Networking Performance   5

       Improved Multi-VM Performance   5

       Improved Suspend/Resume and Snapshot Performance   6

       Isochronous USB Support   6

       Improved Memory Utilization   7

       Teams   7

       New Guest Operating System Support   7

       New Host Operating System Support   8

       New Command-Line Interface   8

       Movie Record and Playback   8

       NX Bit Support   9

       WMware Tools Improvements   9

       WMware Virtual Machine Importer   9

       Experimental Support for Guest ACPI S1 Sleep   9

       Windows Upgrade Installs   9

What Was New in Version 4.x?   9

   What Was New in Version 4.5?   10

   What Was New in Version 4.5.2?   11

Installation System Requirements   11

Supported Guest Operating Systems   12

Virtual Machine Hardware Overview   13

VMware Workstation Resources   14

Conventions Used in this Book   14

2   **Installing VMware Workstation**   **15**

Installation Requirements   15

Installing VMware Workstation on a Windows Platform   16

Uninstalling VMware Workstation on a Windows Platform   21

Unattended Installation of VMware Workstation   22

   Extracting the Installation Image   22

Installing VMware Workstation on a Linux Platform   25

   RPM Installation   25

   Tar Archive Installation   28

Configuring VMware Workstation on a Linux Platform   31

Uninstalling VMware Workstation   33

3   **Quick Tour of VMware Workstation**   **35**

VMware Workstation Control Center   35

Working with the Menu Bar   36

   The File Menu   37

   The Edit Menu   38

   The View Menu   43

   The VM Menu   48

   The Team Menu   52

   The Windows Menu   53

   The Help Menu   53

Working with the VMware Workstation Toolbar 56

The Virtual Machine Settings 57

Windows Systems Virtual Settings 57

About Workstation Tabs 63

About the Status Bar 63

4 Upgrading VMware Workstation 65

Upgrading VMware Workstation 4.x to 5 on a Windows Host 66

Upgrading VMware Workstation 4.x to 5 66

Run Legacy 4.x Virtual Machines Under 5 Without Upgrading 66

Running the Installer 66

Upgrading VMware Workstation 4.x to Workstation 5 on a Linux Host 70

About the Tar Installer 70

About the RMP Installer 71

5 Creating Virtual Machines 73

Anatomy of a Virtual Machine 73

Creating a Virtual Machine with a Windows Host Computer 76

Creating a Virtual Machine with a Linux Host Computer 83

6 Installing Windows and Linux Guest Operating Systems 87

CD-ROM versus ISO Image 88

Booting from an ISO Image 89

Installing Windows XP Professional/Windows 2003 Server 91

Starting Your Virtual Machine 91

Installing Windows XP Professional/Windows Server 2003
with a SCSI Drive 93

Steps to Install Windows XP and Windows Server 2003 94

Installing Windows 98/ME 97

Creating Virtual Floppies 97

Preparing the Windows 98 Virtual Machine 99

Starting your Virtual Machine   100

Installing Longhorn (Experimental)   103

The Longhorn Installation Process   103

Installing Linux Guest Operating Systems   107

Sun Java Desktop System 2   107

Installing SuSE Linux 9.1   108

Starting Your Virtual Machine   108

Installing RedHat Linux 9.0 and Mandrake Linux 10.0   110

Starting Your Virtual Machine   111

7   **Installing VMware Tools**   **113**

Installing VMware Tools for Windows Guest Operating Systems   113

VMware Tools Configuration Options   116

Installing VMware Tools for Linux   117

Installing VMware Tools via the tar.gz Installer   117

Installing VMware Tools via the RPM Installer   120

8   **Managing and Working with Snapshots**   **121**

Definition of a Snapshot   122

Using Snapshots as Restore Points   122

Using Snapshots in a Tree Structure   123

Creating Your First Snapshot   124

Using the Snapshot Manager   124

Delete a Snapshot   124

Clone a Snapshot   124

Go To Snapshot   126

Edit a Snapshot Name and Description   126

Revert versus Go To a Snapshot   127

Working with Snapshot Settings   127

9   Cloning a VMware Workstation Virtual Machine   **131**

    Creating a Full Clone   132

    Creating a Linked Clone   134

10   Working with Teams   **139**

    What Are Teams?   139

    About Teams   141

        Create a Team   141

        Delete a Team   145

        Power On a Team   145

        Power Off a Team   145

        Open and Close a Team   146

        Suspend/Resume a Team   146

        Individual Snapshots within a Team   148

    Working with the Team Settings   148

        Connections   148

        Virtual Machines   149

        LAN Segments   150

        Options   150

    About Team Console   151

        Active Virtual Machine   152

        Inactive Virtual Machines   152

11   Securing VMware Workstation   **155**

    NTFS Security   155

    About Administrative Lockout   156

        Configuring Administrative Lockout   156

        Removing a Lost or Forgotten Password   158

    Graphical User Interface Security   158

        Restricting the User Interface   159

12   Networking Virtual Machines   163

About VMware Workstation Networking   164

Bridged Networking   164

Host Only   164

Network Address Translation   164

Custom   165

Virtual Switch   165

Bridge   165

Host Virtual Adapter   166

DHCP Server   166

Virtual Network Adapters   166

Configuring a Bridged Network   166

Summary Tab   167

Automatic Bridging   167

Host Virtual Network Mapping   169

Configuring a Host-Only Network   171

About the VMware DHCP Server   171

About Host Virtual Adapters   174

Configuring Network Address Translation   176

Configuring a Custom Network Address Translation   176

About Port Forwarding   178

About Vnetsniffer   181

Working with Vnetsniffer   181

About Virtual MAC Addresses   182

About UUID   183

Manually Assigning a MAC Address   185

Configuring a Custom Virtual Network   186

13   Performance Tuning and Optimization of Virtual Machines   191

VMware Workstation Optimization Settings   191

About the Working Directory or Default Location   192

Memory Optimization 192

Host Disk Defragmentation 194

Shrinking and Defragmenting Virtual Disks 194

Guest Operating System Selection 197

Debugging Mode 198

Remove Unnecessary Virtual Hardware 198

Running Virtual Machines from the Network 199

Snapshots 199

CD-ROM Drive Polling 199

Disable Effects 200

Monitoring Virtual Machines 200

Monitoring VMware Workstation Performance Settings 202

14   **Virtual to Virtual (V2V) Conversion**   **205**

What Is the VMware Virtual Machine Importer? 205

Virtual Machine Importer Requirements 206

VPC Requirements 206

Installing the Virtual Machine Importer 207

Uninstalling the VMware Virtual Machine Importer 208

Converting Virtual PC to VMware Workstation 5 209

Virtual Machine Conversion Options 211

15   **Physical to Virtual Conversion**   **217**

Physical to Virtual (P2V) Conversion Tools 218

Using VMware P2V Assistant 2.0 218

P2V Requirements 218

Installing VMware P2V Assistant 218

Installing the P2V Source Machine Boot CD-ROM 219

The P2V Assistant Wizard 222

About Leostream P>V 226

How Does It Work? 226

Installing the Leostream Host Agent Wizard   226

Installing the Leostream P>V Wizard   230

Performing a Physical to Virtual Conversion via Leostream 231

About Disk Transport Options   235

Leostream Converter   236

Norton Ghost 2003   239

Performing Network P2V Conversion   240

P2V via an Image   247

16   Tips and Tricks   249

Installing VMware Workstation as a Service   249

Requirements   250

Configuring VMware Workstation as a Service   250

Creating the Service   250

Disabling the Shutdown Event Tracker on Windows Server 2003 254

Creating a Screenshot or a Movie of a Virtual Machine   255

About Screenshots   256

About Movies   256

Using BgInfo with Your Virtual Machines   257

Creating Virtual Floppies with WinImage   258

Creating a Virtual Floppy Disk   258

Working with the Virtual Floppy Driver   260

Creating Virtual Floppy Disks   262

Working with the Virtual Disk Manager   264

Virtual Disk Tasks   265

Using the DiskMount Utility   267

About DiskMount Limitations   270

Archiving Virtual Machines   270

Using Raw Disk Partitions in VMware Workstation   272

Using WinISO   275

Working with VMware Workstation from the Command Line   276

Working with the VMrun Command Line   278

Modifying the Tip of the Day   278

Working with Shared Folders   280

    Creating a Shared Folder   280

Keyboard Shortcuts   282

17   High Availability with VMware Workstation   283

Creating the Virtual Environment   284

Adding Network Cards   284

    Private Network Configuration   285

    Public Network Configuration   286

Configuring Shared Disks in VMware Workstation   287

    Editing the VMX File   290

    Booting into the BIOS   294

    Configuring the Drives   294

Configuring the Cluster Service on a Windows 2003 Server   296

    Testing the Windows 2003 Cluster   302

Installing SQL Server 2005   304

Installing SQL Server 2005 on the Second Instance   312

18   High Availability with GSX Server   315

Creating a Shared Disk   316

    Viewing the Shared Disks   320

Attaching the Shared Disks to an Additional Computer   320

Editing the .vmx File   323

About the CD-ROM   325

Index   327

Acknowledgments

It has always been a goal of mine to write a book. I love to write and I love it even more when it helps people. I enjoy writing articles and hearing how an article I wrote really simplified something a reader had been trying to conquer. I live for that. I have a very simplified writing style that most people enjoy because I get right to the point and show how to get things done with plenty of supporting examples.

About three years ago I started playing around with VMware products and instantly was attracted to the idea of virtualization. I have written many articles about VMware products and finally decided to take the knowledge I have gathered and create a single unified source for people to use with VMware Workstation. Out of this desire, I molded this book on VMware's next release: Version 5. I have really enjoyed writing this book and hope you enjoy it as well.

I would like to thank VMware for creating a fantastic product and giving me the support necessary to write this book. Additionally, I would like to thank my agent, Neil Salkind , for his advice and experience during this process. To Charles River Media, my publisher, thank you for giving me a medium to express myself and to my wife, Danna, thanks for your patience, kindness, and total support throughout this project. The amount of editing and time you have put into this book is a true testament to your love for me. This is as much your accomplishment as it is mine. I couldn't have done it without you

And to my daughter Catie-Charlotte, your Daddy is back, let's go play. I watched you go from a high chair to a booster seat during the writing of this book. You are growing up so quickly. I love you, little angel. And finally, to Dain, my son, you have gone from dependency to crawling around and getting into everything. You are such a joy!

1 Introduction

In This Chapter

- What's Inside?
- What Is VMware Workstation?
- What's New in Version 5?
- What Was New in Version 4.x?
- Installation System Requirements
- Supported Guest Operating Systems
- Virtual Machine Hardware Overview
- VMware Workstation Resources
- Conventions Used in This Book

Welcome to the world of virtualization! The book you are about to read holds the key to a different way of thinking. If you have never worked with virtualization software or are new to VMware Workstation, you are going to be amazed or become a VMware junkie. Imagine one computer containing multiple operating systems loaded on a single PC, each of which functions as a separate OS on a separate physical machine. VMware Workstation 5 does just that by creating and managing one or more virtual machines on a single, physical host PC. Every virtual machine is a fully functioning virtual computer, where you can install a guest operating system of your choice, with network configuration and a full suite of PC software. Once you install the software and reboot your computer, you will begin your quest of transforming your IT infrastructure into a virtual infrastructure. As you read this book further, you will see what makes virtualization so powerful and useful. This chapter is an overview of VMware Workstation, and it will provide you with the optimal system requirements of VMware Workstation 5 to install the software.

WHAT'S INSIDE?

The *VMware Workstation 5 Handbook* will teach you the nuts and bolts of VMware Workstation. Material will be presented in a step-by-step fashion that will allow you to work with the product as you read along. We will provide you with plenty of examples and screenshots to reinforce what you need to learn in each chapter. If you already have VMware Workstation experience, you will be able to skip ahead to the more advanced chapters and not get lost. This book will teach you how to configure, run, and troubleshoot virtual machines by showing you in a hands-on tutorial how to:

- Install\upgrade VMware Workstation on a Windows platform and a Linux platform.
- Troubleshoot and trace common problems with VMware Workstation.
- Configure complex virtual networks.
- Work with the Snapshot Manager.
- Deploy virtual machines quickly and easily.
- Performance tune your virtual machines.
- Image virtual machines.
- Ensure high availability.
- Archive virtual machines.
- Perform physical to virtual (P2V) conversion.
- Perform virtual to virtual (V2V) conversion.

WHAT IS VMWARE WORKSTATION?

Simply stated, VMware Workstation is a computer inside a computer. It allows you to run multiple operating systems simultaneously on a single PC. You can install VMware on multiple platforms such as Microsoft Windows and Linux. After you install VMware Workstation, you can configure the virtual machine with memory, virtual hard disks, Ethernet adapters, USB controllers, and more. Once the hardware configuration is complete, you can install the selected operating system and turn it on as if it were a physical PC on your network. You can assign it an IP address, access the Internet, and do all of the functions of a real, physical PC. Examples of how VMware Workstation is used include help desk support, quality assurance, training, and software development.

History of VMware

According to VMware's Web site, VMware was first founded in 1998 with the main goal of bringing mainframe class virtualization technology to the public. Its first product, VMware Workstation, was released in 1999 and met with huge success. VMware GSX Server and VMware ESX Server were introduced in 2001. GSX Server is the Enterprise-Class Virtual Infrastructure for Intel-based servers and ESX Server is the Mainframe-Class product for environments such as corporate IT and data centers. As the server market gained momentum, VirtualCenter and VMotion were introduced in 2003, making VMware a leader in the virtualization market. Currently, VMware has more than 3 million registered users and more than 10,000 customers. In recent news, VMware was acquired by EMC in early 2004. This acquisition creates a symbiotic relationship for EMC and VMware. It allows VMware to accelerate its growth and reach more people while allowing EMC to help its customers lower costs by deploying virtualization technologies across their existing infrastructures. Additionally, VMware introduced VMware ACE to extend the virtual infrastructure to the enterprise desktop. VMware is headquartered in Palo Alto, California.

WHAT'S NEW IN VERSION 5?

Whether you're a seasoned veteran of VMware Workstation or completely new to the software, the list of enhancements dating back to 4.x will help you quickly get up to speed with what VMware Workstation has to offer. With the release of VMware Workstation 5, the following features have been added:

- Multiple snapshots
- Cloning virtual machines
- A redesigned Linux user interface
- Enhanced networking performance
- Improved multi-VM performance
- Improved suspend/resume and snapshot performance
- Isochronous USB support
- Improved memory utilization
- Teams
- New guest operating system support
- New host operating system support
- New command line interface
- Movie record and playback

■ NX bit support
■ VMware Tools improvements
■ VMware Virtual Machine Importer
■ Experimental support for guest ACPI S1 Sleep
■ Windows upgrade installs

Multiple Snapshots

With VMware Workstation 5, you can take an unlimited number of snapshots. This allows you to capture the state of a virtual environment at different points in time. This added functionality allows you to switch very quickly between configurations and accelerates testing and debugging. Furthermore, the new snapshot console displays a thumbnail of each snapshot and gives you the ability to revert to a previously saved snapshot. Figure 1.1 illustrates the Snapshot Manager. For more information see Chapter 8.

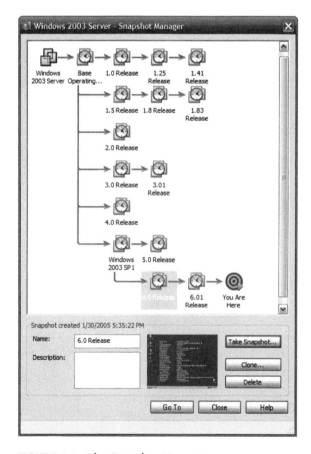

FIGURE 1.1   The Snapshot Manager.

Linked and Full Clones

In this release, you can make a linked or full clone of a virtual machine (see Figure 1.2). A linked clone is a copy of a virtual machine that has a reference to the original virtual machine. Changes that are made are saved locally in a format that a group or team can collaborate on. A full clone makes a complete standalone copy of the virtual machine. For more information see Chapter 9.

FIGURE 1.2   Linked and full clones.

Linux User Interface

VMware Workstation 5 offers a gtk2-based user interface on the Linux platform (see Figure 1.3). This provides an improved user experience with enhanced usability.

Enhanced Networking Performance

In this release, VMware enhances networking performance by leveraging its custom network driver. Once you install or upgrade the new VMware Tools, the network drivers improve VMware Tools networking performance.

Improved Multi-VM Performance

When multiple virtual machines are running concurrently, VMware Workstation 5 improves memory utilization, which allows the virtual machine to run more efficiently and with less memory.

FIGURE 1.3   The new and improved Linux interface.

Improved Suspend/Resume and Snapshot Performance

VMware has drastically reduced the amount of time it takes to suspend/resume and take snapshots. The difference in speed from VMware Workstation 4.x to 5 is like night and day. For more information see Chapter 8.

Isochronous USB Support

VMware now supports isochronous USB input devices. Examples include Web cameras, microphones, and output devices such as speakers. You now have the ability to use a webcam or work with multitrack audio all in the same guest operating system.

Improved Memory Utilization

The VMware Workstation 5 release includes vast improvements in memory utilization when you are running multiple virtual machines. This provides you with virtual machines that are running more efficiently with less memory.

Teams

VMware Workstation 5 introduces teams with this release (see Figure 1.4). The concept behind teams is to simulate the real world multitier configurations. An end user can create a collection of virtual machines and assemble them into a team. Within this team the user can configure network bandwidth and the percentage of packet loss. For more information see Chapter 10.

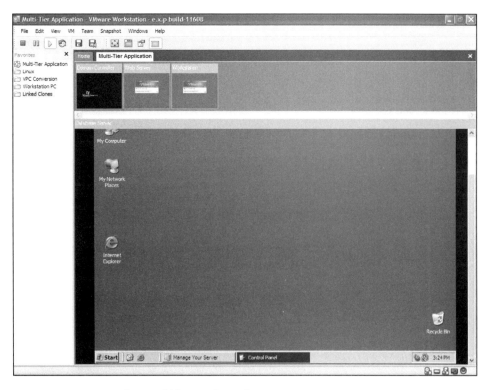

FIGURE 1.4   A team is a multitier configuration.

New Guest Operating System Support

This release supports Windows Small Business Server, Red Hat Linux Advanced Server 3.0 and 4.0, SuSE Linux Pro 9.2, SuSE Linux Enterprise Server 9.0, Mandrake

Linux 10, Novell NetWare 6.5 SP3, Novell NetWare 5.1 SP8, Novell Linux Desktop 9, Sun's Java Desktop System, Windows Server 2003 SP1 beta (experimental support), Red Hat Enterprise Linux 4.0 beta (experimental support), and SuSE Linux Enterprise Server 9 SP1 (experimental support).

New Host Operating System Support

This release supports SuSE Linux Pro 9.2, SuSE Linux Enterprise Server 9.0, Mandrake Linux 10.0, Windows Server 2003 SP1 beta (experimental support), Red Hat Enterprise Linux 4.0 (experimental support), 64-bit host hardware and operating system support for Windows XP, Red Hat Enterprise Linux 3.0, SuSE Linux Enterprise Server 9, SuSE Linux Enterprise Server 8, Windows Server 2003 SP1 (experimental support), and Red Hat Enterprise Linux 4.0 (experimental support). Finally, the 64-bit hardware supported is AMD Opteron, AMD Athlon 64, and Intel EM64T.

New Command-Line Interface

A new command-line interface, as shown in Figure 1.5, is introduced in this release. It enables users to create scripts to automate certain steps. For more information see Chapter 16.

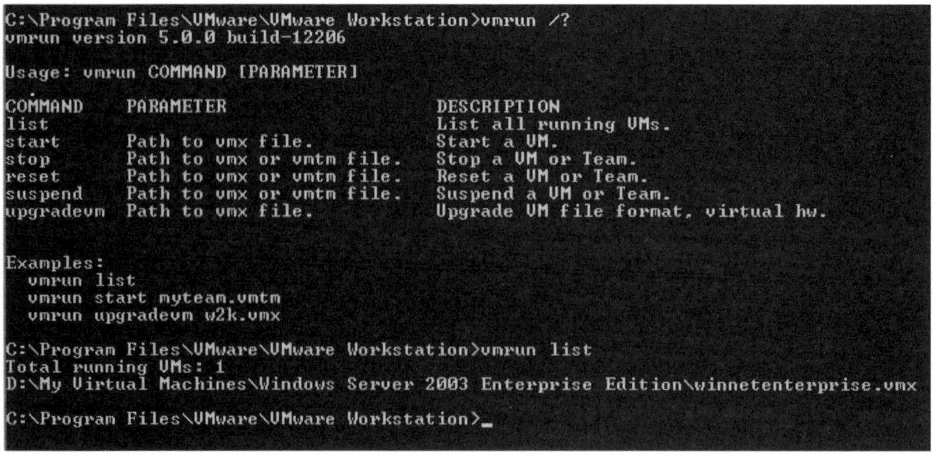

```
C:\Program Files\VMware\VMware Workstation>vmrun /?
vmrun version 5.0.0 build-12206

Usage: vmrun COMMAND [PARAMETER]

COMMAND    PARAMETER                    DESCRIPTION
list                                    List all running VMs.
start      Path to vmx file.            Start a VM.
stop       Path to vmx or vmtm file.    Stop a VM or Team.
reset      Path to vmx or vmtm file.    Reset a VM or Team.
suspend    Path to vmx or vmtm file.    Suspend a VM or Team.
upgradevm  Path to vmx file.            Upgrade VM file format, virtual hw.


Examples:
  vmrun list
  vmrun start myteam.vmtm
  vmrun upgradevm w2k.vmx

C:\Program Files\VMware\VMware Workstation>vmrun list
Total running UMs: 1
D:\My Virtual Machines\Windows Server 2003 Enterprise Edition\winnetenterprise.vmx

C:\Program Files\VMware\VMware Workstation>_
```

FIGURE 1.5   The VMrun command line.

Movie Record and Playback

You now have the ability to record your activity within a virtual machine and save it in an .AVI format. This file can be played back on any computer running

VMware Workstation 5 or by downloading the codec available on VMware's Web site. For more information on movie record and playback see Chapter 16.

NX Bit Support

This version of VMware Workstation supports NX bit for guest operating systems.

VMware Tools Improvements

After upgrading your virtual machines on a Windows platform, VMware Tools installation uninstalls the previous release and installs the current release of VMware Tools. VMware Tools for Linux allows you to install VMware Tools without exiting the X session. For more information see Chapter 7.

VMware Virtual Machine Importer

This VMware utility allows you to convert a Microsoft Virtual PC or Microsoft Virtual Server machine into a VMware Workstation 4.x or 5 virtual machine. For more information on this feature see Chapter 14.

Experimental Support for Guest ACPI S1 Sleep

This release has experimental support for guest operating systems that support ACPI S1 Sleep.

Windows Upgrade Installs

On a Windows host you can install the release right on top of an existing release. The VMware install automatically detects a previous release and prompts you to uninstall before installing the new release.

WHAT WAS NEW IN VERSION 4.X?

Snapshots: Snapshots, introduced in Version 4, give you the ability to take a point-in-time picture or image of your virtual machine's current working state and save it to disk. You can lock a snapshot, prevent a new snapshot from occurring, or revert back to a previous snapshot at any given point in time. The ability to use snapshots makes testing and debugging a snap because you can test a specific scenario repeatedly. (VMware 4.x supported only one snapshot per virtual machine.)

Drag and Drop: You have the ability to drag and drop files and folders between your Windows host and your Windows virtual machines.

Shared Folders: Using shared folders allows you to quickly share files between your host system and your virtual machines.

Full Debug Support: Programmers can debug a virtual machine with support for both user and kernel debuggers.

Sound and Video: VMware added a new sound device by emulating Creative Labs Sound Blaster AudioPCI. This allows your virtual machines to have high performance graphics and lets you display streaming video.

New Operating System Support: This release includeed support for the following operating systems:

- Microsoft Windows 2003
- Red Hat Linux 8.0
- Red Hat Linux 9.0
- Red Hat Linux Advanced Server 2.1
- Red Hat Enterprise Linux Workstation 2.1
- SuSE Linux 8.0, 8.1 ,8.2
- SuSE Enterprise Server 8.0
- Mandrake Linux 9.0

New Graphical User Interface: The Linux GUI contains a redesigned virtual machine settings editor, and the Windows GUI has an updated Favorites list. You now have the ability to run multiple virtual machines in the same window, and tab using VMware Workstation's new quick switch mode.

Network Settings: On Windows virtual machines, the Virtual Network Editor now provides you with a GUI to change the configuration of DHCP servers running on your virtual networks. You can also configure the NAT device and host virtual adapters.

What Was New in Version 4.5?

The features of Version 4.5 included:

Increased Memory Size for Virtual Machines: With this release you can create a single virtual machine with a maximum of 3600 MB as well as use up to 4 GB of memory for all of your running virtual machines.

Experimental Support for Longhorn: This release supports the beta install of the next release of Microsoft Windows. The code name for this next release is Longhorn.

Improved Support for Guests Using Linux Kernels in the 2.6 Series: With this release, virtual machines that are running the 2.6 kernel will see better performance.

PXE Support: This release supports the Preboot Execution Environment (PXE) to boot and install operating systems into new virtual machines.

Tip of the Day: With each initial launch of the program, a pop-up tip is displayed that will inform you of a new feature of VMware Workstation.

USB Device Installation: If you have a user account on a Windows PC that hosts VMware Workstation, you no longer have to have administrative rights to connect a USB device to a virtual machine.

Automatic Check for Product Updates: Workstation now has the ability to automatically check for new updates. This new function can be adjusted to check for new updates by the user or be turned off if necessary.

New Operating System Support: This release added support for the following:

- Novell NetWare 5.1
- Novell NetWare 6.0
- Novell Netware 6.5
- SuSE Linux 9.0

What Was New in Version 4.5.2?

The new features in Version 4.52 included:

VMware Virtual Disk Manager: Using this utility, you can use the command line or create scripts to create, manage, and modify virtual disk files.

Experimental Support for 64-bit Host Computers: With this release, you can install Workstation on a 64-bit host computer that uses an AMD64 Opteron, Athlon, or Intel 32e CPU.

Experimental Support for Solaris Guest Operating Systems: The x86 edition of Solaris 9 and Solaris 10 beta as guest operating systems are supported in this release.

Support for SuSE LINUX 9.1 Guest: You can install SuSE Linux 9.1 as a guest operating system in this release.

Enhanced VPN Support over NAT: Workstation supports PPTP over NAT.

INSTALLATION SYSTEM REQUIREMENTS

In order to successfully install and work with VMware Workstation 5, you need to be aware of the minimum system requirements necessary to run the software. The following requirements are just a guideline to get started. If you plan on running more than two virtual machines simultaneously, you should look to expanding your memory and processor past the minimum requirements.

VMware Workstation will run on a standard 500 MHz or faster x86 processor with at least 256 MB of memory. The basic installation of Workstation requires 150 MB for Windows and 80 MB for Linux during the installation.

As far as performance is concerned, increasing processor speeds and the memory will allow you to run additional virtual machines and see a performance boost. The latest computer on the market today combined with 1–2 GB of memory will give you plenty of virtual machines to work with and great performance. We will discuss the host system requirements further in Chapter 2.

SUPPORTED GUEST OPERATING SYSTEMS

As of Version 4.5 of VMware Workstation, the following operating systems are supported:

- Windows Longhorn experimental support
- Windows 2003 Enterprise, Standard, and Web Editions
- Windows XP Professional, Windows XP Home Edition, Windows 2000 Professional
- Windows 2000 Advanced Server and Windows 2000 Server
- Window NT Workstation 4.0 SP 6a, Windows NT 4.0 Server SP 6a, and Windows NT 4.0 Terminal Server Edition SP 6
- Windows 98, Windows 98 SE, Windows ME, Windows 95 SP1 (includes OSR releases)
- Windows for Workgroups 3.11, Windows 3.1
- MS-DOS 6.x
- Novell NetWare 5.1, 6, 6.5
- FreeBSD 4.0-4.6.2, 4.8, 5
- Solaris X86 Edition 9 experimental, 10 beta experimental support
- Mandrake Linux 8.2, 9.0
- Red Hat Linux 7.0, 7.1 ,7.2, 7.3, 8.0, 9.0
- Red Hat Enterprise Linux 2.1, 3.0
- Red Hat Linux Advanced Server 2.1
- SuSE Linux 7.3, 8.0, 8.1, 8.2, 9.0, 9.1
- SLES 7, 7 patch 2, 8
- TurboLinux Server7.0, Enterprise Server 8, Workstation 8

VIRTUAL MACHINE HARDWARE OVERVIEW

When you create a virtual machine, Workstation provides you with the following virtual hardware:

Processor: Your virtual machine uses the same processor that your operating system uses. For example, if a computer is using a 1.80 GHz Pentium 4 processor, then the virtual machine will take advantage of the same platform.

Chip Set: The Workstation chip set is an Intel 440BX motherboard with NS338 SIO chip and 82093AA IOPIC.

Memory: A single virtual machine can have a maximum of 3600 MB. A total of 4 GB is the maximum for running on all virtual machines.

Bios: Any virtual machine in Workstation that you create will run the PhoenixBIOS 4.0 Release 6 with Vesa BIOS.

Graphic: VMware Workstation supports both VGA and SVGA.

IDE Drives: You can have a maximum of four devices. It can be a combination of disks, CD-ROM/DVD-ROM. Your hard disks can be either virtual or physical disks. Furthermore, you can have a virtual disk with a maximum of 128 GB.

SCSI Devices: With VMware Workstation, you can have up to seven SCSI devices and each SCSI disk can have a maximum of 256 GB.

Floppy Drives: You can have a maximum of two 1.44 MB floppy devices. Workstation gives you the ability to use either a physical floppy driver or a floppy image.

Serial COM Ports: VMware Workstation supports up to four serial COM ports.

Parallel LPT Ports: You can have a maximum of two bidirectional parallel LPT ports.

USB Ports: VMware Workstation uses a two-port USB 1.1 UHCI controller and supports devices such as USB printers, scanners, hard disk drives, memory card readers, and digital cameras.

Keyboard: VMware Workstation uses a 104-key Windows 95/98 enhanced keyboard.

Ethernet Card: You can have a maximum of three virtual Ethernet cards per virtual machine. They are AMD PCnet-PCI II compatible.

Sound: Each virtual machine emulates Creative Labs Sound Blaster AudioPCI.

Virtual Networking: You can have nine virtual Ethernet switches. Three are configured by default. They include bridged, host only, and NAT networking.

VMWARE WORKSTATION RESOURCES

If you are looking to get further resources from the Internet, there are several available to you. You can search VMware's knowledge base at *http://www.vmware.com/kb* or search their online community at *http://www.vmware.com/community/index.jspa*. Topics on their community discussion forum are moderated by VMware. For general newsgroups, you can visit the VMware NNTP news server at *news.vmware.com*.

CONVENTIONS USED IN THIS BOOK

The following conventions and terms are used in this book:

- Vertical bars are used to separate menu choices. For example, select **VM | Settings.**
- When we refer to the Control Center, we are referring to the VMware Workstation summary window where you see all of the virtual machines.
- Whenever we mention the host system, we mean the operating system that has VMware Workstation installed.
- The guest system refers to the virtual machine running within VMware Workstation. Examples include a Windows XP virtual machine or a SuSE Linux virtual machine running within VMware Workstation.

By using VMware Workstation, more companies than ever before are able to run multiple applications on a single computer. With the ability to move virtual systems around as necessary and the small amount of overhead needed to run this technology, virtualization is becoming more and more popular and cost effective. In this chapter we have reviewed the requirements to run VMware Workstation and have given you a brief overview of what the software can do. In the next chapter, you will get your feet wet by installing VMware Workstation on either a Windows or a Linux platform.

2 Installing VMware Workstation

In This Chapter

- Installation Requirements
- Installing VMware Workstation on a Windows Platform
- Uninstalling VMware Workstation on a Windows Platform
- Unattended Installation of VMware Workstation
- Installing VMware Workstation on a Linux Platform
- Configuring VMware Workstation on a Linux Platform
- Uninstalling VMware Workstation

The installation of VMware Workstation will be discussed in this chapter as well as upgrading and uninstalling the product. The chapter will be divided into two sections. The first section will discuss how to install and uninstall VMware Workstation on a Windows platform. You will be provided with all the necessary details to successfully install VMware Workstation in a Windows environment. The second section will discuss how to install, upgrade, and uninstall VMware Workstation on a Linux platform. Upon completion of this chapter, you will have the ability to perform this installation on both environments with confidence.

INSTALLATION REQUIREMENTS

Prior to installing VMware Workstation, it is recommended that your host PC has at least a 500 MHz or faster processor and enough memory to run your host operating and virtual machines. VMware Workstation supports the Intel and AMD family of processors such as Pentium II–IV (M, Centrino, Xeon, Prestonia), and AMD Athlon (MP, XP, Duron, Opteron).

You should have enough memory to run your guest operating system as well as the minimum required to run your virtual machines. If you plan to run multiple virtual machines, you should have at least 1–2 GB of total RAM. This will give you the ability to run multiple virtual machines on one desktop and not decrease the performance of your operating system.

VMware recommends a 16-bit color display or better for running virtual machines on a Windows platform. For Linux installations, an X Server should meet the X11R6 specifications to run Linux as well as a video adapter supported by your server to run virtual machines in full-window mode.

Currently, VMware Workstation requires 150 MB of disk space on a Windows platform and 80 MB of space on a Linux platform. In addition, each guest OS should have a minimum of 1 GB of space to install the OS and applications, but 3–4 GB per OS is recommended. VMware Workstation supports IDE and SCSI hard drives in addition to a CD-ROM and DVD-ROM.

INSTALLING VMWARE WORKSTATION ON A WINDOWS PLATFORM

It is a very straightforward process to install VMware Workstation on a Windows platform. The first step in the installation process is to make sure you are logged in as an administrator or a user that belongs to the administrator's group. This could be the local administrator's group or a domain administrator.

If you are installing VMware Workstation on a Windows XP or Windows 2003 host computer, it is highly recommended that you be logged in as a local administrator to successfully install VMware Workstation.

Next, place the CD in the CD-ROM and the Workstation 5 splash screen appears. Click Install and you will be presented with the welcome window of the installation as shown in Figure 2.1.

Click Next to read the VMware Workstation End User License Agreement (see Figure 2.2). After reading the license agreement, select the Yes, I accept the terms in the license agreement. Then you can continue. Click **Next**, as shown in Figure 2.3, to choose the destination of your VMware Workstation installation. The default destination is C:\Program Files\VMware\VMware Workstation. To change the default path, simply click the **Change** button and provide an alternate path.

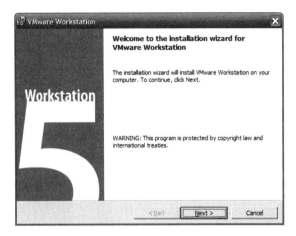

FIGURE 2.1   The VMware Workstation welcome window.

VMware recommends that you refrain from installing VMware Workstation on a network drive.

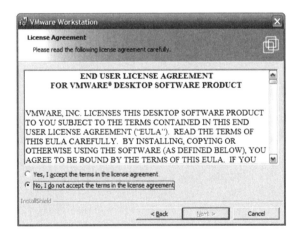

FIGURE 2.2   The End User License Agreement.

Now you are ready to configure your shortcuts as shown in Figure 2.4. A default check is placed on the following: `Desktop`, `Start Menu Programs folder`, and `Quick Launch toolbar`. Click **Next** to accept the defaults or deselect any option you desire.

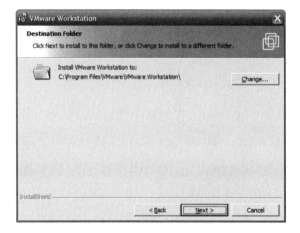

FIGURE 2.3 The Destination Folder window.

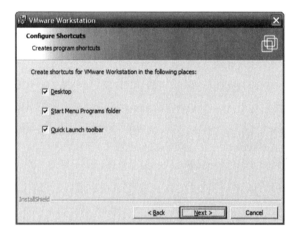

FIGURE 2.4 Configuring shortcuts.

If your computer currently has CD-ROM autorun enabled, as shown in Figure 2.5, unexpected results might happen with any virtual machines that you create or that exist. Accept the defaults to disable autorun and click **Next**. On the Ready to Install the Program window, choose **Install** to begin the VMware Workstation installation (see Figure 2.6). A status bar with a blue indicator logs the progress until completion.

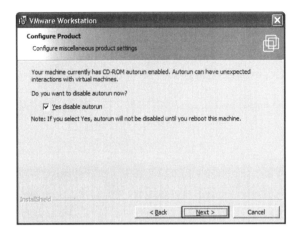

FIGURE 2.5   Disable autorun.

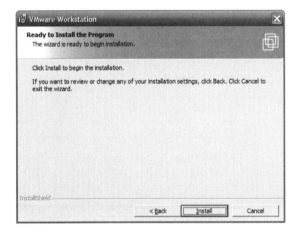

FIGURE 2.6   Your VMware Workstation installation
begins after you choose the **Install** button.

Once the installation is complete (see Figure 2.7), you have the option of entering your user name, company name, and serial number and choosing **Enter**. If you decide to skip this step, you can enter this information the first time you run the VMware Workstation product by choosing **Help | Enter Serial Number** as shown in Figure 2.8. Finally, click **Finish** (see Figure 2.9) to complete the installation and reboot if necessary.

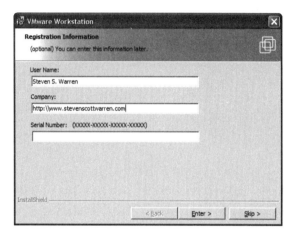

FIGURE 2.7   The VMware Workstation registration window.

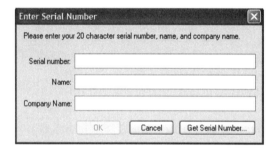

FIGURE 2.8   Entering the serial number.

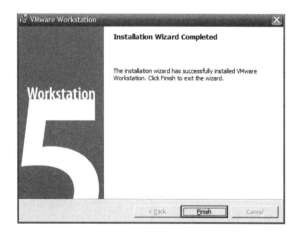

FIGURE 2.9   Finishing the installation.

UNINSTALLING VMWARE WORKSTATION ON A WINDOWS PLATFORM

Uninstalling VMware Workstation requires you to remove the program from `Add/Remove Programs`. Click **Start | Control Panel | Add or Remove Programs** and choose **VMware Workstation** from the currently installed programs (see Figure 2.10). Next, click **Remove** and you are prompted with a dialog box that asks you if you are sure you want to remove this program. Choose **Yes** and the Windows Installer removes VMware Workstation.

FIGURE 2.10   Removing VMware Workstation from your computer.

During the uninstall process, you are prompted with a dialog box (see Figure 2.11) that asks you if you want to keep your VMware license from within the computer's registry. If you plan on reinstalling VMware Workstation, choose **Yes** and the Windows Installer finishes the uninstall process and prompts you to reboot your computer. If you choose **No**, highlight the license and click **OK** to remove, as shown in Figure 2.12. You are prompted one last time with a warning message stating the following: "Removing this license may prevent you from installing upgrade versions of VMware products. Are you sure you want to remove this license. Click **No** to keep the license file."

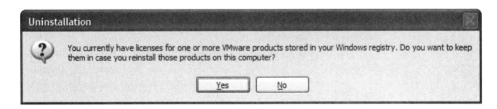

FIGURE 2.11   VMware Workstation license uninstalled.

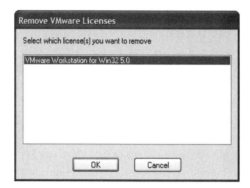

FIGURE 2.12   Removing the VMware license.

UNATTENDED INSTALLATION OF VMWARE WORKSTATION

In a corporate environment, you might have to install VMware Workstation on many host computers. In order to quickly install VMware Workstation, you will want to take advantage of the unattended installation feature of the Windows Installer. In order to correctly perform an unattended installation, you must be currently running Version 2.0 or above of the Windows Installer.

Windows Installer 2.0 is available with Windows XP and can be downloaded for versions prior to Windows XP and Windows 2003 Server at http://www. microsoft.com/downloads/details.aspx?displaylang=en&FamilyID=4B6140F9-2D36-4977-8FA1-6F8A0F5DCA8F.

NOTE

Extracting the Installation Image

Before you can perform an unattended installation, you must first extract the image to a directory of your choice. Before you begin, please check to see what type of VMware Workstation media you are using. If you downloaded the software from VMware's Web site, then your executable file will read VMware-Workstation-xxxx.exe where xxxx represents the version and build number, as shown in Figure 2.13. If you have the CD-ROM media, then the name of the installer is setup.exe.

Next, click **Start | Run |** and type cmd to open a command prompt. Inside the command prompt, Listing 2.1 shows you how to properly extract your installation image. The executable is case sensitive, so make sure you type the listing exactly as it appears in Figure 2.14. Also make sure that you are in the proper directory that houses the VMware-Workstation-5.0-12206 executable.

The actual filename will be different and might be setup.exe. The release of VMware Workstation on the CD-ROM is VMware-workstation-5.0.0–13124.exe.

VMware-workstation-5.0.0-12544.exe   55,041 KB   Application
VMware-workstation-5.0.0-12888.exe   57,303 KB   Application

FIGURE 2.13 The VMware release number.

LISTING 2.1 Extracting the VMware Workstation Image Syntax

```
VMware-Workstation-5.0-12206.exe /a /s /v" /qn TARGETDIR=c:\vm-image"
```

```
C:\>cd downloads

C:\Downloads>dir
 Volume in drive C has no label.
 Volume Serial Number is 0C37-B817

 Directory of C:\Downloads

02/16/2005  10:12 PM    <DIR>          .
02/16/2005  10:12 PM    <DIR>          ..
01/28/2005  03:00 PM        55,423,920 VMware-workstation-5.0.0-12206.exe
               1 File(s)     55,423,920 bytes
               2 Dir(s)  56,363,540,480 bytes free

C:\Downloads>VMware-workstation-5.0.0-12206.exe /a /s /v" /qn TARGETDIR=c:\vm-image"
```

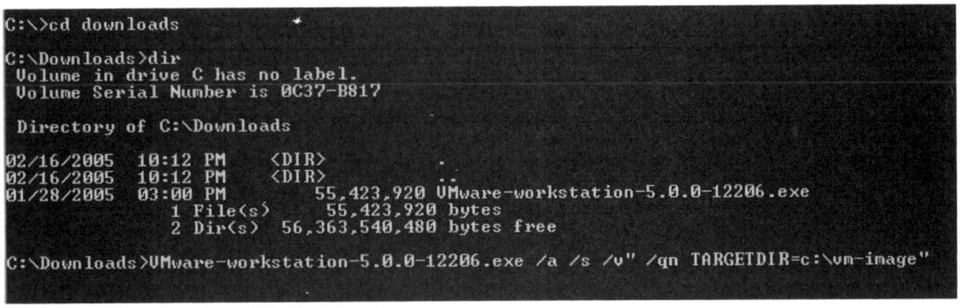

FIGURE 2.14 Proper command line for extracting the image.

After you type the path in Listing 2.1, press **Enter** on your keyboard. Figure 2.15 displays your image that will be used for all unattended installations.

FIGURE 2.15 The VMware Workstation administrative installation image.

Now that you have successfully extracted your image, let's run an unattended installation of VMware Workstation on your computer by using the syntax in Listing 2.2. The REMOVE= value allows you to skip certain parts of the unattended installation as shown in Table 2.1. The Property= value allows you to further customize the unattended installation by adding the parameters shown in Table 2.2.

LISTING 2.2   The MSIEXEC Installation Syntax

```
Msiexec —i "<Installation Path>\VMware Workstation.msi"
[INSTALLDIR="<ProgramPath>"] ADDLOCAL=ALL,[Remove=<Feature=featurename,
featurename>] /qn
```

TABLE 2.1   The Remove Parameters

Value	Description
Authd	The VMware authorization service.
Network	Remove networking components such as the virtual bridge and the host adapters for host-only networking. Do not remove if you plan on using NAT and DHCP with VMware Workstation.
DHCP	The virtual DHCP server.
NAT	The virtual Nat device.

TABLE 2.2   The Property Parameters

Property	Outcome
DESKTOP_SHORTCUT	This parameter puts a VMware Workstation shortcut on your desktop. A 1 in quotes means true and a 0 in quotes means false. For example, DESKTOP_SHORTCUT="1" places a shortcut on the desktop. If you did not want a shortcut, you would use Desktop_Shortcut="0".
DISABLE_AUTORUN	This parameter disables autorun on your host machine. A 1 in quotes means true and a 0 in quotes means false.
REMOVE_LICENSE	This parameter removes all VMware Workstation licenses upon uninstallation.
SERIALNUMBER	The value is the serial number, including the hyphens.

Now that we have gone over the parameters of an unattended install, let's show you a real-world example of how to use it (see Figure 2.16). In this example, VMware Workstation is installed to a specified location with all networking components. Additionally, we set the parameters to add a VMware Workstation desktop shortcut, disable the autorun feature to prevent problems with the virtual machine, and automatically enter the serial number.

```
c:\>Msiexec -i "c:\vm-image\vmware workstation.msi" INSTALLDIR="d:\VMware\VM\" ADDLOCAL=ALL
SERIALNUMBER="xxxxx-xxxxx-xxxxx-xxxxx" DISABLE_AUTORUN="1" /qn
```

FIGURE 2.16 Example of a VMware Workstation unattended installation.

Remember to use the command prompt to run the Msiexec syntax.

INSTALLING VMWARE WORKSTATION ON A LINUX PLATFORM

In this section, we will discuss how to install VMware Workstation on a Linux platform. There are many distributions of Linux available on the market today, and each distribution might handle installing VMware Workstation in a slightly different way. In order to appeal to all distributions, we are going to document the universal way to install VMware Workstation via the terminal. Installing VMware Workstation can be a real sticking point, so this will be an in-depth look at getting VMware Workstation installed on a Linux machine. If you are an advanced user, you can skip ahead if you are comfortable with the installation process.

Depending on how you purchased VMware Workstation, you will either have a CD-ROM or a downloaded version of the product. VMware Workstation allows you to choose whether you want to install the program by using an RPM version or a compressed Tar archive. Let's first discuss how to install VMware Workstation using the RPM version.

RPM Installation

The RPM version can be downloaded from VMware's Web site, or you can insert the CD-ROM. Many distributions will automatically recognize your CD-ROM and perform a mount command. If your distribution does not take care of this automatically, open a terminal window and type the command shown in Listing 2.3. Prior to mounting your CD-ROM, you must become root to install the product. You can either log in to Linux as root or in a terminal window type su and type your root password as shown in Figure 2.17.

LISTING 2.3   Mounting Your CD-ROM

```
Mount /dev/cdrom/
```

Now that you have mounted your CD-ROM (see Figure 2.18), you are ready to run the command to unpack the RPM file; see Listing 2.4. If you are new to Linux, most distributions allow you to simply double-click the RPM file, which kicks off the installation.

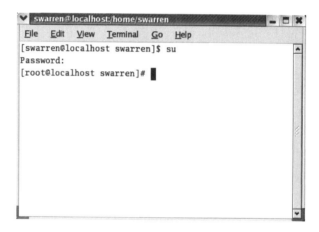

FIGURE 2.17   Login as super user.

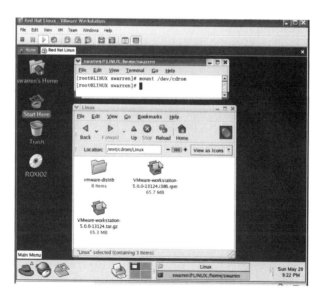

FIGURE 2.18   Mounting the CD-ROM.

When typing commands in the terminal window, pay close attention to the case. Commands are case sensitive.

LISTING 2.4 Extracting the RPM File

```
rpm —Uhv filename.rpm/
```

After typing this command in the terminal window, as shown in Figure 2.19, change your directory to /usr/bin by typing cd /usr/bin in a terminal window and run the command found in Listing 2.5. The VMware-config.pl is discussed in the next section.

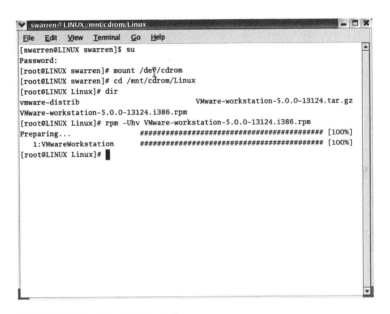

FIGURE 2.19 The RPM installer.

The location of the RPM file on the CD-ROM is shown in Listing 2.5.

LISTING 2.5 Configuring VMware Workstation

```
./Vmware-config.pl
```

When the installation is complete, do not forget to unmount the CD-ROM by typing the unmount command. Figure 2.20 shows you exactly how you should type this command in the terminal window.

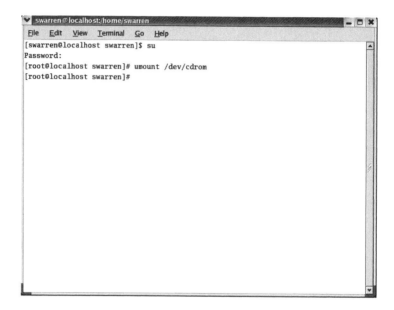

FIGURE 2.20 Unmounting the CD-ROM.

Tar Archive Installation

The Tar archive installation is very similar to the RPM installation. One major difference is that the Tar archive needs to be extracted. Your Tar archive is similar to a zipped file in Windows. Let's walk through the process.

Start by opening a terminal window in your Linux distribution. Log in as SU and mount the CD-ROM. After you mount the CD-ROM, copy the tar.gz to the /tmp directory. Figure 2.21 shows the commands to accomplish logging in as SU, mounting your CD-ROM, and copying the contents to the /tmp directory.

Now it is time to point to the directory where you unpacked the archive. To change to that directory, type cd /tmp and unpack the archive. Figure 2.22 shows you the command to type in the terminal window to properly unpack the archive.

The final steps include changing the directory to the vmware-distrib directory and running the installation program vmware-install.pl. Figure 2.23 shows you the command necessary to finally install VMware Workstation. At this point you will be asked a series of questions (see Listing 2.6). Accept all of the default directories of the binary files, library files, documentation files, and init script. Once the installation is complete, you have to run the configuration program that is discussed in detail in the next section.

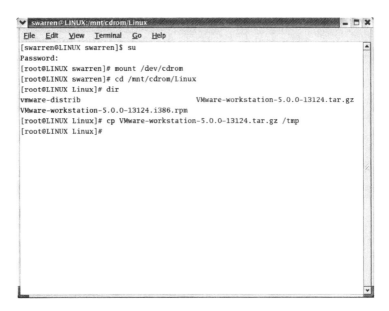

FIGURE 2.21 Tar archive installation of VMware Workstation.

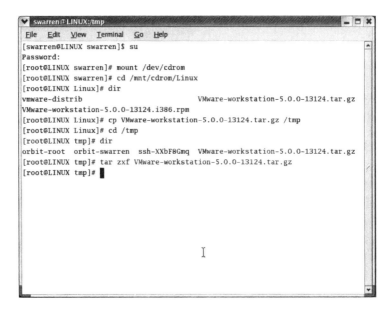

FIGURE 2.22 The Tar archive needs to be unpacked prior to installing VMware Workstation.

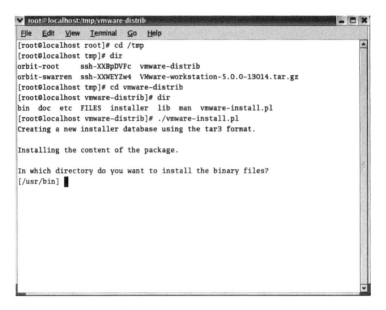

FIGURE 2.23   Installing VMware Workstation via the vmware-install.pl.

If you installed VMware Workstation with the RPM installer, then you need to run the vmware-config.pl *after the install. If you use the Tar archive, you have the option of the installer launching the configuration program for you by choosing* **Yes**.

LISTING 2.6   Installer Questions

```
In which directory do you want to install the binary files? [/usr/bin]

What is the directory that contains the init directories (rc0.d/ to
rc6.d/)? [/etc/rc.d]

What is the directory that contains the init scripts?
[/etc/rc.d/init.d]

In which directory do you want to install the library files?
[/usr/lib.vmware]

In which directory do you want to install the manual files?
[/usr/share/man]

In which directory do you want to install the documentation files?
[/usr/share/doc/vmware]
```

The path "/usr/share/doc/vmware" does not exist currently. This program
is going to create it, including needed parent directories. Is this
what you want? [Yes]

The installation of VMware Workstation 5 build-12888 for Linux
completed successfully. You can decide to remove this software from
your system at any time by invoking the following command:
"/usr/bin/vmware-uninstall.pl."

Before running VMware Workstation for the first time, you need to
configure it by invoking the following command: "/usr/bin/vmware-
config.pl." Do you want this program to invoke the command for you now?
[Yes]

CONFIGURING VMWARE WORKSTATION ON A LINUX PLATFORM

Now that we understand how to install both the RPM and the Tar archive installers, let's discuss the configuration of VMware Workstation needed to run the program successfully. To start the program, open a terminal window, log in as SU and type cd /usr/bin followed by ./vmware-config.pl as shown in Figure 2.24.

```
[root@localhost cdrom]# cd /usr/bin
[root@localhost bin]# ./vmware-config.pl
Making sure services for VMware Workstation are stopped.

Stopping VMware services:
    Virtual machine monitor                              [  OK  ]

You must read and accept the End User License Agreement to continue.
Press enter to display it. █
```

FIGURE 2.24   Configuring VMware Workstation networking using vmware-config.pl.

First, you must read and accept the End User License Agreement to continue the configuration. Press **Enter** to display the EULA and accept the EULA by typing Yes. At this point, the configuration program will search for a suitable vmmon module for your running kernel. When it finds the appropriate module, a message is displayed. Figure 2.25 displays the message that the installation program displays.

```
Trying to find a suitable vmmon module for your running kernel.

The module up-2.4.20-8.i686-RH9.0 loads perfectly in the running kernel.

Trying to find a suitable vmnet module for your running kernel.

The module up-2.4.20-8.i686-RH9.0 loads perfectly in the running kernel.
```

FIGURE 2.25   A suitable vmmon module has been found.

Next, you are asked to install networking for your virtual machines. Choose **Yes** and the program configures a bridged network for vmnt0 and a Network Address Translation (NAT) network on vmnet8.

The program automatically searches for an unused private subnet when you choose **Yes** (see Figure 2.26). Next, accept the default answer of **No** for configuring a host-only network in your virtual machines. You can always add this later if you decide you need a host-only network.

```
Do you want this program to probe for an unused private subnet? (yes/no/help)
[yes]
```

FIGURE 2.26   Searching for an unused private subnet.

The last question asks you if you want to allow your virtual machines to access the host's file system. If you choose **Yes**, VMware Workstation configures SAMBA for you. Finally, the configuration program starts the VMware services (see Figure 2.27) and you are ready to run VMware Workstation.

```
Starting VMware services:
    Virtual machine monitor                             [  OK  ]
    Virtual ethernet                                    [  OK  ]
    Bridged networking on /dev/vmnet0                   [  OK  ]
    Host-only networking on /dev/vmnet1 (background)    [  OK  ]
    Host-only networking on /dev/vmnet8 (background)    [  OK  ]
    NAT service on /dev/vmnet8                          [  OK  ]

You have successfully configured VMware Workstation to allow your virtual
machines to access the host's filesystem.  Would you like to add a username and
password for accessing your host's filesystem via network interface vmnet1 at
this time? (yes/no/help) [yes]
```

FIGURE 2.27   Samba access for your virtual machines.

After the services start, you can add a username and password for accessing the host's file system. Once you have added the users, click **No** and the configuration program tells you to access VMware Workstation by typing the command `cd /usr/bin` followed by `vmware` (see Figure 2.28).

FIGURE 2.28   Opening VMware Workstation.

UNINSTALLING VMWARE WORKSTATION

Uninstalling VMware Workstation from a Linux machine is a very simple process. If you are using the RPM installer, you can remove the software by opening a terminal window, logging in as root and typing `rpm -e VMwareWorkstation`. Figure 2.29 shows the command to type in the terminal window.

This command is case sensitive. Type it exactly as it is displayed or you will not be able to uninstall.

If you are using the Tar installer, you can remove the software simply by opening a terminal window, logging in as SU and running the `vmware-uninstall.pl`. Figure 2.30 shows you the command necessary to uninstall VMware Workstation using the Tar installer.

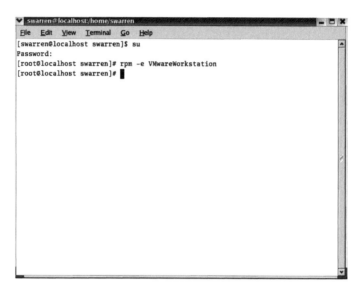

FIGURE 2.29 RPM uninstall of VMware Workstation.

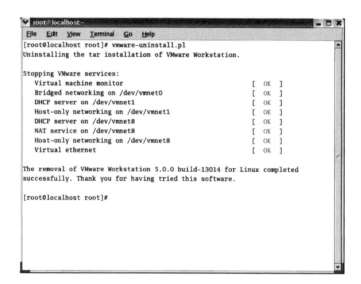

FIGURE 2.30 The Tar uninstall.

This chapter explained how to install VMware Workstation on a Windows and a Linux operating system. In our next chapter we will provide you with a quick tour of the user interface (UI) so that you can become more familiar with the product.

3 Quick Tour of VMware Workstation

In This Chapter

- VMware Workstation Control Center
- Working with the Menu Bar
- Working with the VMware Workstation Toolbar
- The Virtual Machine Settings
- About Workstation Tabs
- About the Status Bar

Now that we have installed VMware Workstation 5, let's explore the look and feel of its interface. In this chapter, we will show you the new interface and briefly highlight how each feature works. In later chapters, these features will be discussed in detail.

VMWARE WORKSTATION CONTROL CENTER

The VMware Workstation main window or Control Center is where you will create and work with virtual machines. The Control Center allows you to create, stop, start, pause, suspend, and perform all functions as they relate to administering your virtual machines. Let's go over the composition of the Control Center to help you feel more comfortable when working with the product. See Figure 3.1 for a view of the Control Center panel.

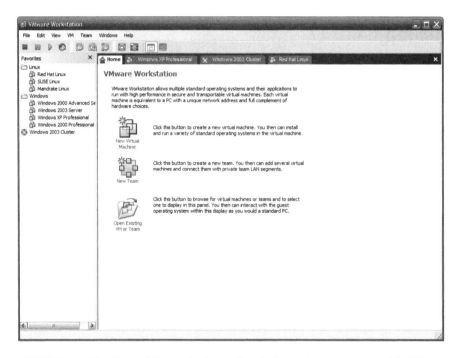

FIGURE 3.1   The Control Center is the main window when you work with VMware Workstation.

WORKING WITH THE MENU BAR

The menu in VMware Workstation allows you to control every aspect of the virtual machines that you create. The VMware menu item is composed of seven pull-down menus that give you access to all of the VMware Workstation functionality; see Figure 3.2. We will now discuss each menu item in detail.

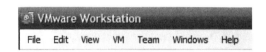

FIGURE 3.2   The VMware Workstation menu bar.

The File Menu

The File menu (see Figure 3.3) allows you to perform the following tasks:

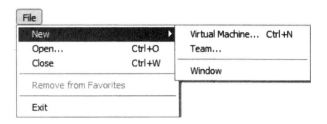

FIGURE 3.3   The File menu.

New Virtual Machine

When you choose **File | New | Virtual Machine**, the New Virtual Machine wizard will walk you through the creation of your first virtual machine as shown in Figure 3.4. For a more detailed explanation of the New Virtual Machine wizard, refer to Chapter 5.

New Team

When you choose **File | New Team**, the New Team wizard (see Figure 3.5) will walk you through the creation of a team. For more a more detailed explanation of the New Team wizard, refer to Chapter 10.

FIGURE 3.4   The New Virtual Machine Wizard.

FIGURE 3.5   The New Team Wizard.

New Window

Choose **File | New | Window** and a new Control Center opens up. This gives you the ability to have multiple Control Centers or VMware Workstation windows open at one time.

Open...

File | Open Virtual Machine allows you to open an existing and configured virtual machine. For example, if you moved the locations of your virtual machines or copied a virtual machine image down from the network to your local machine, you could simply open the new virtual machine by browsing to the correct path.

Close

File | Close exits you out of the current virtual machine you are working with.

Add to Favorites

In order to add a virtual machine to the Favorites window, open the virtual machine and make it active (click its tab) and choose **File | Add to Favorites**.

Remove from Favorites

In order to remove a virtual machine from the Favorites window, highlight a virtual machine in the Favorites window and choose **File | Remove from Favorites**. The virtual machine is no longer visible in the Favorites window, but it still exists. You can add the virtual machine back by choosing **File | Open** and browsing to the virtual machine's *.vmx configuration file. Once you have opened the virtual machine, right-click on the applicable virtual machine's tab and choose **Add to Favorites**. If you want to permanently remove the virtual machine, right-click on a virtual machine from the Favorites window and choose **Delete from Disk**.

Exit

File | Exit will exit you out of the VMware Workstation program. If you have any virtual machines running, you will be prompted first to make sure you want to power off and close the virtual machine.

The Edit Menu

The Edit menu (see Figure 3.6) allows you to perform five tasks:

Cut, Copy, and Paste

Edit | Cut, Copy, Paste allows you to cut, copy, and paste text when working in the Control Center or Summary view. An example includes copying and pasting text in the Notes field of the Control Center.

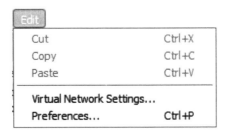

FIGURE 3.6   The Edit menu.

Virtual Network Settings

Edit | Virtual Network Settings is where you will configure your virtual network. Configuring complex virtual networks is discussed in Chapter 12.

Preferences

Edit | Preferences gives you the following additional tabs to work with: Workspace, Input, Hot Keys, Display, Memory, Priority, and Lockout.

Workspace

The Workspace tab (see Figure 3.7) allows you to choose the default location of your virtual machines when they are first created. The default location is C:\ Documents and Settings\Administrator\My Documents\My Virtual Machines. **Opened Tabs** is set by default, to remember opened virtual machines between sessions so that each of your chosen virtual machine tabs will display the next time you open the Control Center. **Software Updates** allows you to choose how often VMware Workstation checks for new updates. You have the option of choosing **Never, Daily, Weekly**, or **Monthly**.

Input

The Input tab (see Figure 3.8) allows you to change how the virtual machine controls and releases the keyboard, mouse, and cursor. In addition, you have the ability to select whether you want to be able to copy and paste text between the host and guest.

The VMware Tools must be installed in order to receive the benefits of the copy/paste and cursor functionality.

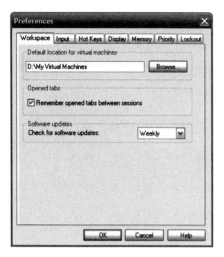

FIGURE 3.7   The Workspace tab.

FIGURE 3.8   The Input tab.

Hot Keys

The Hot Keys tab (see Figure 3.9) allows you to specify which hot-key sequence will allow you to switch between virtual machines, send commands, and leave full screen mode. You can customize this as you see fit. Table 3.1 describes the default hot keys if you do not want to customize.

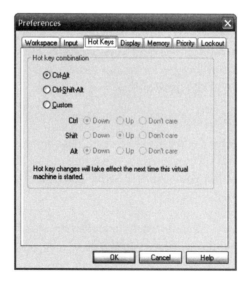

FIGURE 3.9   The Hot Keys tab.

TABLE 3.1 Hot Key Preferences

Hot-Key Sequence	Description
Alt-Tab	Changes between applications within the virtual machine (vm).
Alt-Esc	Shifts between application windows within the vm.
Ctrl-Alt-Delete	Lets you shut down or (depending upon the operating system) log off the operating system. This command is received by both the host operating system and the virtual machine, even when VMware Workstation has control of input. You can cancel the ending of the host operating system's session, then return to the virtual machine and log off or shut down the guest operating system, or perform administrative tasks.
Ctrl-Alt-Insert	Lets you shut down or (depending upon the guest operating system) log off the guest. This command is received solely by the virtual machine.

Note: Changing the hot-key combination changes the sequence you need to use. For instance, if you change the hot-key combination to Ctrl-Shift-Alt, you must press Ctrl-Shift-Alt-Insert to end the guest operating system session.

Ctrl-Alt	Takes the virtual machine out of full screen mode; if the virtual machine is not in full screen mode, this hot-key combination releases the mouse and keyboard from the virtual machine.

Note: Changing the hot-key combination changes the sequence you need to use. For instance, if you change the hot-key combination to Ctrl-Shift-Alt, you must press Ctrl-Shift-Alt to take the virtual machine out of full screen mode or release the mouse and keyboard.

Ctrl-Alt-Enter	Expands the current virtual machine into full screen mode; when running several virtual machines and repeating the command, it switches the next virtual machine into full screen mode. This command provides a useful way to move between virtual machines.

Note: Changing the hot-key combination changes the sequence you need to use. For instance, if you change the hot-key combination to Ctrl-Shift-Alt, you must press Ctrl-Shift-Alt-Enter to enter full screen mode.

Ctrl-Alt-<space>	Sends any command into the virtual machine so that VMware Workstation does not process it. Hold down Ctrl-Alt as you press the space bar and continue to hold those keys down as you press the next key in the sequence. For example, follow these steps to send Ctrl-Alt-Esc to the virtual machine, bypassing Workstation:

1. Press Ctrl-Alt.
2. Press and release <space>.
3. Press and release Esc.
4. Release Ctrl-Alt.

Note: Changing the hot-key combination changes the sequence you need to use. For instance, if you change the hot-key combination to Ctrl-Shift-Alt, you must press Ctrl-Shift-Alt-<space> to have Workstation not process a command.

Display

The Display tab allows you to configure how VMware Workstation displays your virtual machines. You can tweak these settings to suit your needs. Figure 3.10 illustrates how the Display window appears.

Memory

The Memory tab (see Figure 3.11) allows you to set how much host memory you want to reserve to run all of your virtual machines and how your system should allocate this memory for virtual machines.

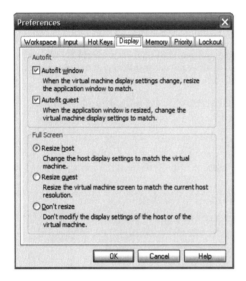

FIGURE 3.10 Configuring the display of the Control Center.

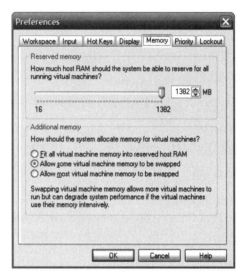

FIGURE 3.11 Choose the appropriate option to allocate additional memory for your virtual machines.

Priority

The Priority tab allows you to establish the priority that the Windows host gives to your virtual machines. You can choose either **Normal** or **High** as shown in Figure 3.12.

The settings above are global settings. To change the setting for a single virtual machine, choose VM | Setting | Options |Advanced and choose the appropriate priority.

Lockout

The Lockout tab is a global setting that lets you lock down the following tasks with a password:

- Creating new teams and virtual machines
- Editing team and virtual machine configurations
- Managing virtual networks

In order to lock down the above settings, select **Enable administrative lockout**, type a password, and choose from one, all, or a combination of the above as shown in Figure 3.13. Please refer to Chapter 11 for a detailed explanation.

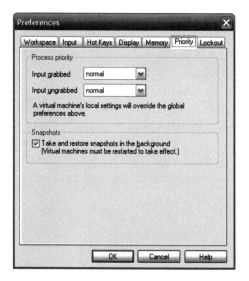

FIGURE 3.12 Choose the appropriate option to configure the desired priority.

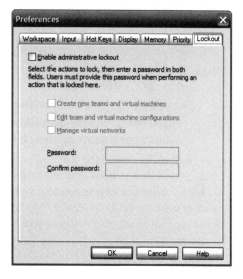

FIGURE 3.13 Locking down your virtual machines is easy with VMware Workstation 5.

The View Menu

The View menu (see Figure 3.14) allows you to perform 12 tasks.

Full Screen

View | Full Screen allows you to switch your virtual machine to full screen mode. You can also use the hot key Ctrl-Alt-Enter to switch a virtual machine to full

FIGURE 3.14 The View menu.

screen mode. In order for your virtual machines to support a better screen resolution in full screen mode, you must remember to install VMware Tools. Without it, you will not be able to choose a better screen resolution and color depth.

When you are ready to leave fullscreen mode, simply choose the hot-key combination Ctrl-Alt to return to the Control Center.

Quick Switch

View | Quick Switch, as shown in Figure 3.15, allows you to switch between virtual machines in a full screen mode. This is a very convenient way to switch between virtual machines in a quick and easy fashion.

Current View

View | Current View allows you to toggle between the console and the Control Center (Summary window). If you power on a virtual machine, you can switch between the powered-on virtual machine and its Control Center administration.

Autofit Window

View | Autofit will automatically fit your virtual machine within the Control Center. With **Autofit** checked, you will not be able to resize the Control Center. If you want the ability to resize your Control Center, uncheck the **View | Autofit** option.

FIGURE 3.15 The Quick Switch window enables you to move from virtual machine to virtual machine with an easy transition via tabs.

Autofit Guest

View | Autofit Guest automatically resizes the guest display when you drag the Workstation window to a new size.

Fit Window Now

View | Fit Window Now allows you resize your Control Center at any time and have the ability to fit your virtual machine within the Control Center when you deem necessary. By choosing this option, all black space in your virtual machine is eliminated.

Fit Guest Now

View | Fit Guest Now allows you to fit the guest operating system within the confines of the windows immediately.

Go to Home Tab

This option allows you to return to the VMware Workstation Home tab in the Control Center. On this tab you can create a new virtual machine or open an existing virtual machine.

Favorites

View | Favorites allows you to view all of your virtual machines in a treelike structure. On this tab you can see all of the virtual machines that you created and create folder structures for all of your virtual machines. For example, you can create a folder called Domain Controllers and put all of your virtual machine domain controllers in this window.

In order to create folders, right-click on the white space in the Favorites work area and choose **New Folder** as shown in Figure 3.16. After you create your new folder, you can simply drag and drop virtual machines into your folder.

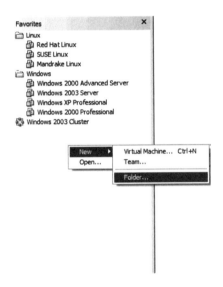

FIGURE 3.16 The Favorites workspace allows you to organize the structure of your virtual machines.

Toolbars

View | Toolbars allows you to choose which toolbars will appear in the toolbar window underneath the menu bar. The toolbars that are available to you are Power, Snapshot, and View.

Status Bar

View | Status bar will add or remove the status bar at the lower-righthand corner of the VMware Control Center.

Tabs

View | Tabs will add or remove the tabs across the VMware Control Center, as shown in Figure 3.17 and Figure 3.18.

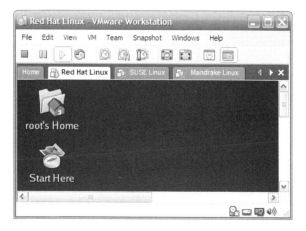

FIGURE 3.17   The VMware Control Center with tabs.

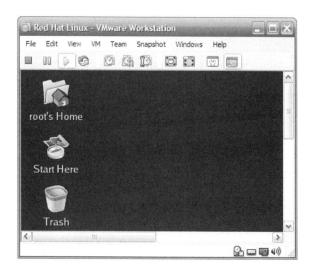

FIGURE 3.18   The VMware Control Center without tabs.

The VM Menu

The VM menu (see Figure 3.19) allows you to perform the following tasks:

Power

VM | Power allows you to perform the following tasks (see Figure 3.20):

FIGURE 3.19   The VM menu.   **FIGURE 3.20**   The Power menu.

Power On

Power | Power On allows you to power on a virtual machine.

Power Off

Power | Power Off shuts down your virtual machine without shutting down the operating system. This is similar to your pushing the power off button on your computer without shutting it down.

Suspend

Power | Suspend allows you to pause or suspend your virtual machine at whatever point you choose. For example, if you are in the middle of writing a Word document and you are not ready to shut down your virtual machine, you can simply choose to suspend or freeze your computer right where it is and continue at a later date. Suspending is quicker than a shutdown and power up. Then, when you are ready to continue your work, click **Power | Resume** to continue working where you left off.

Reset

Power | Reset powers down your virtual machine and restarts it. This is similar to pressing the reset button on your physical computer.

When you attempt to do this, you are prompted with a dialog box asking you if you are sure you want to reset your virtual machine in this fashion.

Shut Down Guest

Power | Shut Down Guest will first shut down your guest operating system and then shut down the virtual machine. This is similar to shutting down your computer via **Start | Turn off Computer** and then powering your computer off. You must have VMware Tools installed in order to perform this.

Restart Guest

Power | Restart Guest powers off your guest operating system and restarts it. This is similar to choosing **Restart** on your PC. You must have VMware Tools installed in order to perform this.

Suspend after Running Script

Power | Suspend after Running Script will run a virtual machine script and then go into a suspend state mode. You must have VMware Tools installed in order to perform this.

Resume and Run Script

Power | Resume and Run Script will run a virtual machine script and then resume activity or leave its suspended state. You must have VMware Tools installed in order to perform this.

Power On and Run Script

Power | Power On and Run Script powers on your virtual machine and executes a virtual machine script. You must have VMware Tools installed in order to perform this.

Removable Devices

VM | Removable Devices allows you to connect and disconnect devices such as audio, floppy drives, CD-ROM, NIC, and USB ports.

Snapshot

The Snapshot menu allows you to perform the following tasks:

Take Snapshot. . .

Take Snapshot … takes a snapshot or picture of your virtual machine and saves the data as it existed at that point in time. You can create a snapshot when the virtual machine is running, is suspended, or is not running. You can have as many snapshots as your work requires. This release supports multiple snapshots.

Revert to Snapshot

Snapshot | Revert to Snapshot discards all changes made on your virtual machine and reverts to data from when the snapshot was taken. For example, if you wanted to test a particular installation on a new Windows XP machine, you could take a snapshot of the blank operating system and wait until it completes. Once the snapshot is complete, you would load the software for testing purposes. If you had problems, you could revert back to your snapshot and start again until all issues were resolved. Snapshots are a great feature within Workstation and can be very powerful for testing any type of PC scenario. For further information on snapshots, refer to Chapter 8.

Snapshot Manager

Snapshot Manager is a graphical tool that allows you to manage your multiple snapshots in one place. For more information on Snapshot Manager, see Chapter 8.

Install VMware Tools

This option allows you to install VMware Tools, which is necessary to take full advantage of VMware Workstation. The installation of VMware Tools is discussed in Chapter 7.

Upgrade Virtual Hardware

If you upgraded from a previous release of VMware Workstation, this option will be available to upgrade your virtual machine. If you created the virtual machine with the current version of VMware Workstation, this option will be dimmed out. Please refer to Chapter 4 for a detailed explanation on upgrading VMware Workstation 4.x to 5.

Send Ctrl-Alt-Del

When you choose **Send Ctrl-Alt-Del**, you send this command to the virtual machine to either log in to the virtual machine on boot or to bring up Windows Task Manager.

Grab Input

By choosing **VM | Grab Input** or typing Ctrl-G, you are immediately given control of the virtual machine that you are currently running.

Capture Screen...

VM | Capture Screen allows you to take a screenshot of any virtual machine window at any given point in time. The file defaults to a bitmap file on a Windows host and a PNG file on a Linux host.

Capture Movie...

VM | Capture Movie... allows you to capture movies of any actions you are performing on the window. For more information on this feature, refer to Chapter 16.

Clone

VM | Clone allows you to make either a linked or full clone of a virtual machine. See Chapter 9 for more information.

Delete from Disk

Highlight the applicable virtual machine in the Favorites window to delete it from the disk. Deleting from disk not only removes the virtual machine from the Favorites window but deletes the entire virtual machine contents from the disk. Figure 3.21 describes the warning message you get before you delete a virtual machine from disk.

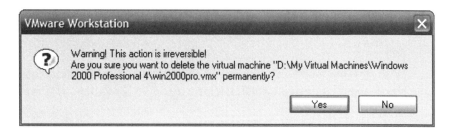

FIGURE 3.21   Deleting a virtual machine from disk.

Settings

VM | Settings allows you to configure your virtual machine hardware and options. For example, you can configure extra memory, hard disks, and NICS in addition to configuring shared folders, snapshots, and priority. These settings will be discussed in detail later in this chapter.

The Team Menu

The Team menu (see Figure 3.22) allows you to perform the following tasks:

FIGURE 3.22 The Team menu.

Power

Team | Power allows you to power on, power off, suspend, and resume all virtual machines within a team.

Switch To

Team | Switch To allows you to switch the main focus to any virtual machine in the team.

Add

With this menu option you can add a new virtual machine, an existing virtual machine, a new clone of a virtual machine, and a LAN segment to simulate bandwidth and packet loss.

Remove

Team | Remove allows you to remove a virtual machine from a team.

Delete from Disk

Team | Delete from Disk allows you to delete a team only or delete the team and virtual machines.

Settings…

Team | Settings allows you to view and configure connections, virtual machines, LAN segments, and options. For a detailed description of these tasks, refer to Chapter 10.

The Windows Menu

This menu allows you to switch between all of your currently open virtual machines as shown in Figure 3.23. For example, if you were running three virtual machines and wanted to switch to the next virtual machine, you could choose **Windows | Next Window** or choose the virtual machine in the Windows display.

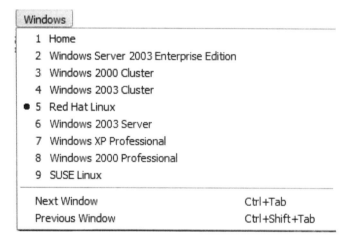

FIGURE 3.23   The Windows menu.

The Help Menu

The Help menu (see Figure 3.24) allows you to perform the following tasks:

Help Topics

Help | Help Topics allows you to peruse the VMware Workstation online help as shown in Figure 3.25.

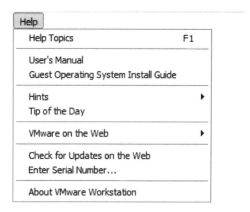

FIGURE 3.24   The Help menu.

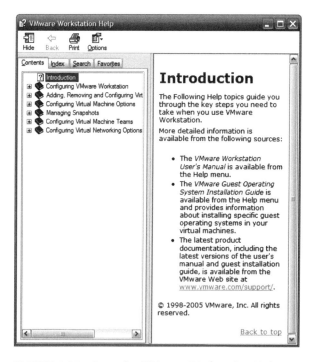

FIGURE 3.25   Browsing VMware Workstation Help.

User's Manual

Help | User's Manual allows you to peruse the VMware Workstation manual on-line.

Guest Operating System Install Guide

By choosing **Help | Guest Operating System Install Guide**, you can get a tutorial on installing a guest operating system in VMware Workstation.

Hints

Help | Hints gives you the ability to hide or show hints in VMware Workstation. This is especially useful if you have turned off some hints and want to turn all hints back on.

Tip of the Day

Help | Tip of the Day will give you a VMware Workstation Tip as shown in Figure 3.26. Otherwise, every time you open VMware Workstation, you are presented with a tip.

You can customize the Tip of the Day to suit your needs. For detailed steps on how to customize the Tip of the Day, see Chapter 16.

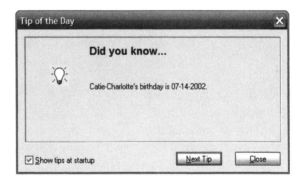

FIGURE 3.26   Example of a Tip of the Day.

VMware on the Web

By choosing this option from the Help menu, you are able to perform the following:

- Access the VMware home page.
- Obtain online support.
- View the VMware product line.
- Obtain licenses.
- Register.
- Request support.

Check for Updates on the Web

Help | Check for Updates on the Web will immediately check to see whether there is an updated VMware Workstation build for you to download. Furthermore, VMware Workstation will check for updates automatically based on your selection in **Edit | Preferences | Workspace | Software Updates**.

Enter Serial Number

Help | Enter Serial Number allows you to input the serial number of your purchased version of VMware Workstation.

About VMware Workstation

Help | About VMware Workstation gives you pertinent information in a dialog box, such as product, version, and build numbers.

WORKING WITH THE VMWARE WORKSTATION TOOLBAR

The VMware Workstation toolbar, as shown in Figure 3.27, allows you to perform various tasks with the click of a button. With the VMware Workstation toolbar you can:

- Power off this virtual machine
- Suspend this virtual machine
- Power on this virtual machine
- Reset this virtual machine
- Take a new snapshot of this virtual machine
- Revert to this virtual machine's parent snapshot
- Manage snapshots for this virtual machine
- Enter full screen mode
- Enter quick switch mode
- View summary
- View console

To get a description of each toolbar icon, hover your mouse over the button for a description.

FIGURE 3.27   The VMware Workstation toolbar.

THE VIRTUAL MACHINE SETTINGS

The Virtual Machine Settings window allows you to take greater control of the hardware that exists in your virtual machine. On the Hardware tab you have the ability to expand or decrease memory, configure hard disks, and add additional network cards, as well as change other VMware preferences that will be discussed below.

The Virtual Machine Settings window in Linux and Windows can be accessed from **VM | Settings** or by selecting the name of the virtual machine tab and choosing **Edit virtual machine settings**.

Windows Systems Virtual Machine Settings

There are two tabs in the Virtual Machine Settings window of VMware Workstation. They are:

- Hardware
- Options

Hardware

On the Hardware tab (see Figure 3.28), you can further customize your virtual machine setup. Let's go over these options so you can be familiar as we progress through this book. When you first look at this window, you will notice that you have specific devices listed such as memory, hard disk, CD-ROM, floppy, NIC, USB Controller, and audio. At any point, you can add and remove devices by clicking the **Add** or **Remove** button. If you click on the **Add** button, the Add Hardware wizard appears to walk you through adding new hardware. Furthermore, by clicking on each device, you can change the settings. For example, if you select the memory device, you can move the slider and increase or decrease the memory as you see fit. Under the hard disk device, you can browse to your disk file or defrag the virtual disk, which is a great tool to keep the performance of your virtual machine at top speed. The CD-ROM device allows you to use either a physical CD-ROM or an ISO image. ISO images are very handy to use with VMware because you can keep them on external media or the hard drive. The floppy drive also allows you to use a physical floppy or a floppy image.

Your NIC hardware is a little more advanced in that you can choose up to four options. They are Bridged, NAT, Host-Only, and/or Custom. A Bridged network allows the virtual machine to appear as an additional computer on the same Ethernet network as the host. This option will allow your virtual machine to quickly be able to access network resources. It is also the most popular method of connecting virtual machines to your network. Next, Network Address Translation (NAT) allows you to connect to the Internet or a network using the host computer's dial-up networking connection or broadband connection. If you cannot give your virtual machine an IP address on the external network, this is a great way to give your virtual machine access. The virtual machine does not have its own IP address but gets its IP address from a VMware virtual DHCP server. Finally, a Host-Only connection is only connected to the host operating system on a virtual private network, which cannot be seen outside the host.

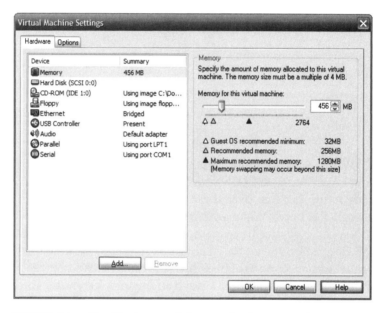

FIGURE 3.28 The Hardware tab lets you further customize your virtual machine.

Options

On the Options tab (see Figure 3.29) you can change the name of a virtual machine, change the type of guest operating system you are using, and change the location of the working directory where your snapshots and redo logs are stored. Additionally, you can configure your power options, enable shared folders, and configure dragging and dropping of files from host to guest and the virtual machine priority.

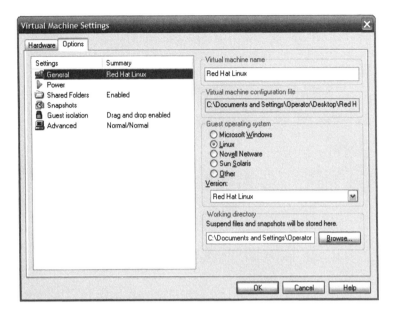

FIGURE 3.29   Configuring the virtual machine settings options.

General

On the General setting (see Figure 3.29) you can change the name of the virtual machine and specify a directory other than the default where suspend (.vmss) and snapshots (.vmsn) will be stored. The default location is in the folder where the virtual machine was created.

Power

The Power options (see Figure 3.30) allow you to set the defaults when you power up a virtual machine, configure how you want your toolbar to work, and choose what options you want to configure with your VMware Tools scripts.

Shared Folders

VMware Workstation has a unique way of sharing folders with a host PC. For more information refer to Chapter 16.

Snapshots

You have the ability to completely disable snapshots by choosing . **Snapshots | Disable snapshot.** If the screen is dimmed, it is because your virtual machine already has a snapshot. You must first delete the snapshot prior to disabling snapshots for a particular virtual machine (see Figure 3.31).

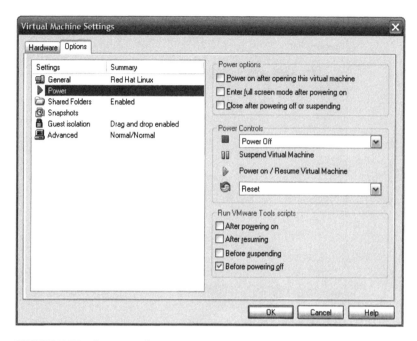

FIGURE 3.30   Power options.

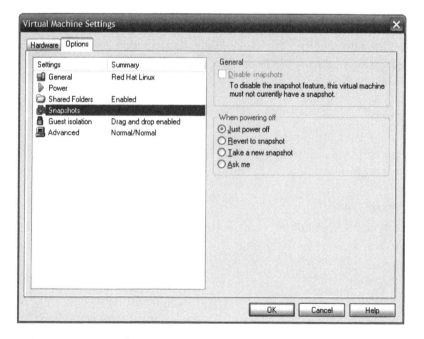

FIGURE 3.31   Snapshot options.

You can also specify what will happen when you power off your virtual machine. Do you want to just power off, revert to a snapshot, take a new snapshot, or be asked? Choose the appropriate setting applicable to you.

Guest Isolation

You have the ability, as shown in Figure 3.32, to disable the drag and drop feature between virtual machines and the host.

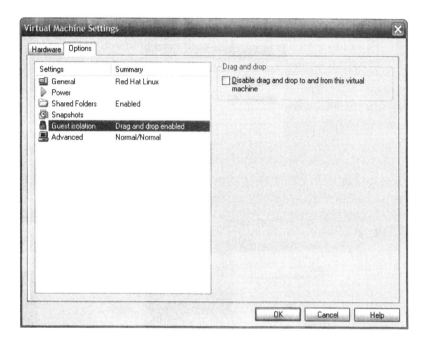

FIGURE 3.32   Guest isolation options.

Advanced

With the advanced options (see Figure 3.33), you can perform the following:

■ **Process priorities:**   You can change the default priority of your virtual machines in Windows so that some virtual machines have a higher priority than others. The settings on this window override the settings under Edit | Preferences | Priority. When you change the default settings, the change is active only on the virtual machine you are working with.

■ **Settings:**   Place a check in Run with debugging information to turn debugging on for troubleshooting. A log gets created in the directory where your configuration files reside. When you run in DEBUG mode, you might experience a slowdown because of the additional logging. Next, select Disable acceleration if the software you load in a virtual machine seems to hang. In many cases, disabling acceleration will help with such issues. For more information, refer to VMware Workstation KB article 901 at *http://www.vmware.com/support/kb/enduser/std_adp.php?p_sid=dRNvQiBh&p_lva=&p_faqid=901&p_created=1039560336&p_sp=cF9zcmNoPTEmcF9ncmlkc29ydD0mcF9yb3dfY250PTEmcF9zZWFyY2hfdGV4dD05MDEmcF9zZWFyY2hfdHlwZT03JnBfcHJvZF9sdmwxPX5hbnl_JnBfcHJvZF9sdmwyPX5hbnl_JnBfc29ydF9ieT1kZmx0JnBfcGFnZT0x&p_li=*. In this section, you can also log virtual machine progress periodically to increase debugging and logging information. Finally, you have the ability to enable the template mode for cloning. Refer to Chapter 9 for more information on cloning and enabling the template mode.

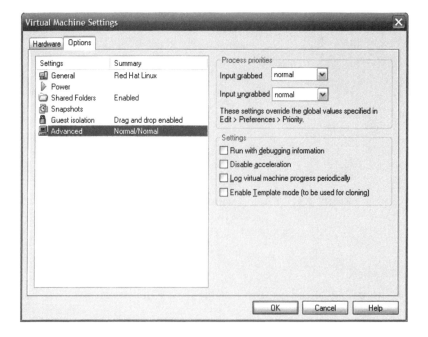

FIGURE 3.33   Advanced options.

ABOUT WORKSTATION TABS

In the Control Center of VMware Workstation, the virtual machine tabs provide you redundant information if you simply right-click on a tab as shown in Figure 3.34. Right-click on a tab to view your options. Most are also accessible from the menu and toolbar of Workstation. It is up to you to decide whether you want to right-click or use the menu and toolbar.

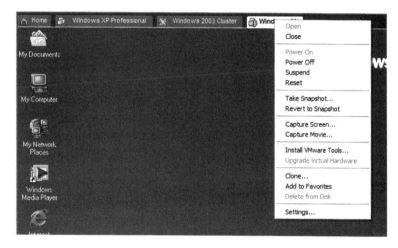

FIGURE 3.34   Right-click on a Workstation tab to perform similar options to the menu bar.

ABOUT THE STATUS BAR

The Status bar, as shown in Figure 3.35, allows you to right-click on a removable device to disconnect or edit its configuration. For example, you can right-click on the CD-ROM device and edit its settings by connecting to a different physical drive or loading a different ISO image.

FIGURE 3.35   The status bar of VMware Workstation.

In this chapter we have provided you with a brief overview of how VMware Workstation is designed. Now that you have a better understanding of the Graphical User Interface (GUI), let's move on to the next chapter where we will explain how to upgrade VMware Workstation from 4.x to 5.

4

Upgrading VMware Workstation

In This Chapter

- Upgrading VMware Workstation 4.x to 5 on a Windows Host
- Upgrading VMware Workstation 4.x to 5 on a Linux Host

To take advantage of the new features of VMware Workstation 5, you must upgrade your virtual hardware. Installing VMware Workstation 5 is a simple process that requires minimal time as long as you follow some recommendations. For example, if you currently run virtual machines prior to 5, it is recommended that you make sure all virtual machines are powered off prior to installing VMware Workstation 5. Additionally, make sure all snapshots of your legacy virtual machines have been removed and that no virtual machines are in a suspended state. If any virtual machines that you want to upgrade are in a suspended state, resume the virtual machine and power it off prior to upgrading to VMware Workstation 5. For more information on snapshots and the suspend and resume feature, refer to Chapter 8. Finally, it is very important to back up your virtual machines in case the upgrade presents problems. Refer to Chapter 16 for information on how to properly back up and archive your virtual machines. In this chapter we will discuss how to upgrade a VMware Workstation 4.x legacy virtual machine to VMware Workstation 5 on both a Windows and a Linux platform.

UPGRADING VMWARE WORKSTATION 4.X TO 5 ON A WINDOWS HOST

You have two upgrade scenarios when working with virtual machines that are currently running VMware Workstation 4.x.

- Upgrade with all VMware Workstation 5 functionality.
- Run your legacy Workstation 4.x virtual machine under Workstation 5 without upgrading.

Upgrading VMware Workstation 4.x to 5

If you choose to upgrade, your virtual machine will have all of the functionality that is available with the new release, but any virtual machine in Workstation 4.x that is upgraded to Workstation 5 will no longer have the ability to run under VMware Workstation 4.x. With that being said, archive your Workstation 4.x virtual machines in case you ever need to go back to them. For information on how to archive your virtual machines, see Chapter 16.

Run Legacy 4.x Virtual Machines under 5 Without Upgrading

If you choose not to upgrade to VMware Workstation 5, you can run your virtual machine under 5, but you will not be able to reap the benefits that are provided with the new release. For example, you will not be able to take advantage of the Snapshot Manager feature that allows you to have multiple snapshots or the ability to create linked and full clones. Please see Chapter 1 for a definition of these features.

Running the Installer

Once you have made the decision to upgrade, execute the VMware Workstation 5 installer from your CD-ROM or from the directory where you downloaded the software. With this release, you can run the upgrade on top of the release. The installer recognizes that a previous version exists, as shown in Figure 4.1, and uninstalls before installing its current version. At the end of the installation click **Finish** and reboot.

At this point you have VMware Workstation 5 installed with Workstation 4.x virtual machines. You can choose to upgrade your virtual machines or run them in legacy mode. In order to upgrade a virtual machine, right-click (see Figure 4.2) on

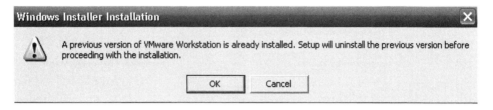

FIGURE 4.1 VMware automatically uninstalls a previous version.

the applicable virtual machine in the Favorites window and choose **Upgrade Virtual Hardware**. You can also right-click on the tab in the Control Center (see Figure 4.3) and choose **Upgrade Virtual Hardware**. When you choose to upgrade the virtual hardware, you are presented with a warning message that tells you that you cannot reverse this process. Click **Yes** to upgrade your configuration.

A virtual machine must be powered off when you run Upgrade Virtual Hardware. If the virtual machine is not powered off, this function will not be available.

FIGURE 4.2 You can upgrade the virtual hardware from the Favorites window.

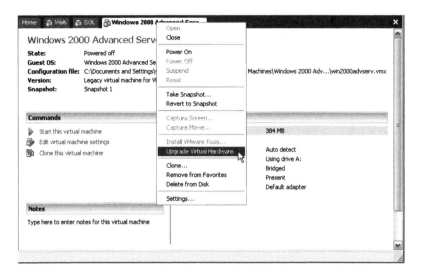

FIGURE 4.3 You can upgrade the virtual hardware from the VMware Workstation tabs.

Another cool feature of VMware Workstation 5 is that you can tell what version of VMware Workstation you are on by simply looking at the version in the Control Center (see Figure 4.4). In this example, Figure 4.4 is a legacy virtual machine running in VMware Workstation 5 or a virtual disk that has not been upgraded yet. After you upgrade your virtual hardware, the version is updated to the current release, as shown in Figure 4.5. Once the virtual hardware is upgraded, the version reads as follows: Current virtual machine for VMware Workstation 5.

Windows 2000 Advanced Server

State: Powered off
Guest OS: Windows 2000 Advanced Server
Configuration file: C:\Documents and Settings\Operator\My Documents\My
Version: Legacy virtual machine for VMware Workstation 5.0.0
Snapshot: Snapshot 1

FIGURE 4.4 Legacy virtual machine running in VMware Workstation 5.

State:	Powered off
Guest OS:	Windows 2000 Advanced Server
Configuration file:	C:\Documents and Settings\Operator\My Documents\My Virtual
Version:	Current virtual machine for VMware Workstation 5.0.0
Snapshot:	Snapshot 1

FIGURE 4.5 Current or upgraded virtual machine running in VMware Workstation 5.

VMware Workstation 5 is very intuitive. If you try to power on a legacy virtual machine, you are presented with a message box (see Figure 4.6) that reminds you to upgrade your virtual hardware. If you do not want to upgrade your legacy virtual machine, just continue to power on the virtual machine.

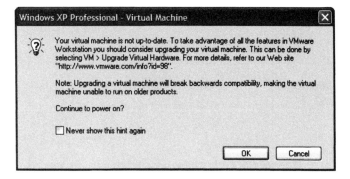

FIGURE 4.6 Powering on a legacy virtual machine will generate a hint about upgrading.

If you do want to upgrade, choose **VM | Upgrade Virtual Hardware**. After choosing **VM | Upgrade Virtual Hardware**, a warning message (see Figure 4.7) says that you are about to upgrade. Choose **Yes** and you are presented with a dialog box saying that you have successfully upgraded your virtual hardware. Figure 4.8 displays the upgrade success dialog.

It is now necessary to power on the virtual machine and install the newest version of VMware Tools. Please see Chapter 7 for instructions on how to load VMware Tools on a Windows host.

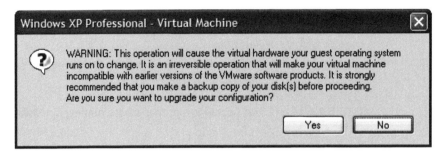

FIGURE 4.7   Upgrading your virtual hardware.

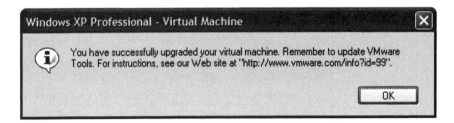

FIGURE 4.8   The upgrade has been a success.

UPGRADING VMWARE WORKSTATION 4.X TO WORKSTATION 5 ON A LINUX HOST

Upgrading from version Workstation 4.x to Workstation 5 is a very simple process. You can upgrade using the following installers:

- Tar installer
- RPM installer

About the Tar Installer

When using the Tar installer, refer to Chapter 2 on installing VMware using the Tar installer. The Tar installer automatically removes the previous version and installs the current version.

About the RPM Installer

Prior to upgrading to VMware Workstation 5, you must uninstall the current version of VMware by opening a terminal session, as shown in Figure 4.9, and typing the command as shown in the figure.

```
rpm[root@localhost root]# rpm -e VMwareWorkstation
[root@localhost root]#
```

FIGURE 4.9   Use the proper syntax to uninstall VMware Workstation with the RPM installer.

Once the uninstall is complete, you can install VMware Workstation 5 by running the RPM installer as shown in Figure 4.10.

```
[root@localhost root]# mount /dev/cdrom
mount: No medium found
[root@localhost root]# cd /mnt/cdrom
[root@localhost cdrom]# dir
VMware-workstation-5.0.0-12206.i386.rpm  VMware-workstation-5.0.0-12206.tar.gz
[root@localhost cdrom]# rpm -Uhv VMware-workstation-5.0.0-12206.i386.rpm
Preparing...                ######################################### [100%]
   1:VMwareWorkstation       ######################################### [100%]
[root@localhost cdrom]# 
```

FIGURE 4.10   Installing VMware Workstation 5.

Upgrading from Workstation 4.x to Workstation 5 is a piece of cake. If you need to upgrade from a version that is earlier than Workstation 4.x, refer to the VMware online documentation at *http://www.vmware.com/support/pubs/*.

Now that we have learned how to upgrade from Workstation 4.x to Workstation 5, we are ready to create virtual machines.

5 Creating Virtual Machines

In This Chapter

- Anatomy of a Virtual Machine
- Creating a Virtual Machine with a Windows Host Computer
- Creating a Virtual Machine with a Linux Host Computer

Now that VMware Workstation is installed, you are ready to begin creating virtual machines. In this chapter, we will describe how to properly create new virtual machines using both a Windows and a Linux platform. Included with the installation of VMware Workstation is a wizard that allows you to create a virtual machine very quickly. We will discuss this in detail, but first let's go over the components that make up a virtual machine.

ANATOMY OF A VIRTUAL MACHINE

After walking through the wizard, a set of files will be located in the default directory of VMware Workstation (which you chose during the installation in Chapter 2). A virtual machine is simply a set of relative files that contain the computer's pertinent information. These files can be moved from computer to computer and will open up and work fine. This is a great feature because if you have a computer catastrophe, a simple backup will give you the entire computer back again if you are working from within a virtual machine. The virtual machine is made up of the files in Table 5.1 (also see Figure 5.1).

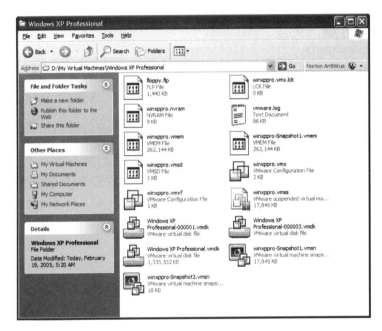

FIGURE 5.1 The anatomy of a virtual machine.

TABLE 5.1 VMware File Extensions and Names

VMware Extension	Name of File	Description
.flp	Floppy	If you attach a Floppy Image through the Add Hardware Wizard Under VM | Settings | Hardware | Add, a blank Floppy.flp image is created in this directory.
		→

VMware Extension	Name of File	Description
.vmx.lck	Lock	When you select a virtual machine from the Favorites tab or when you choose File | Open and browse to a virtual machine, the lock file is created. As soon as you close the VMware Workstation tab that represents the opened VM or exit VMware Workstation, the lock file disappears.
.log	vmware.log	This is a log file that tracks the activity of the virtual machine in question. It is very helpful when debugging and troubleshooting issues that might arise.
.nvram	[VM Name] .nvram	Just as a PC has a BIOS, every virtual machine must have a BIOS as well. The .nvram file is, simply stated, the file that stores the BIOS.
.vmem	[VM- Name-Name of Snapshot]	When you take a snapshot, a vmem or virtual memory file is created to store the memory of the snapshot.
.vmsd	[VM Name].vmsd	This file stores metadata and snapshot information in one centralized location.
.vmx	[VM Name].vmx	The .vmx file is the configuration file that stores all of the settings that are selected when you create a new virtual machine via the wizard. You can open the .vmx file with Notepad to view its contents. Inside you will see such things as the guest OS you are running. Once you get the hang of creating virtual machines, you can modify the settings in the .vmx file to more advanced configurations, such as clustering and starting VMware Workstation as a service.
vmdk	[VM Name].vmdk	The .vmdk is the actual hard drive of your virtual machine. All of the data is stored in this file. During the wizard, you can either configure a set amount of space for your virtual hard drive or have it auto-grow; it is your choice. Additionally, you can have the data split in 2 GB chunks as well, which helps out if you ever have to zip or backup the virtual files to media.

→

VMware Extension	Name of File	Description
.vmdk	[VM Name]-xxxxx.vmdk	When you have snapshots, a redo log file is created. The redo log file stores changes to the virtual disk while the virtual machine is in a running state. Furthermore, if you are splitting your disks into 2 GB files, the naming convention becomes more complex.
.vmsn	[VM Name] – Snapshot.vmsn	This file is the VMware Workstation virtual machine snapshot. This file stores the running state of your virtual machine at the point-in-time that you take the snapshot.
.vmss	[VM Name].vmss	When you click the suspend toolbar button to suspend a virtual machine, the information about VMware Workstation virtual machine's suspended state is stored in this file.
.vmxf	[VM Name].vmxf	When you create a virtual machine team and add a virtual machine to the team, the .vmxf team configuration file is added to the virtual machine directory. For more information about teams refer to Chapter 10.

CREATING A VIRTUAL MACHINE WITH A WINDOWS HOST COMPUTER

We are now ready to create our first virtual machine. Let's walk through the steps of the virtual machine wizard by opening VMware Workstation from the Start menu. Choose **Start | Programs | VMware | VMware Workstation**. From the menu, choose **File | New Virtual Machine** or type Ctrl-N. The New Virtual Machine Wizard Welcome window appears as shown in Figure 5.2.

The VMware Workstation wizard gives you the option of choosing a Typical or Custom configuration (see Figure 5.3) of a virtual machine. Let's walk through the Custom configuration.

When choosing a virtual machine format (see Figure 5.4), you can either choose to create a new Workstation 5 format that has all the latest bells and whistles or you can choose to create a legacy virtual machine that doesn't have all the bells and whistles. Because VMware Workstation 5 isn't compatible with ESX

FIGURE 5.2   The virtual machine Welcome window.

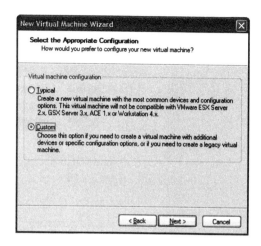

FIGURE 5.3   Select a Typical or Custom installation.

Server 2.x, GSX Server 3.x, VMware ACE 1.x, and Workstation 4.x, having the ability to create virtual machines that these platforms support is extremely helpful.

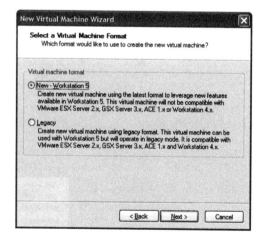

FIGURE 5.4   Choose the appropriate virtual machine format.

On the Select a Guest Operating System window, you have the option of choosing the operating system that you want to install and the version. For example, you could choose Microsoft Windows and then choose Windows Server 2003 Enterprise Edition (see Figure 5.5) for your guest operating system. Let's move on and create a new Workstation 5 virtual machine.

This Wizard simply configures the virtual machine for a specific operating system. Once you have appropriately configured the operating system, you must install that operating system yourself.

Once you have selected a guest operating system, you can either accept the defaults of the name and path of the virtual machine or customize it to suit your needs as shown in Figure 5.6.

FIGURE 5.5 Choosing a virtual operating system is easy with VMware Workstation.

FIGURE 5.6 Choose a location for the virtual machine.

The next window allows you to specify the memory settings for the virtual machine (see Figure 5.7). The legend included on this window is made up of a yellow triangle, green triangle, and blue triangle. The yellow triangle represents the minimum memory requirements to run a virtual machine. This is never a good idea unless you are simply trying to squeeze space to run as many virtual machines simultaneously as possible. The green triangle represents the recommended memory; in almost all scenarios this setting will suffice. Finally, the blue triangle shows you the maximum for best performance.

When learning how to work with VMware Workstation, begin by choosing **Use bridged networking** (see Figure 5.8) because it is the simplest of the networking types. Once you load the virtual machine with the selected operating system, you simply either supply a static IP address or obtain one from a DHCP server, and the virtual machine will have network and Internet access. We will dedicate Chapter 12 to networking virtual machines and discussing these options in detail.

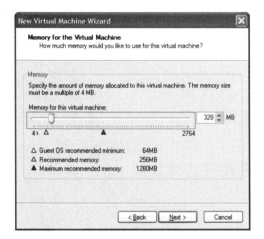

FIGURE 5.7 The amount of memory on this window can be selected or entered in increments of 4 MB.

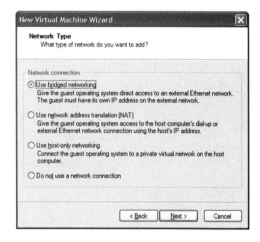

FIGURE 5.8 Choose your network connection.

On the Select I/O Adapter Types window, as shown in Figure 5.9, you have the option of choosing **Buslogic adapter** or **LSI Logic adapter**. All guest operating systems except Windows Server 2003, NetWare, and Red Hat Enterprise Linux 3 default to the **Buslogic adapter** but allow you to choose **LSI Logic** if applicable.

The Select a Disk window (see Figure 5.10) allows you to either create a disk, use an existing disk, or (for advanced users) choose a physical disk. If you were to use an existing disk, you would choose the appropriate radio button and browse to that disk file. Accessing the physical disk is discussed in Chapter 16 of this book. Let's create a new disk and move forward.

It is now time for you to choose (see Figure 5.11) whether you want your disk to be an IDE or a SCSI disk. IDE is supported by all operating systems so it is a safe choice. If you want to use a SCSI disk, this might require some advanced work such as downloading the appropriate driver from the VMware Web site. In Chapter 6, we will show you how to configure a virtual machine using a SCSI drive with a Buslogic adapter.

FIGURE 5.9 Select I/O adapter type.

FIGURE 5.10 Choose your virtual disk configuration.

FIGURE 5.11 Select your virtual disk type.

On the Specify Disk Capacity window (Figure 5.12), you can specify the disk size in GB for your virtual machine in addition to specifying whether you want to allocate the disk space upon completion of the wizard. A handy feature is the ability to split your disk files into 2-GB files. This is highly recommended as it gives you the flexibility to back up your virtual machines to DVD as well as giving you the ability to zip with a zip archiving tool. For more information on archiving your virtual machines, see Chapter 16.

The Specify Disk File window (See Figure 5.13) allows you to specify the name of your .vmdk file. This is the disk file that will hold all of your data. You can think of this drive as a virtual hard drive. When you click on the **Advanced** button, you can configure the location of your virtual hard drive on the IDE or SCSI channel. Furthermore, you can specify advanced configurations on your disks, as shown in Figure 5.14. They are:

■ Independent-Persistent Disk Mode
■ Independent-Nonpersistant Disk Mode

FIGURE 5.12 Split your disk files into 2-GB increments for archiving and DVD backups.

FIGURE 5.13 The Specify Disk File window.

FIGURE 5.14 Specify your advanced options for the virtual disk.

If you accept the default options of the wizard, your virtual hard drive has the ability to be included with snapshots. A snapshot takes a picture of your virtual machine, including drives, and stores it for you to restore at a later date. When you restore a snapshot, it ignores all changes made after the snapshot was created. In some cases, you might not want your virtual hard drives to have snapshots available. If so, choose the **Independent** checkbox and select a mode.

The **Persistent** mode writes all of your data changes directly to the virtual hard drive immediately. This is permanently written and cannot be discarded. The **Non-persistant** mode discards all changes immediately when the virtual machine is powered off or rebooted. This setting is applicable if you create a base machine and want to continue testing it over and over again without having to revert to a snapshot. Once you have made your selection click **Finish** and you have successfully created your first virtual machine, as shown in Figure 5.15. For more information on snapshots, refer to Chapter 8.

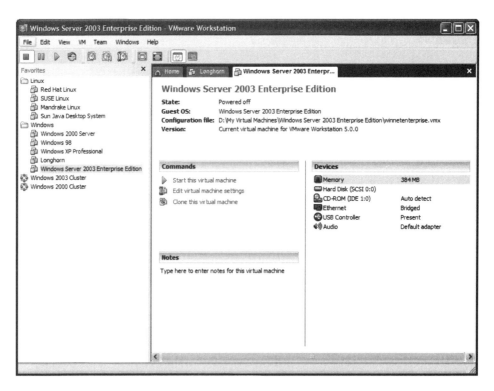

FIGURE 5.15 The Control Center displays your newly created virtual machine.

CREATING A VIRTUAL MACHINE WITH A LINUX HOST COMPUTER

Creating a new virtual machine in Linux is very similar to creating a new virtual machine in Windows. Let's walk through the steps now by opening a terminal window in your Linux distribution and typing `cd /usr/bin` followed by `vmware`. Figure 5.16 shows you the VMware Workstation Control Center on a Linux platform.

From the menu, choose **File | New Virtual Machine** or type `Ctrl-N` and the New Virtual Machine wizard welcome window appears. The only difference in the Linux virtual machine wizard is where you save the data. Just as in Windows, you choose a **Typical** or **Custom** installation. Then you select a guest operating system as shown in Figure 5.17.

Next, you choose where you want to save your new virtual machine (see Figure 5.18). The default installation path for Linux is the home directory of the username which you are currently logged into. The only windows that are different from Microsoft throughout the Linux wizard are the Location and Specify Disk File windows.

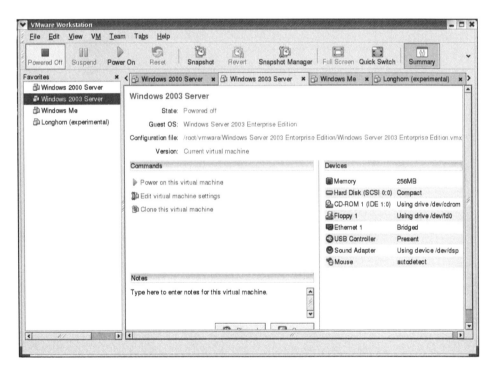

FIGURE 5.16   The Linux user interface in VMware Workstation 5.

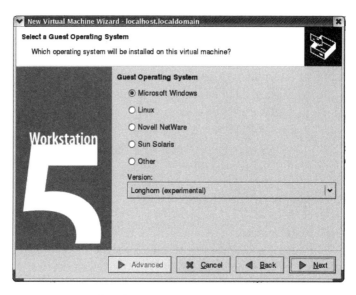

FIGURE 5.17 Choosing your operating system.

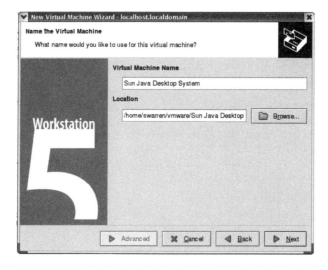

FIGURE 5.18 Specify the location of your virtual machine.

On the Specify Disk File window, you choose the path of your disk file; it defaults to your home directory as well, as shown in Figure 5.19. Once you have walked through the wizard, the Control Center displays the newly created virtual machine. Figure 5.20 shows you the Control Center with several new virtual machines.

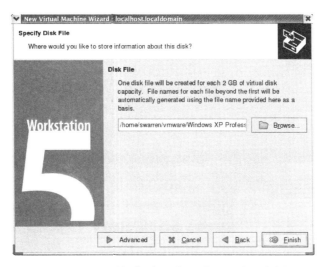

FIGURE 5.19 Specify the location of your virtual drive.

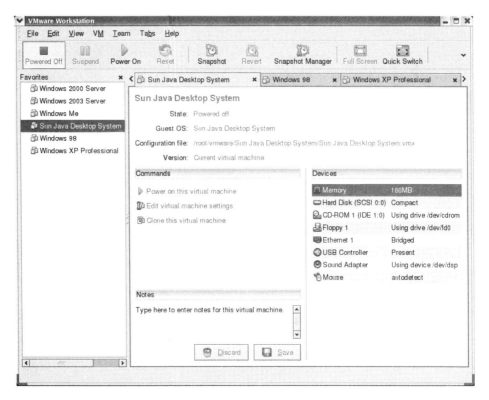

FIGURE 5.20 The Linux Control Center.

At this point we have learned how to create new virtual machines on a Windows host and a Linux host. In our next chapter we will begin to show you how to load Windows and Linux operating systems into new virtual machines.

6 Installing Windows and Linux Guest Operating Systems

In This Chapter

- CD-ROM Versus ISO Image
- Booting from an ISO Image
- Installing Windows XP Professional/Windows 2003 Server
- Installing Windows 98/ME
- Installing Longhorn (Experimental)
- Installing Linux Guest Operating Systems

It is time to install Windows guest operating systems! At this point, you should be able to install VMware Workstation and create new virtual machines. Because of the large number of operating systems supported by VMware, we will show you a tutorial on the most popular or problematic. This chapter covers how to install the following Windows and Linux operating systems:

- Windows XP Professional
- Windows Server 2003 Enterprise Edition
- Windows 98
- Longhorn (experimental)
- SuSE Linux 9.1
- Red Hat Linux 9.0
- Mandrake Linux 10.0

VMware Workstation supports many operating systems. For the purposes of this book, we are going to show you how to install the operating systems that require additional information other than the default installation.

CD-ROM VERSUS ISO IMAGE

When installing virtual machines, you have two options. You can either install the operating system via the CD-ROM or you can install the operating system via an .ISO image. The speed of your CD-ROM will determine how fast the installation completes.

If you are installing via CD-ROM, start your virtual machine and boot to the BIOS. Additionally, check to make sure the BIOS is configured properly from the Boot menu. The default options are set for a CD-ROM to boot automatically.

For quick installations, create an .ISO image of your CD-ROM and save it to either an external USB 2.0 hard drive or your local hard drive. Examples of .ISO image programs include WinISO and Undisker.

With WinISO, you simply have to place your CD in your CD-ROM drive and choose **Actions | Make ISO from CD-ROM** (see Figure 6.1). Next, you are presented with a Create ISO from CD-ROM. Click **Make** and an ISO image is created minutes later. You can download a trial copy at *http://www.winiso.com.*

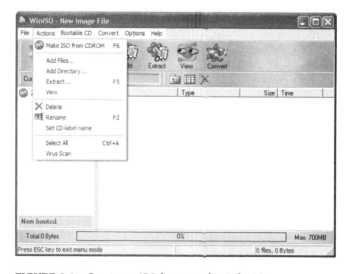

FIGURE 6.1 Create an ISO image using WinISO.

BOOTING FROM AN ISO IMAGE

In order to boot your new virtual machine from an ISO image, highlight the virtual machine you want to work with and click **Edit virtual machine settings**. Figure 6.2 describes how to edit your virtual machine settings.

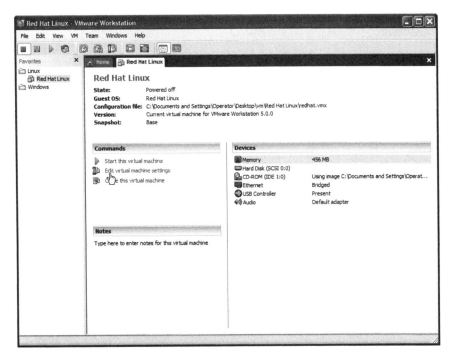

FIGURE 6.2   Editing the settings of a new virtual machine.

On the Hardware tab highlight **CD-ROM** and choose **Use ISO image**. You now have the ability to browse the location of your ISO images. Figure 6.3 shows the process of choosing an ISO image over a physical CD-ROM drive. Click **OK** and you are ready to begin the installation of your virtual machine. The Control Center now has the CD-ROM connected to the ISO image as shown in Figure 6.4.

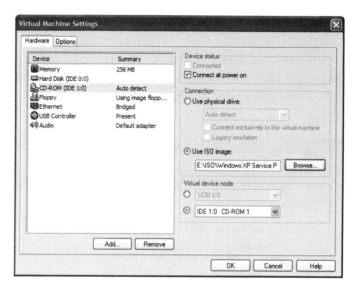

FIGURE 6.3   Using an ISO image for your virtual machine.

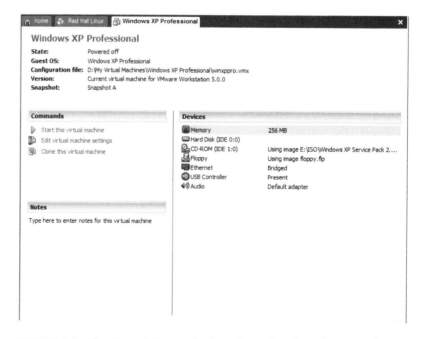

FIGURE 6.4   The Control Center displays the updated ISO image path.

INSTALLING WINDOWS XP PROFESSIONAL/
WINDOWS 2003 SERVER

You can install Windows XP Professional via the CD-ROM or ISO image. If you are installing via a CD-ROM, place the CD-ROM in your tray to begin. If you are installing via an ISO image, see the previous section in this chapter on booting from an ISO image.

Starting Your Virtual Machine

Open **VMware Workstation** from the Start menu and highlight the **Windows XP Professional** virtual machine from your Favorites window. If the Favorites window does not appear, choose **View | Favorites** from the menu. Inside the Favorites window, highlight your virtual machine and click **Start this virtual machine.**

If your virtual machine does not appear in the Favorites windows, choose File | Open Virtual Machine and browse to your new virtual machine's .vmx file and choose Open. This places a tab in the Control Center with the virtual machine's name. Right-click on the tab and choose Add to Favorites. Your virtual machine is now displayed in the Favorites window.

Next, you are presented with a dialog box stating that Windows XP Professional requires product activation (see Figure 6.5) and that you should configure your final memory and install VMware Tools prior to activating Windows XP Professional. Product activation can be done via the Internet or the telephone. Once you click **OK**, you are reminded to install VMware Tools, (discussed in Chapter 7), and the virtual machine boots to either your CD-ROM or ISO image (see Figure 6.6).

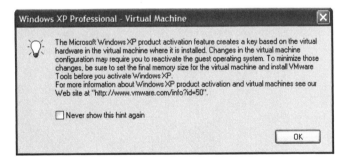

FIGURE 6.5 The Windows XP activation process.

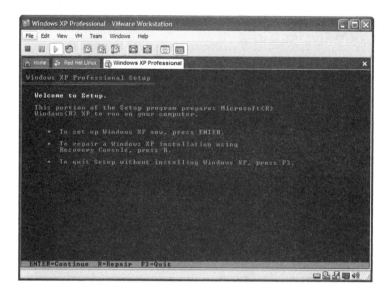

FIGURE 6.6   The Windows XP Setup window.

Next, you will install Windows XP Professional just as if you were installing it on a physical computer. The end result is Windows XP Professional running in a virtual machine, as shown in Figure 6.7.

FIGURE 6.7   Windows XP Professional

Installing Windows XP Professional/Windows Server 2003 with a SCSI Drive

When you create a Windows XP Professional virtual machine, the default configuration creates an IDE drive instead of a SCSI drive. If you want to create a SCSI drive, it will be necessary for you to download the SCSI disk driver. VMware provides this driver for use with the BusLogic virtual SCSI adapter. The BusLogic virtual SCSI adapter can be used with Windows XP Professional, Windows 2000, and Windows Server 2003. If your virtual machine does not use a SCSI driver or you configure the virtual machine to use the LSI Logic virtual SCSI adapter, this driver is not needed. You can download the SCSI disk driver at *http://www.VMware.com/download/downloadscsi.html.*

The file that you download is a floppy image; it requires you to add hardware to your virtual machine. To do this, highlight your Windows XP Professional virtual machine from the Favorites window in the Control Center and choose **Edit virtual machine settings**.

On the Hardware tab, select **Add** and the Add Hardware wizard appears. Click **Next** and highlight **Floppy Drive** as shown in Figure 6.8. You have the option of choosing to use a physical floppy drive, a floppy image, or a blank floppy image. The easiest method is to use a floppy image (see Figure 6.9).

FIGURE 6.8 Adding a floppy drive image.

FIGURE 6.9 Selecting to use a floppy image.

On the Choose Floppy Image window, browse to the location where you downloaded your SCSI disk driver floppy image. Remember to make sure the **Device status** is deselected. If you have the **Device status** selected, the virtual machine boots from the floppy image instead of the CD-ROM or ISO image. Click **Finish** and you have a floppy drive listed under your Hardware devices. Figure 6.10 shows the floppy image path.

FIGURE 6.10   A floppy image attached to the virtual machine.

Steps to Install Windows XP and Windows Server 2003

Now that we have downloaded and created our floppy image in our virtual machine, let's load the operating system via either CD-ROM or ISO. Once you have chosen your preferred method, highlight your virtual machine in the Favorites windows and choose **Start this virtual machine**.

Next during the setup, a message appears to press F6 if you need to install a third-party driver (see Figure 6.11). After the Windows setup files load, you are presented with a Setup window to specify your SCSI adapter (see Figure 6.12).

Remember to be active inside the virtual machine before pressing F6. If you are not active (click inside the virtual machine), you will have to rerun setup.

Before proceeding with loading the driver, press Ctrl-Alt to release the mouse and choose **VM | Settings** from the Control Center menu toolbar. Next, highlight the **Floppy device** on the Hardware tab and select **Connected** in the Device Status box. This connects the virtual floppy image that stores the SCSI driver information. Figure 6.13 displays a connected floppy image. Finally, click **OK** and you are ready to continue the operating system installation by loading the SCSI driver.

Click inside the virtual machine window, then on the Setup window, select the letter **s** on your keyboard. A window appears asking you to insert your disk into A:. This is why it is necessary to connect your virtual floppy image prior to this step.

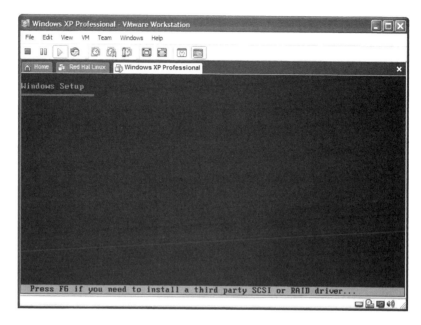

FIGURE 6.11   Press F6 to load third-party drivers.

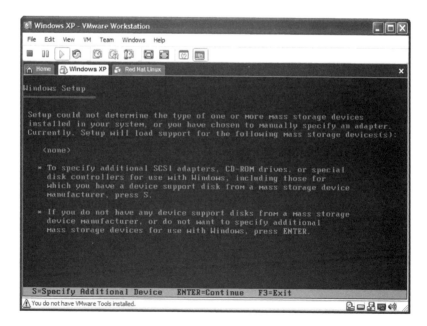

FIGURE 6.12   Specifying your SCSI adapter.

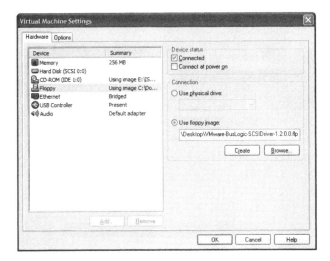

FIGURE 6.13   Connecting your floppy image.

Next, press **Enter** on your keyboard and the Setup window verifies (see Figure 6.14) that you want to load the VMware SCSI Controller. Press **Enter** twice to continue installing Windows XP\2003 Server. At this point, you would install the operating system as if it were a physical computer.

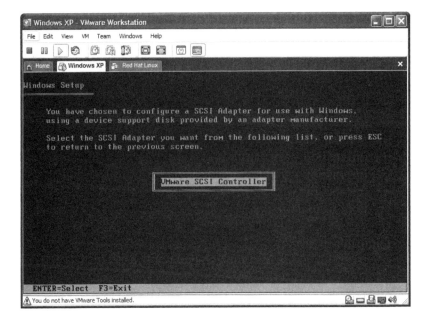

FIGURE 6.14   Installing the SCSI driver.

*During the installation of your operating system, several messages appear warning you that the driver has not passed Windows logo testing. Ignore the messages and click **Yes** to continue.*

INSTALLING WINDOWS 98/ME

Installing Windows 98/ME can be a little tricky in VMware Workstation. In order to make it a successful installation, we will use several tools to aid in the installation process. When installing one of these operating systems, you can either work with an ISO image or a CD-ROM. For the fastest installation, prior to loading the operating system, we will need to boot to the Windows 98 or ME boot disk.

The easiest way to grab the appropriate boot disk if you do not have one handy is to open a browser to *http://www.bootdisk.com*. This Web site allows you to download the appropriate boot disk for the operating system you want to install. A very cool feature of VMware Workstation is the ability to work with virtual floppy images as opposed to a physical floppy drive. Once you have a boot disk, you can use a tool such as Floppy Image or WinImage to convert the contents on the floppy disk to an image file. For more information on creating virtual floppies, refer to Chapter 16. Let's walk through this process.

You can download a trial copy of Floppy Image at http://www.rundegren.com/ products/floppyimage/.

Creating Virtual Floppies

The first step in creating a virtual floppy is to download and create the boot disk for the operating system you would like to install. For example, if you want to create a Windows 98 virtual machine, download the Windows 98 boot disk from *http://www.bootdisk.com*. After the files are downloaded, place a floppy disk in your floppy drive and double-click the **boot98.exe** (see Figure 6.15). See Figure 6.16 for an example of how your floppy disk is created.

Next, download the appropriate third-party utility, such as Floppy Image, that allows you to convert floppy disks to floppy images. Download the Floppy Image program and follow these steps to create a boot disk image. We will begin by selecting **Start | Programs | Floppy** for Floppy Image as shown in Figure 6.17.

FIGURE 6.15 Creating a Windows 98\ME boot disk.

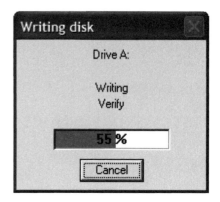

FIGURE 6.16 Writing the boot disk to a floppy drive.

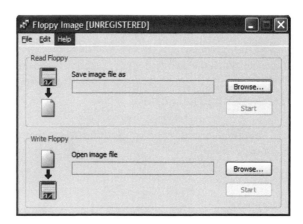

FIGURE 6.17 Floppy images.

Next, click **Browse** in the Read Floppy box and browse to a location where you want to save your floppy image (see Figure 6.18). For example, we save all of our floppy images in a folder called Floppy Images. Additionally, when saving the location of your floppy image, remember to choose **Uncompressed Image File (IMG)** instead of the default. **Compressed Image File (IMZ),** as shown in Figure 6.19. Finally, click **Start** to create your floppy image, as shown in Figure 6.20.

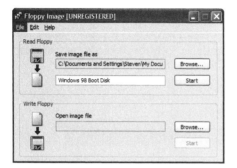

FIGURE 6.18 Save your bootdisk to a specified location.

FIGURE 6.19 Select the uncompressed image file.

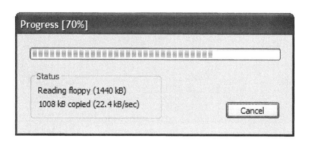

FIGURE 6.20 Writing your virtual floppy for use with VMware Workstation.

Preparing the Windows 98 Virtual Machine

You can install Windows 98 via the CD-ROM or ISO image. If you are installing via a CD-ROM, place the CD-ROM in your tray to begin. If you are installing via an ISO image, please see the section in this chapter on booting from an ISO image.

Prior to starting the Windows 98 virtual machine for the first time, you have to add a virtual floppy drive. In order to do this, highlight the **Windows 98 virtual machine** in the Favorites window and choose **Edit virtual machine settings** from the Control Center.

On the Hardware tab, click **Add** and the Add Hardware wizard appears. As you walk through the Add Hardware wizard, choose **Floppy Drive**. On the Floppy

Media Type window, choose **Use a Floppy Image** and browse to the Windows 98 floppy image you created earlier in this chapter (see Figure 6.21). Click **Finish** and you have properly configured a virtual floppy drive to boot to the newly created Windows 98 boot disk.

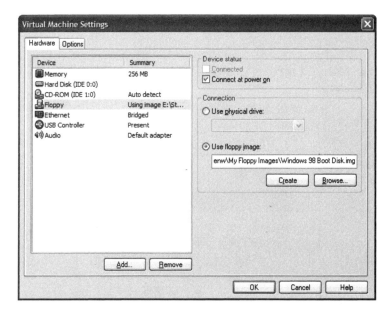

FIGURE 6.21 Using a floppy image.

Starting your Virtual Machine

Open VMware Workstation from the Start menu and highlight the **Windows 98 virtual machine** from your Favorites window. If the Favorites window does not appear, choose **View | Favorites** from the menu. Inside the Favorites window, highlight your virtual machine and click **Start this virtual machine.**

*If your vrtual machine does not appear in the Favorites window, choose **File | Open Virtual Machine** and browse to your new virtual machine's .vmx file and choose **Open**. This places a tab in the Control Center with the virtual machine's name. Right-click on the tab and choose **Add to Favorites**. Your virtual machine is now displayed in the Favorites window.*

Because you chose to boot to a floppy image, your operating system will boot to the Windows 98 boot disk. Click inside the virtual machine window, then choose to start the virtual machine with CD-ROM support as shown in Figure 6.22.

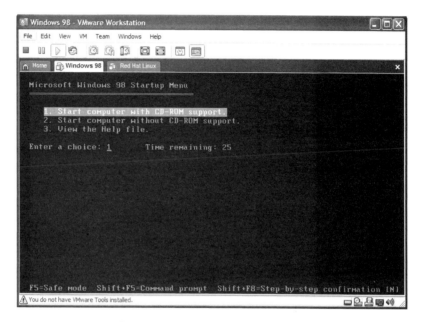

FIGURE 6.22   Starting your Windows 98 installation with CD-ROM support.

From the DOS prompt, type fdisk and enable large disk support if applicable. Now, create your Primary Dos Partition and reboot your virtual machine once again to the floppy with CD-ROM support. After the reboot, type format c: and type Y to properly format your c: drive for the Windows 98 installation (see Figure 6.23).

Next, type a label name and reboot your virtual machine with CD-ROM support. Upon reboot, browse to your CD-ROM drive via the DOS prompt and run the setup.exe to begin your Windows 98 installation. Finally, run through the setup of Windows 98 as if it were a physical PC. Figure 6.24 shows a fully operational installation of Windows 98 in a virtual machine.

If you are using an ISO image, reboot your computer with CD-ROM support and make sure you connect your Windows 98 ISO image from VM | Settings | Hardware. For more information, refer to the section on booting from an ISO image.

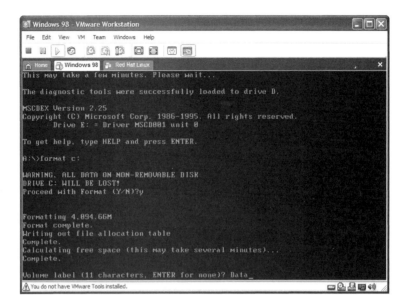

FIGURE 6.23   Formatting your virtual hard drive.

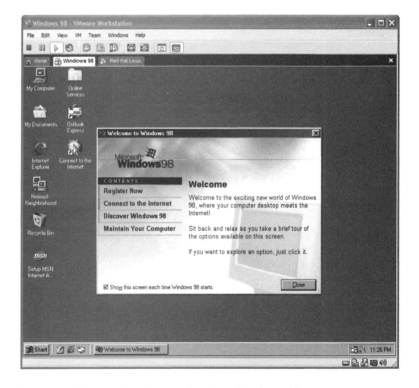

FIGURE 6.24   Windows 98 running in a virtual machine.

INSTALLING LONGHORN (EXPERIMENTAL)

Longhorn will be the next major release of the Windows operating system. Before loading Longhorn, (Build 4074), you must obtain a copy from Microsoft. In the New Virtual Machine wizard, make sure you allocate a minimum of 512 MB of memory to this virtual machine. The more memory you can allocate the better performance you will have when you are running Longhorn. Other than choosing a **10 GB** disk partition, you can accept the remaining defaults. Figure 6.25 shows the newly created virtual machine. Next, either place the DVD in the DVD-ROM or edit the virtual machine settings and select **CD-ROM** and choose **ISO image** to load the Longhorn operating system.

FIGURE 6.25   A new Longhorn virtual machine.

The Longhorn Installation Process

When installing Longhorn for the first time, be very patient as this release is still in its early stages. Be prepared to wait at least 75 minutes before you have the product completely up and running. Let's now power on the virtual machine and boot to the Longhorn setup program. The first thing you will see is the Longhorn splash window (see Figure 6.26) followed by the Windows Setup (see Figure 6.27). The installation appears hazy but is readable. When the installation is complete we will install VMware Tools, which will fix the haziness.

FIGURE 6.26   The Longhorn splash window.

FIGURE 6.27   Windows Setup.

If you cannot use the mouse during the installation, please use the keyboard commands.

Next, continue through the install until completion. At times throughout the installation, it seems as if the install is not responding. Please be patient as the install is still recognizing hardware and is working. Once the installation is complete and Longhorn is loaded (see Figure 6.28), we will install VMware Tools to clear up all of the remaining display and networking issues. A more detailed discussion on VMware Tools is available in Chapter 7.

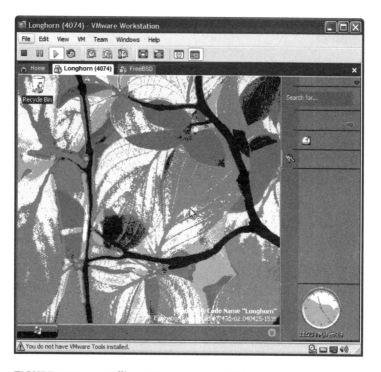

FIGURE 6.28   Installing VMware Tools within Longhorn to correct display issues.

Longhorn uses a new method to install drivers within its operating system. During the installation of VMware Tools, several warning messages appear at different intervals during the installation of the guest operating system. These messages are hidden behind windows and the system might appear to hang. If you press Alt-Tab, you can bring the warning message to the front and continue. You will see the following messages:

■ A message that says the driver is not Authenticode signed. When you see this message, click **Install Now** to continue installing VMware Tools.

■ A message that says the driver package is not compatible with Longhorn. When you see this message, click **Cancel** to continue installing VMware Tools.

■ You might not see any messages at all and the VMware Tools installation will complete without error.

Furthermore, when you choose **VM | Install VMware Tools**, the VMware Tools installer might not automatically start. If it does not start, browse the CD-ROM and run the setup.exe. You might also see a message asking you to restart before the VMware Tools installer has finished. Do not restart the guest operating system until the VMware Tools installation is complete. Figure 6.29 illustrates a successful installation of Longhorn Build 4074.

FIGURE 6.29 Longhorn Build 4074.

Once the installation is complete and Longhorn is loaded, shut down the virtual machine and open the .vmx file and add the following line: `Ethernet.virtualDev = "vmxnet"`. In order to get networking to work with Longhorn, you will have to remove `ethernet0.present = "True"` and replace it with `Ethernet.virtualDev = "vmxnet"` (see Figure 6.30). This will allow networking to run properly. The .vmx file is located in the directory where you created your virtual machine. Now power on your Long-horn virtual machine and when the operating system boots up, the Found New Hardware wizard appears with your Ethernet Controller. The driver is located in the VMware Tools ISO image. You can load the image by choosing **VM | Install VMware Tools** and allowing the Found New Hardware to search the CD-ROM.

FIGURE 6.30 Modifying the .vmx configuration file.

INSTALLING LINUX GUEST OPERATING SYSTEMS

Now that we have gone over some of the caveats of installing Windows operating systems, let's cover some of the gotchas of installing Linux operating systems. We are going to concentrate on the most popular Linux distributions. They are:

- Sun Java Desktop System 2
- SuSE Linux 9.1
- Mandrake Linux 10.0
- Red Hat 9.0

Sun Java Desktop System 2

Installing Sun Java Desktop System 2 is a snap. You can use ISO images or a CD-ROM to install. Once you have the media available, power on the virtual machine and start installing Sun Java Desktop 2 as shown in Figure 6.31. Once the installation is complete, install VMware Tools. For more information on how to install VMware Tools on a Linux platform, refer to Chapter 7.

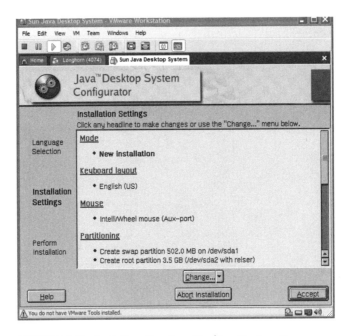

FIGURE 6.31   Installing Sun Java Desktop System 2.

Installing SuSE Linux 9.1

You can install SuSE Linux 9.1 via the DVD-ROM or ISO image. If you are installing via an ISO image, please see the previous section in this chapter on booting from an ISO image. You can download an evaluation edition from *http://www.suse.com.*

Starting Your Virtual Machine

Open **VMware Workstation** from the Start menu and highlight the **SuSE Linux 9.1** virtual machine from your Favorites window. If the Favorites window does not appear, choose **View | Favorites** from the menu. Inside the Favorites window, highlight your virtual machine and click **Start this virtual machine**.

*If your virtual machine does not appear in the Favorites window, choose **File | Open Virtual Machine** and browse to your new virtual machine's .vmx file and choose **Open**. This places a tab in the Control Center with the virtual machine's name. Right-click on the tab and choose **Add to Favorites**. Your virtual machine is now displayed in the Favorites window.*

Next, the Linux operating system boots from the CD-ROM and you have the following choices:

- Boot from hard disk
- Installation
- Installation – ACPI disabled
- Installation – safe settings
- Manual installation
- Rescue system
- Memory test

In order for you to properly install SuSE Linux 9.1, you must choose **F2** (see Figure 6.32) and select **Text Mode** and then choose **Installation** (see Figure 6.33) and follow the text installer through to completion as if you were installing the operating system on a physical machine. Figure 6.34 displays a SuSe Linux installation completed, with user login. Installing VMware Tools on a Linux and on a Windows guest operating system is discussed in Chapter 7.

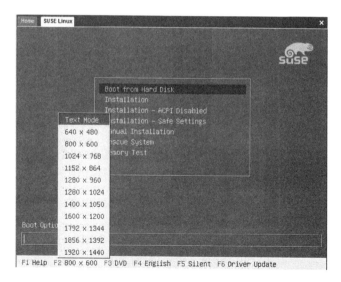

FIGURE 6.32 Installing SuSE 9.1 via text mode.

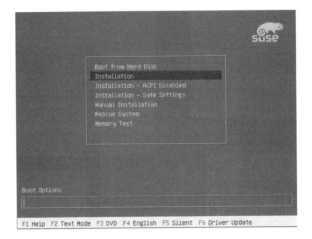

FIGURE 6.33 Selecting Installation for a successful SuSE 9.1 install.

FIGURE 6.34 The SuSE 9.1 desktop.

Installing Red Hat Linux 9.0 and Mandrake Linux 10.0

You can install Red Hat Linux 9.0/Mandrake Linux via the CD-ROM or ISO image. If you are installing via an ISO image, please see the previous section in this chapter on booting from an ISO image.

Starting Your Virtual Machine

Open **VMware Workstation** from the Start menu and highlight the **RedHat/Mandrake Linux** virtual machine from your Favorites window. If the Favorites window does not appear, choose **View | Favorites** from the menu. Inside the Favorites window, highlight your virtual machine and click **Start this virtual machine**. At this point, you can install RedHat/Mandrake Linux as if you were installing it on a physical machine. Figure 6.35 displays a Red Hat Linux installation completed, with user login, and Figure 6.36 displays a Mandrake Linux installation completed, with user login. For more information on how to install other operating systems, please visit VMware's Web site at *http://www.VMware.com/support/guestnotes/doc/index.html* or from the Help menu (Help | Guest Operating System Install Guide).

In many cases Workstation 5 requires you to install Linux guest operating systems via the text-mode installer. You can experiment with the graphical and text mode installer, as some distributions work just fine via the graphical installation.

FIGURE 6.35 The Red Hat Linux desktop.

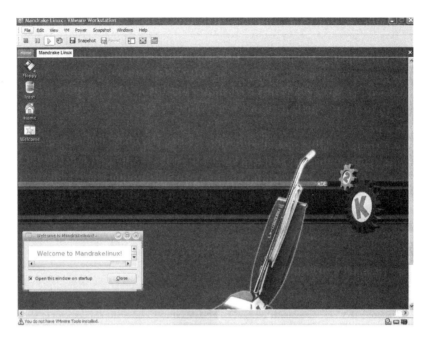

FIGURE 6.36 The Mandrake Linux desktop.

Now that we have exposed you to creating virtual machines in VMware Work-station, let's drive the concepts home by teaching you how to install the VMware Tools on both a Windows and a Linux platform.

7 Installing VMware Tools

In This Chapter

- Installing VMware Tools for Windows Guest Operating Systems
- VMware Tools Configuration Options
- Installing VMware Tools for Linux

Now that you have learned how to install guest operating systems on the Windows and Linux platforms, you are ready to install VMware Tools. We will break this chapter into two sections: VMware Tools for Windows and VMware Tools for Linux. At the end of the chapter you will be able to successfully load VMware Tools.

INSTALLING VMWARE TOOLS FOR WINDOWS GUEST OPERATING SYSTEMS

Currently VMware Tools for Windows supports the following guest operating systems: Windows XP, Windows 2000 Professional, Windows 95, Windows 98, Windows ME, Windows NT 4.0, Windows 2000 Server, and Windows 2003 Server.

It is recommended that you are logged in as an Administrator prior to installing VMware Tools.

The installation of VMware Tools is a straightforward process. Once you have installed your virtual machine, you simply choose **VM | Install VMware Tools** from the Control Center menu bar.

Prior to VMware Tools being installed, a message box appears that states the following: "Installing VMware Tools package will greatly enhance graphics and mouse performance in your virtual machine..." Click **Install** to begin VMware Tools installation.

Once you have selected the option, the VMware Tools ISO file is loaded automatically as your CD-ROM and the installer kicks off. If the installer does not automatically start, browse to the CD-ROM in Explorer and double-click the **VMware Tools** icon as shown in Figure 7.1.

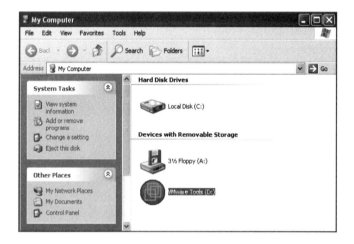

FIGURE 7.1 Double-click VMware Tools CD-ROM icon to begin VMware Tools installation.

Next, you are introduced to the Welcome window. The wizard asks you if you want to choose a **Typical**, **Complete**, or **Custom** installation and then prompts you to click **Install**, as shown in Figure 7.2. Throughout the installation you might be prompted with dialog boxes that state the software you are installing has not passed the Windows Logo testing. Click **Continue Anyway**, as shown in Figure 7.3. At the completion of VMware Tools installation, you will be prompted to reboot your computer.

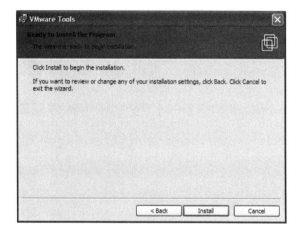

FIGURE 7.2   Click Install to install VMware Tools.

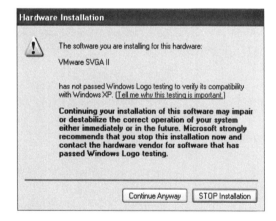

FIGURE 7.3   Select Continue Anyway to install
VMware Tools.

*The ISO files for VMware Tools are located in \Program Files\VMware\VMware
Workstation directory.*

VMWARE TOOLS CONFIGURATION OPTIONS

Once you have installed VMware Tools, you can verify that it has been installed because the VMware Tools icon will show up in the system tray in the form of the VMware logo (see Figure 7.4). In order to remove the VMware Tools icon from the system tray, right-click on the **VMware Tools** icon and choose **Disable Icon**. Additionally, in order to view the VMware configuration options, right-click on the **VMware Tools** icon and choose **Open VMware Tools**, or use your mouse to navigate to **Start | Control Panel | VMware Tools** (see Figure 7.5).

FIGURE 7.4 VMware Tools icon in the system tray.

FIGURE 7.5 VMware Tools properties.

The VMware Tools feature set includes the ability to configure shared folders, shrink a virtual hard drive, and perform time synchronization between the host operating system and the guest operating system. Additionally, you can drag and drop files using your mouse. The Properties window has the following six tabs:

■ **Options:** This checks whether the guest operating system time is lagging behind the host operating system time. Basically, it keeps the time on the virtual machine and the time on the host in synchronization.

- **Devices:** When the flag is turned on or enabled, these devices appear in the taskbar.
- **Scripts:** This tab helps when you want to automate guest operating system operations associated with the virtual machine's power state.
- **Shared Folders:** VMware Workstation has a unique way of handling shared folders from the host to the guest operating system. For more information refer to Chapter 16.
- **Shrink:** Shrinking a virtual disk reclaims unused space in the virtual disk.
- **About:** The About tab provides the copyright and build information for the version of VMware Tools installed in the guest.

INSTALLING VMWARE TOOLS FOR LINUX

VMware Tools installation for Linux is a bit more complicated than installing VMware Tools for Windows. To make this process as simple as possible, we are going to walk you through the steps of installing VMware Tools on a Linux platform. With this release, you now have the choice of installing VMware Tools with the RPM or tar.gz package. Furthermore, you no longer have to exit the X session to install VMware Tools. Let's start by going over the installation with the tar.gz installer.

Installing VMware Tools via the tar.gz Installer

Let's begin choosing **VM | Install VMware Tools**. The RPM and tar.gz packages are automatically mounted as shown in Figure 7.6. Next, open a terminal session, log in as root and copy the package to the temp directory. Figure 7.7 illustrates the commands for these steps.

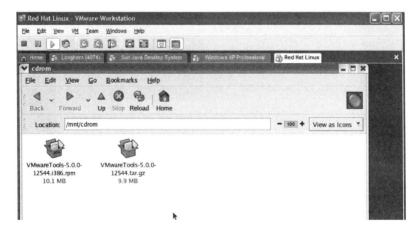

FIGURE 7.6 Mounting VMware Tools ISO.

```
swarren@LINUX:/mnt/cdrom                                    _ □ ✕
File   Edit   View   Terminal   Go   Help
[swarren@LINUX swarren]$ su
Password:
[root@LINUX swarren]# cd /mnt/cdrom
[root@LINUX cdrom]# dir
VMwareTools-5.0.0-13124.i386.rpm  VMwareTools-5.0.0-13124.tar.gz
[root@LINUX cdrom]# cp VMwareTools-5.0.0-13124.tar.gz /tmp
[root@LINUX cdrom]# ▮
```

FIGURE 7.7   Copying VMware Tools tar.gz package to the tmp directory.

Next, let's change directories to the tmp directory and extract the package as shown in Figure 7.8. The final step is to run the vmware-install.pl, as shown in Figure 7.9, to install VMware Tools and choose the appropriate display resolution.

It is best to unmount the ISO image before running the Tar installer.

```
swarren@LINUX:/tmp                                          _ □ ✕
File   Edit   View   Terminal   Go   Help
[swarren@LINUX swarren]$ su
Password:
[root@LINUX swarren]# cd /tmp
[root@LINUX tmp]# dir
orbit-root  orbit-swarren  ssh-XXbF8Gmq  VMwareTools-5.0.0-13124.tar.gz
[root@LINUX tmp]# tar zxf VMwareTools-5.0.0-13124.tar.gz
[root@LINUX tmp]#
```

FIGURE 7.8   Extracting the VMwareTools tar.gz package.

```
orbit-swarren  ssh-XXwMvKIU  vmware-tools-distrib
[root@localhost tmp]# cd vmware-tools-distrib
[root@localhost vmware-tools-distrib]# dir
bin  doc  etc  FILES  INSTALL  installer  lib  sbin  vmware-install.pl
[root@localhost vmware-tools-distrib]# ./vmware-install.pl▮
```

FIGURE 7.9   Executing the vmware-install.pl script.

To begin the installation, type the command ./vmware-install.pl. You are prompted with the following questions, in which you can accept the default values:

```
In which directory do you want to install the binary files? [/usr/bin].
What is the directory that contains the init directories (rc0.d/ to
rc6.d/)? [/etc/rc.d]
What is the directory that contains the init scripts?
[/etc/rc.d/init.d]
In which directory do you want to install the daemon files? [/usr/sbin]
In which directory do you want to install the library files?
[/usr/lib/vmware-tools]
The path "/usr/lib/vmware-tools" does not exist currently. This program
is going to create it, including needed parent directories. Is this
what you want? [yes]
In which directory do you want to install the documentation files?
[/usr/share/doc/vmware-tools]
The path "/usr/share/doc/vmware-tools" does not exist currently. This
program is going to create it, including needed parent directories. Is
this what you want? [yes]
Unmounting The Tools ISO image mnt/cdrom. The installation of VMware
Tools 4.52 build 8848 for Linux completed successfully. You can decide
to remove this software from your system at any time by invoking the
following command: "/usr/bin/vmware-uninstall-tools.pl."
Before running VMware Tools for the first time, you need to configure
it by invoking the following command: "/usr/bin/vmware-config-
tools.pl." Do you want this program to invoke the command for you now?
[Yes]
When you press the Enter key, you are asked to choose your display
size. You have the following choices:
```

- 640×480
- 800×600
- 1024×768
- 1152×864
- 1152×900
- 1280×1024
- 1376×1032
- 1600×1200
- 2364×1773

After you choose your resolution, VMware Tools services is started in your virtual machine and the configuration is complete. Reboot your computer and once you are logged back into Linux, open a terminal and type `/usr/bin/vmware-toolbox` to see the VMware Tools options as shown in Figure 7.10.

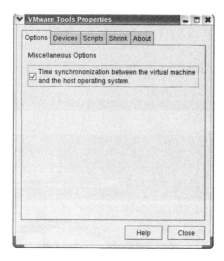

FIGURE 7.10   The VMware Toolbox.

Installing VMware Tools via the RPM Installer

The RPM installer is much easier and preferable. You can either double-click to install the package or run it from the terminal. If you run it from the terminal, make sure you are logged in as root, and type the following command:

```
rpm -Uhv VMwareTools-5.0-13124.i386.rpm
```

Now type `cd /usr/bin` to browse to the vmware-config-tools.pl. The syntax is as follows:

```
/usr/bin/vmware-config-tools.pl.
```

Next, choose your resolution and reboot your virtual machine. Your virtual machine will now be updated to the appropriate resolution. At any point if you want to bring up VMware Tools options, simply open a terminal, log in as root, and type: `/usr/bin/vmware-toolbox`.

In our next chapter, we are going to talk about snapshots, one of the coolest features of VMware Workstation 5. You now have the ability to take multiple snapshots of a virtual machine instead of a single snapshot.

8 Managing and Working with Snapshots

In This Chapter

- Definition of a Snapshot
- Using Snapshots as Restore Points
- Using Snapshots in a Tree Structure
- Creating Your First Snapshot
- Working with Snapshot Settings

One of the great features of VMware Workstation is the ability to take snapshots of your virtual machines at any point in time. Previous to VMware Workstation 5, you were allowed to take only one snapshot per virtual machine. VMware Workstation 5 offers you the ability to take multiple snapshots and manage them with the Snapshot Manager. This adds a whole new layer to your testing and installations. You can create snapshots with specific service packs installed. For example, you might have two snapshots for your Windows XP virtual machines, one with a baseline for service pack 1 and one with a baseline for service pack 2. Furthermore, you might have test plans for training that have 10 snapshots,with each snapshot representing part of the lesson. The functionality this presents can be used in a vast number of ways, depending on your needs.

In addition to taking multiple snapshots, you also have the ability to suspend and resume the state of your virtual machine with VMware Workstation 5. This is very helpful when you want to save the current state of your virtual machine and re-sume at a later date to continue your installation and/or testing. If you have worked before with any release of VMware Workstation, you will notice the increase in speed of the suspend/resume feature. You can suspend or resume and take snap-shots of virtual machines in seconds. For more information on the suspend/resume feature, see Chapter 16.

In this chapter, we are going to provide a definition of what a snapshot is and walk you through some of the functionality that multiple snapshots and Snapshot Manager have to offer. By the end of the chapter, you should feel very comfortable working with snapshots.

DEFINITION OF A SNAPSHOT

When you decide to take a snapshot or "picture" of your virtual machine, the mem-ory, settings, and virtual disk are captured and frozen in time at that specific mo-ment. At any time, you can revert back to that original configuration, losing all changes you made since that snapshot was taken. This is very helpful when you want test specific scenarios over and over again without having to reinstall the op-erating system. Currently, when you take a snapshot, the snapshot is saved in the directory where the virtual machine was created using the wizard.

Now that you have the ability to take multiple snapshots, you can save snap-shots in a linear or treelike structure. Let's go over this in more detail.

USING SNAPSHOTS AS RESTORE POINTS

Let's suppose you are a classroom instructor teaching a Windows 2003 Server course. Each chapter lesson plan contains a specific configuration that you want your students to have in order for the lesson to be effective. You have each student running VMware Workstation 5 in the classroom. By creating snapshots in a linear fashion, you can have each lesson preloaded with the correct configuration. This is an extremely effective way of saving time and effort when you create classroom scenarios. Figure 8.1 shows visually what this might look like in VMware Worksta-tion 5. The lesson plan starts off with a Base Installation of Windows ME.

 When using snapshots as restore points, you can go to any of the lesson plans but you cannot restore to the label Windows ME, as this is simply the name of the vir-tual machine.

NOTE

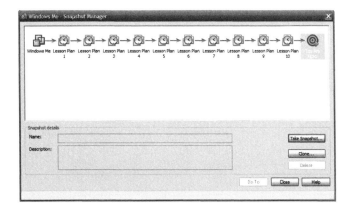

FIGURE 8.1 A visual interpretation of the linear process using the Snapshot Manager.

USING SNAPSHOTS IN A TREE STRUCTURE

Now, let's suppose you work in the Quality Assurance (QA) department for swTechworks Company and your primary job is to test its Web application. With VMware Workstation 5, you can create a treelike testing plan with snapshots as shown in Figure 8.2.

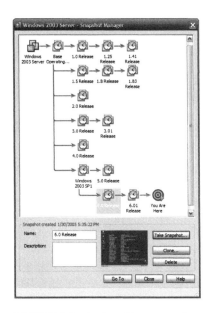

FIGURE 8.2 A visual interpretation of the tree structure in the Snapshot Manager.

CREATING YOUR FIRST SNAPSHOT

Now that we have gone over how snapshots work, let's create our first snapshot by choosing **VM | Snapshot | Take Snapshot**. You can also click the **Take Snapshot** button as shown in Figure 8.3 to take a snapshot of this virtual machine. Once the snapshot is complete, choose **Snapshot | Snapshot Manager** to manage your snapshots. For a detailed description of the toolbar, refer to Chapter 3.

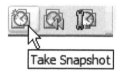

FIGURE 8.3 The Snapshot toolbar.

Using the Snapshot Manager

The Snapshot Manager lets you manage and review all of the snapshots for a particular virtual machine.

With the Snapshot Manager, you can take, clone, and delete snapshots (and delete their children), as well as edit snapshot names and descriptions. Let's take a look first at deleting a snapshot.

Delete a Snapshot

You can delete a snapshot from the Snapshot Manager by highlighting the snapshot and clicking the **Delete** button (see Figure 8.4). You will be prompted with a dialog box asking you if you are sure you want to delete this snapshot. Choose **Yes** and the snapshot is permanently deleted. Another method of deleting a snapshot is to right-click on the snapshot you want to delete as shown in Figure 8.5. Not only can you delete the snapshot but you can also delete all of its children. For example, If you right-click on the **Clean OS** snapshot, and choose **Delete Snapshot and Children**, all of the snapshots will be deleted.

Clone a Snapshot

You can create a linked clone or a full clone of a snapshot. To do this, you must be active on the snapshot you want to clone and the virtual machine must be powered off when the snapshot takes place. If you take a snapshot when the virtual machine

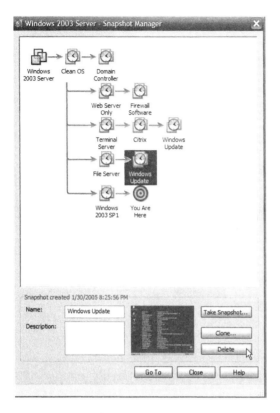

FIGURE 8.4 Deleting a snapshot.

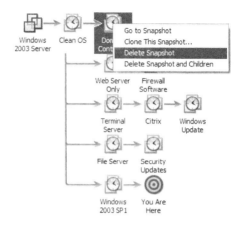

FIGURE 8.5 Right-click to delete a snapshot.

is powered on, you will not be able to clone the snapshot. To test this, take a snapshot with the virtual machine powered on or running. Next, right-click and choose **Clone This Snapshot**. You will get a a message saying that you cannot make a clone of a virtual machine or snapshot that is powered on or suspended (as shown in Figure 8.6).

In order to correctly clone a snapshot, prepare your virtual machine and then power it off. Now take your snapshot while the virtual machine is powered off. Inside Snapshot Manager, right-click on the snapshot you just took and choose **Clone This Snapshot…** or click the **Clone** button. The Clone Virtual Machine wizard appears and allows you to choose a clone source from the current state or from a snapshot. If you have multiple snapshots, click on the applicable snapshot, as shown in Figure 8.7. At this point you can either create a linked clone or a full clone. For more information on cloning a virtual machine, see Chapter 9.

FIGURE 8.6 You cannot clone a snapshot that is powered on.

FIGURE 8.7 Choose a snapshot to clone.

Go To Snapshot

When you right-click on a snapshot and choose **Go To Snapshot**, it takes you to that snapshot. You can also just double-click the snapshot. This functionality makes it very easy to maneuver between multiple snapshots.

Edit a Snapshot Name and Description

You can edit the name and the description of a snapshot by highlighting the snapshot and changing them. Figure 8.8 illustrates where you can edit the name and description.

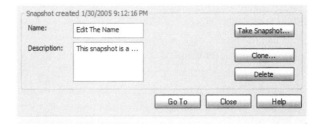

FIGURE 8.8 Editing the name and description of a snapshot.

Revert Versus Go To a Snapshot

When working with Snapshots, it is important to understand the difference between **Revert** and **Go To Snapshot**. Simply stated, **Revert** reverts to the parent snapshot of the current running state, whereas **Go To Snapshot** allows you to go to any snapshot you desire. Inside Snapshot Manager, you will always know where you are by the You are Here icon (see Figure 8.9). When you click the **Revert** button (see Figure 8.10), you are always taken to the immediate left of the You Are Here icon in Snapshot Manager. VMware makes it even easier, because when you click on the **Revert** button, you are told what snapshot you are reverting to, as shown in Figure 8.11.

FIGURE 8.9 The You are Here icon tells your current location in Snapshot Manager.

FIGURE 8.10 When you revert to a previous snapshot, you are always taking its parent (immediate left) snapshot.

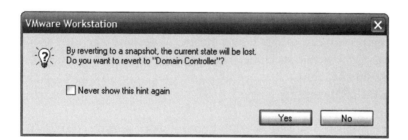

FIGURE 8.11 You will always know what snapshot you are reverting to by reading the informative message.

WORKING WITH SNAPSHOT SETTINGS

You can globally configure the options for snapshots per virtual machine. Highlight the virtual machine of your choice from the Favorites window, and edit the virtual machine setting from the VMware Control Center. On the Virtual Machine Settings window, select the **Options** tab and highlight **Snapshots,** as shown in Figure 8.12.

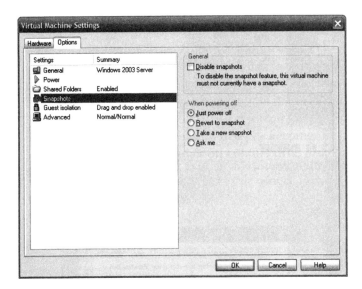

FIGURE 8.12 Configuring the snapshot options.

On this window, you can disable snapshots to increase performance of your virtual machines. You cannot disable snapshots if you have snapshots configured on a virtual machine. Remove the snapshots and then disable. Disabling snapshots is useful if you do not use them or you are looking for a slight performance gain. Furthermore, you can specify how VMware Workstation handles snapshots when you power off a virtual machine. These actions will occur whether you power off your computer via the toolbar or shut down your computer. You can have VMware perform the following:

- Just power off: VMware Workstation simply powers off the virtual machine.
- Revert to snapshot: VMware Workstation reverts to the virtual machine's previous state when the virtual machine is powered off or shut down.
- Take a new snapshot: When the machine is powered off or shut down, VMware Workstation takes a new snapshot of the virtual machine.
- "Ask me": With this option, you are presented with the choice. (This is clearly advantageous.) Figure 8.13 illustrates the message box you will see.

Snapshots in VMware Workstation 5 have been enhanced to allow the end user to have more power at their fingertips. Being able to produce multiple snapshots at any point in time gives you the power to bring your testing, training, and development virtual scenarios to life. In our next chapter, we will introduce clones, another new feature included with VMware Workstation 5.

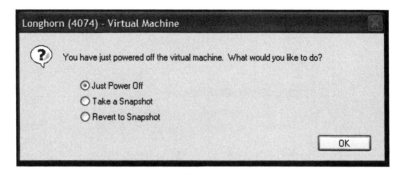

FIGURE 8.13   Choose whether you want the virtual machine to just power off, take a snapshot, or revert to snapshot.

9 Cloning a VMware Workstation Virtual Machine

In This Chapter

■ Creating a Full Clone
■ Creating a Linked Clone

Deploying virtual machines in VMware Workstation 5 has changed since previous releases. In the past, you would configure a virtual machine for each operating system and run the Sysprep utility to prepare it for imaging and duplication. At that point, every time you wanted to test a specific scenario, you would have to browse to your file server and copy down the virtual machine from the network. This process is very lengthy and can become quite tiresome when you need to test or re-create a system quickly. With the release of VMware Workstation 5, you can deploy virtual machines quickly by taking advantage of linked clones.

With the release of VMware Workstation 5, you can clone virtual machines in two ways: full clone and linked clone. If you configure your virtual machines on a file server or shared storage connected to the network, you can create a virtual machine in no time by creating a linked clone of the virtual machine. This is a faster method than copying down a virtual machine from the file server that had Sysprep applied. Once the linked clone is complete, any changes that are made to the linked clone are stored locally. For example, if you are working on a support call and you have to create an environment to test the error, you can create a linked clone very quickly to test the configuration. If you can't solve the problem, you can have the next level of support clone the same virtual machine from the file server or shared storage. Then you can send in your changes and they can apply them and continue where you left off.

Now if you want an exact copy of a virtual machine, VMware Workstation 5 can provide it in the form of a full clone. A full clone is a complete copy of the original virtual machine at its current point in time. The full clone is completely independent and has no links or reference points. The only drawback is that a full clone takes longer to complete and takes up more disk space. Let's move forward and create clones.

CREATING A FULL CLONE

To begin, highlight the applicable virtual machine you want to clone. In most scenarios, you would open a virtual machine from the network shared storage and then select **Clone this virtual machine** from the VMware Control Center, or choose **VM | Clone this virtual machine**. It is important to note that you cannot create a clone from a virtual machine that is powered on or currently suspended. Power off the virtual machine as if you were turning off a physical computer. Now you are ready to run the clone wizard. Figure 9.1 displays the Welcome to the Clone Virtual Machine wizard.

FIGURE 9.1 The Clone Virtual Machine wizard.

The clone source window allows you to clone a virtual machine (see Figure 9.2) from the current state or any applicable snapshot. For more information on cloning snapshots, refer to Chapter 8.

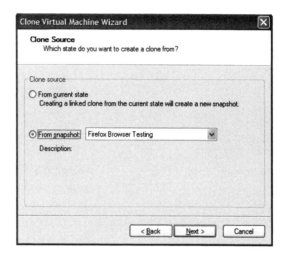

FIGURE 9.2   Choose the applicable state of your virtual machine.

On the Clone Type window (see Figure 9.3) choose from the following two choices:

- **Create a linked clone:**   A linked clone references the original virtual machine and requires less disk space. If the linked clone cannot access the original virtual machine it is linked to, it will fail.
- **Create a full clone:**   This method produces an identical copy of the virtual machine in its current state and requires more disk space to store the files. In our first example, we will create a full clone of a Windows 2003 Domain Controller.

To make a full clone, enter the name and location of the clone as shown in Figure 9.4. Click **Finish** to begin cloning the virtual machine. A progress bar indicator will track the progress of the full clone. The time it takes to complete depends on the size of the virtual machine at the time of cloning. The **Done** button will become enabled when the full clone process finishes. Click **Done** to exit the wizard.

If you are going to use both the cloned virtual machine and the original virtual machine on the same network and they have the same computer name and static IP address, you should change the computer name and IP address of the cloned virtual machine. If you are using DHCP, change the computer name only.

FIGURE 9.3 Choose a linked clone or full clone.

FIGURE 9.4 Choose the location of the full clone.

CREATING A LINKED CLONE

What is great about linked clones is that you can set up a file server with all of your operating systems such as Windows 2000, Windows 2003, Windows XP, SuSE 9.2, Sun Java Desktop System, Windows 98, etc. and lock them down as templates by enabling the template mode feature. When a linked clone of a virtual machine is created, the linked clone depends primarily on the parent virtual machine in order to function. If a linked clone can't find the parent virtual machine or the snapshot on which the linked clone was created, the clone breaks. This can be avoided by enabling the template mode. In general, to clone a virtual machine, you need to have write access to the virtual machine. However, if you designate a virtual machine in template mode, you do not need to have write access to the virtual machine to clone it.

Defining a virtual machine as a template takes just a few clicks. Simply highlight the applicable virtual machine from the Favorites window and select **Edit virtual machine settings** in the VMware Control Center. Now choose the **Options** tab and select **Advanced**. In the Settings box, select **Enable Template mode** (to be used for cloning) as shown in Figure 9.5. When you enable template mode, you are also protecting the parent virtual machine from being added to a team and preventing snapshots on the virtual machine from being deleted.

Now that the template is configured, you must take a snapshot of the system as it stands at that moment in time. If you do not create a snapshot, you will not be able to clone the machine. When you configure a virtual machine in template mode, you can clone only from an existing snapshot.

A best practice would be to create all of your virtual machines on a file server, SAN, or some type of storage device and then enable template mode. This would keep administration at a minimum.

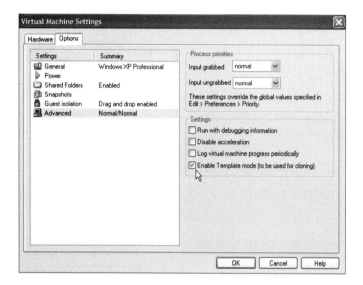

FIGURE 9.5   Enabling template mode.

Let's create a linked clone. In this example, we have a file server with two virtual machines configured (Windows 2003 and Windows XP Professional) and have enabled template mode. The file server has NTFS permissions on the file share, and access over the network to the share is not a problem. Let's begin.

On your workstation, start VMware Workstation 5 and choose **File | Open** and browse to the network share. Browse to the applicable virtual machine's .vmx file and click **Open**. The virtual machine will open in the Control Center as shown in Figure 9.6. You can see the configuration path of the virtual machine in the details.

Now that you have the template virtual machine opened, choose **Clone this virtual machine** in the Control Center. On the Clone Source window, select the snapshot (see Figure 9.7) that you want to link to and choose **Next**. On the Clone Type window, choose **Create a linked clone** and continue through the wizard and enter the location of your linked clone. Whenever you link to clones, you might place them in a folder called Clones to keep all your virtual machines organized. Finally, click **Done** and the linked clone is created as shown in Figure 9.8. Amazing isn't it? Figure 9.9 illustrates the details of the linked clone in the Control Center.

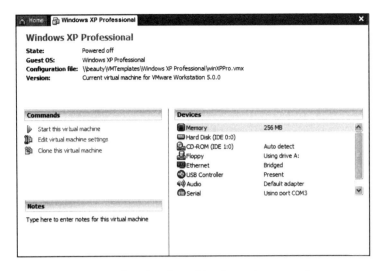

FIGURE 9.6   Open the virtual machine from the network.

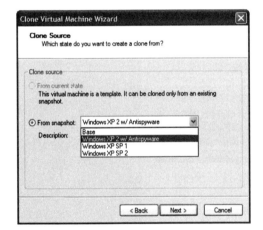

FIGURE 9.7   Choose the applicable snapshot.

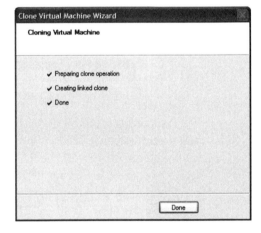

FIGURE 9.8   The linked clone process.

Now we have a linked clone configured, but what happens if you move the linked virtual machine or remove the shared access? Let's test it out, renaming the .vmx file. If the linked clone cannot find the .vmx file on the network, an error message appears as in Figure 9.10.

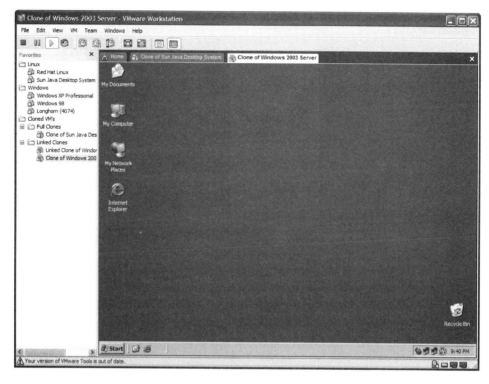

FIGURE 9.9 A properly configured clone.

FIGURE 9.10 .Vmx file not found error.

You should now be very comfortable cloning virtual machines to meet your needs. Let's take some time to practice working with clones before we move on to leveraging teams in VMware Workstation. Of course, if you just can't wait, let's move on.

10 Working with Teams

In This Chapter

- What Are Teams?
- About Teams
- Working with the Team Settings
- About Team Console

WHAT ARE TEAMS?

Teams are a new feature in VMware Workstation 5. With teams you can configure a whole virtual lab on one host computer that allows you to power on all virtual machines within the team. For example, if you configure a clustered environment, you can call the team Windows 2000 Cluster and add all the virtual machines associated with the cluster. Figure 10.1 shows you an example of a team in the VMware Control Center.

What makes a team different from a regular virtual machine is the team's ability to communicate within a private network called a LAN segment. LAN segments are invisible to the host computer's network. With LAN segments you can create a

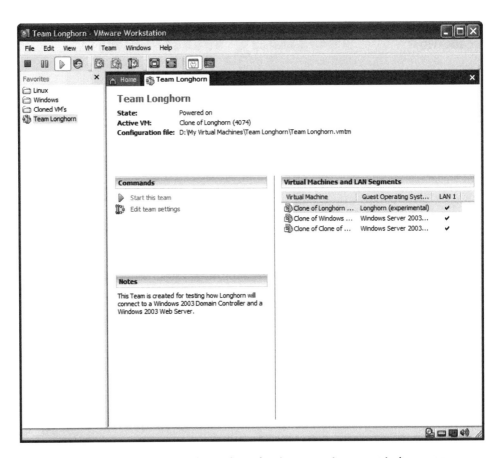

FIGURE 10.1   This team is a Longhorn client that is connecting to a Windows 2003 domain controller.

DMZ or proxy server to bridge the team members to the outside network, allow specific requirements and settings to certain virtual machines within the newly configured team, and control the traffic between the host and team virtual machines. Figure 10.2 shows an example of a LAN segment.

Now that we have given you a brief overview, let's proceed with how to create a Team and add virtual machines to the team.

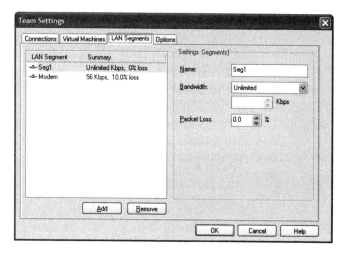

FIGURE 10.2   Creating a LAN segment.

ABOUT TEAMS

In this section, we will describe how to perform the following:

- Create a team
- Delete a team
- Power on a team
- Power off a team
- Open and close a team
- Suspend/resume a team
- Use team snapshots

Create a Team

Creating a team in VMware Workstation 5 can be done by opening VMware Workstation 5 from the Start menu. You can create a new team by going to the Home Tab in the VMware Control Center and choosing the **New Team** button or by right-clicking on the **Favorites window** and choosing **New | Team,** as shown in Figure 10.3.

If the Home tab does not display in the VMware Control Center, select View | Go To Home Tab to have the VMware Control Center home page reappear.

NOTE

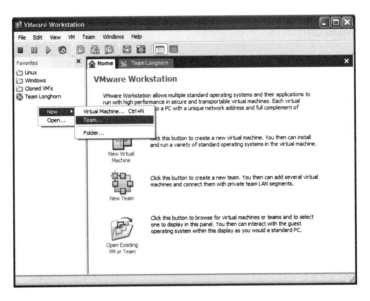

FIGURE 10.3   Creating a new team.

After you choose to create a new team, the New Team wizard window appears (see Figure 10.4) to walk you through the creation of a new team.

FIGURE 10.4   The New Team wizard.

On the Name the Team window (see Figure 10.5), enter the team name and location of a new team. You can browse to a location or type the location.

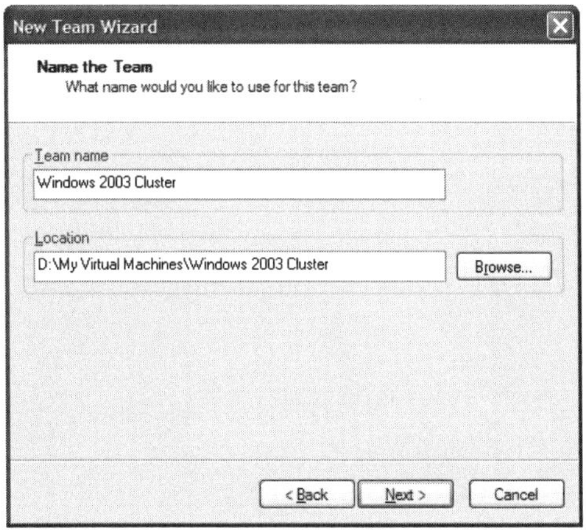

FIGURE 10.5 Naming the team.

The Add Virtual Machines to the Team window (see Figure 10.6) allows you to add virtual machines you have already created to the team, or you can choose to add virtual machines later if you have not created them yet. For purposes of this exercise, we will choose to add virtual machines. The next window (see Figure 10.7) allows you to add a new or existing virtual machine in addition to a new clone of a virtual machine.

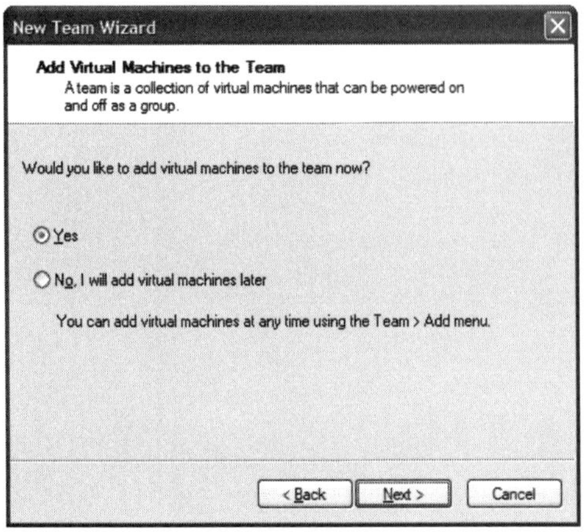

FIGURE 10.6 Adding virtual machines to a team.

FIGURE 10.7 Adding virtual machines to your team.

The Add LAN Segments to the Team window (see Figure 10.8) allows you to add a LAN segment now or at a later time. Let's add a LAN segment now by choosing **Yes**. Click **Add** to add the number of LAN segments that are applicable to the individual needs of your team, as shown in Figure 10.9. The final phase of the wizard allows you to review your options. Click **Finish** to create your new team. The new team is shown in Figure 10.10.

FIGURE 10.8 Do you want to add LAN segments now or later?

FIGURE 10.9 You can decide how many LAN segments you want to create.

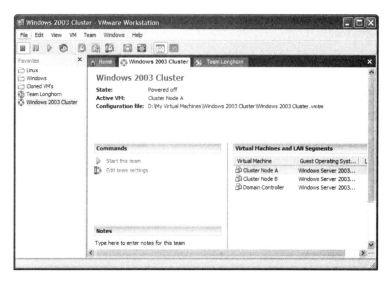

FIGURE 10.10 A Windows 2003 cluster in a team.

Delete a Team

You can delete a team from the disk by selecting the team you want to delete from the Favorites window and choosing **Team | Delete from Disk**. You are then prompted with a dialog box, as shown in Figure 10.11, asking you if you are sure you want to perform this action. You have the ability to delete the team or delete the team and all virtual machines associated with the team. You can also remove a virtual machine from the team without deleting the virtual machine by choosing **Team | Remove** and selecting the appropriate team to remove.

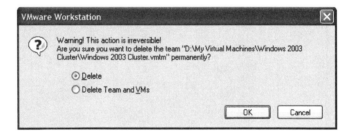

FIGURE 10.11   Deleting a team from disk.

Power On a Team

In order to start a team, simply highlight the applicable team from the Favorites window and choose **Start this team** from the VMware Control Center. You can also choose **Team | Power | Power On** from the menu bar or the **Power On** icon from the toolbar. Figure 10.12 displays a Windows 2003 cluster team prior to starting the team.

Power Off a Team

In order to power off a team, highlight the applicable team from the Favorites window and choose the **Power Off** icon in the toolbar. You can also choose **Team | Power | Power off** from the menu bar. When using teams you have the ability to toggle back and forth between the Control Center and the console by clicking the console and summary buttons from the toolbar. For more information on the toolbar refer to Chapter 3.

Remember that powering off a machine is the same as powering off a physical computer. It is best to shut down the computer rather than power it off. Please see Chapter 3 for a complete description of the user interface.

NOTE

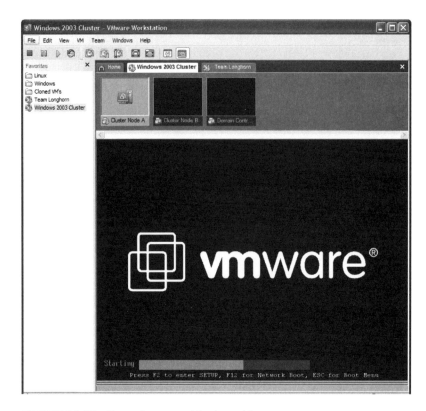

FIGURE 10.12   Powering on a virtual machine.

Open and Close a Team

To open a team, choose **File** | **Open** and browse to the .vmt file for the applicable team. Once you have found the team, as shown in Figure 10.13, click **Open**. The team now appears as a tabbed item in the VMware Control Center and you can right-click on the tab to add the team to your Favorites window.

Suspend/Resume a Team

You can suspend an entire team by simply clicking the **Suspend** button from the toolbar. Once this button is pressed, the entire team suspends simultaneously. Resuming the team is just as easy. Simply click the **Power** button from the toolbar or **Team** | **Power** | **Resume** from the menu bar. Figure 10.14 shows a team that is in a suspended state.

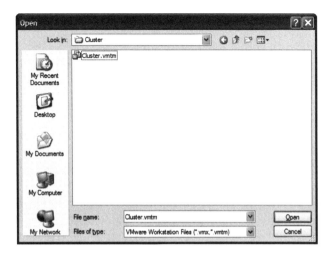

FIGURE 10.13   Opening a team.

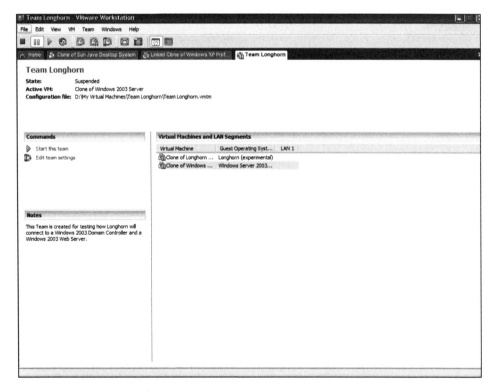

FIGURE 10.14   Suspend an entire team.

Individual Snapshots Within a Team

When you work with a team, snapshots are applied to the individual machine, not the whole team. When you click the **Take Snapshot** toolbar button, you are taking a snapshot of the active virtual machine. For more information on working with snapshots, see Chapter 8.

WORKING WITH THE TEAM SETTINGS

Once you have a team created, you can edit the team settings by highlighting your team and clicking the **Edit Team Settings** link in the VMware Control Center. A Team Settings window appears with the following four tabs:

- Connections
- Virtual Machines
- LAN Segments
- Options

Connections

The Connections tab (see Figure 10.15) allows you to view and add a network adapter to any virtual machine within your team. This is helpful for any custom network configuration you might make. You can change these as applicable. Please see Chapter 12 on networking for a further explanation on how to work with network adapters.

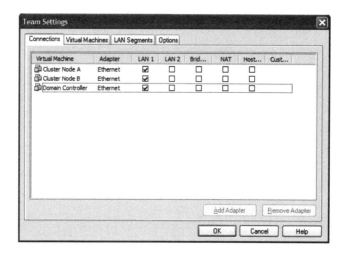

FIGURE 10.15 Assigning network adapters to the applicable LAN segment.

Virtual Machines

The Virtual Machines tab (see Figure 10.16) allows you to add a new virtual machine, an existing virtual machine, or a clone of a virtual machine to your team. When you click **Add | New virtual machine**, the Welcome to the New Virtual Machine wizard appears. When you click **Add | Existing virtual machine**, you can browse to an existing virtual machine and add it to your team. Finally, **Add | New clone of virtual machine** allows you to create a linked or full clone of an existing virtual machine on your network. Please see Chapter 9 for more information on how to configure a linked or full clone of a virtual machine.

Also important is the Startup Details feature, which allows you to configure the delay before each virtual machine in the team powers on. You can specify the number of seconds before each virtual machine starts. Additionally, you can specify the order in which the team virtual machines will start. For example, you might have a domain controller that needs to be running prior to other virtual machines starting. Using the up and down arrows, you make sure the domain controller is at the top of the virtual machine list. The order and delay time is very helpful when you have multitier applications that have many dependencies.

The default delay for all virtual machines in a team is 10 seconds.

NOTE

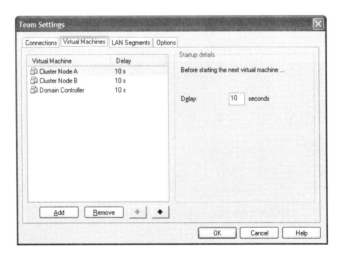

FIGURE 10.16 Assign a boot delay time for each virtual machine in your team.

LAN Segments

The LAN Segments tab (see Figure 10.17) allows you to configure a LAN segment and specify bandwidth and packet loss. This can be very helpful when you are trying to simulate certain environments. You have the ability to configure the following settings:

- **Name:** Enter the name of the LAN segment you are creating. For example, if you are creating a client LAN segment with a dialup modem, call it Modem or Client Modem.
- **Bandwidth:** You can choose the appropriate bandwidth from the drop-down menu as shown in Figure 10.18.
- **KBPS:** You can determine the numeric throughput limit on this field. When you choose the applicable bandwidth, it populates the KPBS, which you can modify.
- **Packet Loss:** This field allows you to specify any percentage of packet loss for testing. You can modify this field as applicable to your specific testing scenario.

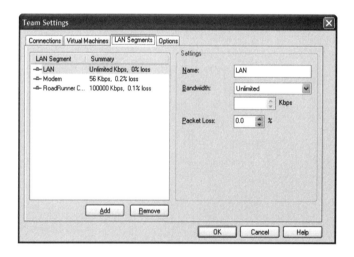

FIGURE 10.17 Editing a LAN segment.

Options

The Options tab (see Figure 10.19) allows you to change the name of the team you created.

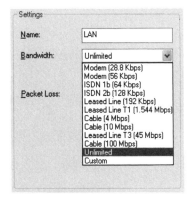

FIGURE 10.18 Choose the bandwidth for your LAN segment.

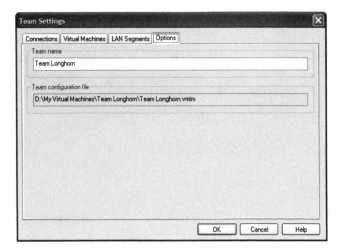

FIGURE 10.19 Changing the team name if applicable.

ABOUT TEAM CONSOLE

The Team Console (see Figure 10.20) consists of three main areas: Favorites window, inactive virtual machines area, and active virtual machines area. Additionally, you have a grab bar that allows you to further size your active/inactive windows. When working with teams, you do not see the team console until you power on the team. Once a team is powered on, you can toggle between the VMware Control Center and the team console by selecting **View | Current View**. Figure 10.21 is what the console of the VMware Control Center looks like when all teams are powered on.

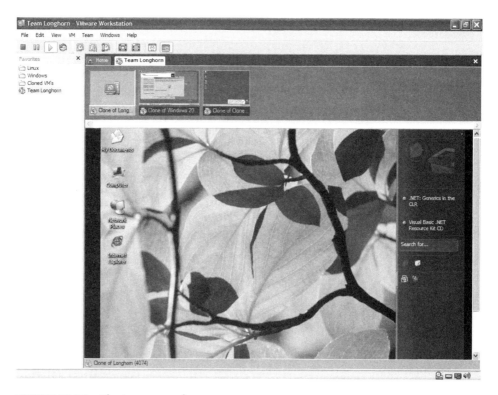

FIGURE 10.20   The team console.

Active Virtual Machine

The active virtual machine is the largest machine in the team console. This virtual machine is located at the bottom of the window and is the only virtual machine that you can work with.

Inactive Virtual Machines

The inactive virtual machines are the row of machines in the team console that appear at the top. To change which virtual machine is active, simply click on one of the smaller inactive virtual machines to make it become active. You can also use the **Team | Switch to** (virtual machine) to perform the same functionality.

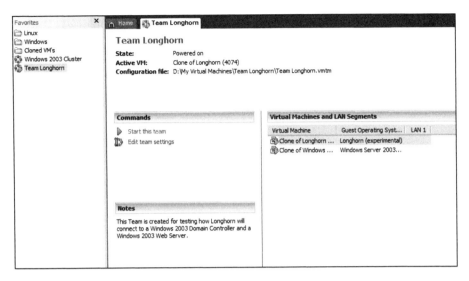

FIGURE 10.21 The team Control Center.

You now have all the information necessary to take off running with teams. You can reinforce these skills by creating many multitier environments and simulating different types of bandwidth and packet loss. In our next chapter we are going to discuss how to secure your virtual machines.

11 Securing VMware Workstation

In This Chapter

- NTFS Security
- About Administrative Lockout
- Graphical User Interface Security

A t times you might need to restrict the VMware Workstation user interface because of a classroom setting, inexperienced users, or multiple users using one Workstation during different shifts. In this chapter, we are going to show you how to secure your VMware Workstation 5 installation.

NTFS SECURITY

A virtual machine in VMware Workstation is basically composed of virtual drives. These virtual drives are just .vmdk files on your operating system hard drives. When you create a VMware Workstation virtual drive, it goes into the default directory that is configured when you install VMware Workstation, for example, my documents\my virtual machines. Thus, your first line of attack is to configure NTFS security on your virtual machine folders.

ABOUT ADMINISTRATIVE LOCKOUT

This feature is a global setting that allows an administrator to set a password for certain global events such as creating new virtual machines, editing virtual machine configurations, and managing virtual networks.

Configuring Administrative Lockout

To begin, open VMware Workstation from the Start menu. From the Control Center, click **Edit | Preferences** from the menu bar and choose the **Lockout** tab as shown in Figure 11.1. Next, select **Enable administrative lockout** and choose the options you want to require a password. When finished click **OK.**

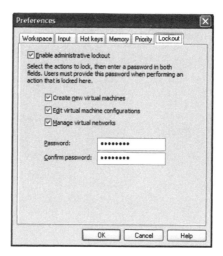

FIGURE 11.1 Enter a password to lock down VMware Workstation globally.

When a user tries to perform one of the global options such as creating a new virtual machine, he will be prompted to enter the password as shown in Figure 11.2. If he types the wrong password or does not have access, he will be told the password is incorrect, as shown in Figure 11.3.

VMware Workstation

VMware Workstation allows multiple standard operating systems and their applications to run with high performance in secure and transportable virtual machines. Each virtual machine is equivalent to a PC with a unique network address and full complement of hardware choices.

New Virtual Machine

Click this button to create a new virtual machine. You then can install and run a variety of standard operating systems in the virtual machine.

New Team

Click this button to create a new team. You then can add several virtual machines and connect them with private team LAN segments.

Open Existing VM or Team

Click this button to browse for virtual machines or teams and to select one to display in this panel. You then can interact with the guest operating system within this display as you would a standard PC.

FIGURE 11.2   Enter the password to create a new virtual machine.

VMware Workstation

VMware Workstation allows multiple standard operating systems and their applications to run with high performance in secure and transportable virtual machines. Each virtual machine is equivalent to a PC with a unique network address and full complement of hardware choices.

New Virtual Machine

Click this button to create a new virtual machine. You then can install and run a variety of standard operating systems in the virtual machine.

New Team

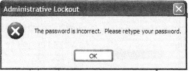

Open Existing VM or Team

operating system within this display as you would a standard PC.

FIGURE 11.3   The administrative lockout window.

Removing a Lost or Forgotten Password

If for some reason you forget or lose the password, VMware Workstation must be uninstalled for you to get access to the functions you locked down. During the uninstall, you are asked if you want to remove the administrative lockout settings. Choose **Yes** to uninstall.

In VMware Workstation 4.x you could do a search for the config.ini, which is located at c:\documents and settings\all users\application data\vmware\vmware workstation. You could see the password by looking at lockout.password. In VMware Workstation 5, the lockout.password is encrypted, as shown in Figure 11.4, so if you have forgotten it, you must reinstall.

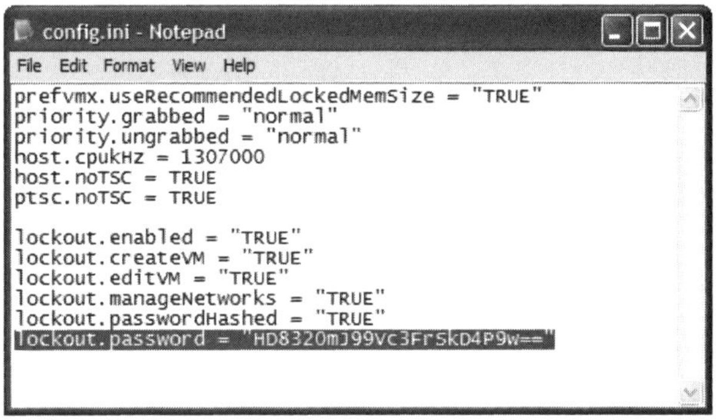

```
config.ini - Notepad
File  Edit  Format  View  Help
prefvmx.useRecommendedLockedMemSize = "TRUE"
priority.grabbed = "normal"
priority.ungrabbed = "normal"
host.cpukHz = 1307000
host.noTSC = TRUE
ptsc.noTSC = TRUE

lockout.enabled = "TRUE"
lockout.createVM = "TRUE"
lockout.editVM = "TRUE"
lockout.manageNetworks = "TRUE"
lockout.passwordHashed = "TRUE"
lockout.password = "HD8320mJ99Vc3FrSkD4P9w=="
```

FIGURE 11.4 The config.ini file.

GRAPHICAL USER INTERFACE SECURITY

Another layer of security you can add affects specific virtual machines. If you add the restricted user interface option to your virtual machines, the following events happen:

- The VMware Workstation toolbar disappears from the Control Center.
- The Power menu is disabled.
- Users have no access to the Control Center.
- Users cannot access virtual network settings.
- The only way a user can start the virtual machine is by double-clicking the *.vmx file.
- When the user has finished working with the virtual machine, he simply clicks File | Close to shut down the virtual machine.

A user must have administrative rights to configure this type of security.

Restricting the User Interface

In order to restrict the user interface, you must first make sure the machine you want to restrict is powered off. Once it is powered off, open the virtual machine's configuration file (.vmx file) in Notepad. You can do this by browsing to the virtual machine directory and right-clicking on the .vmx file and choosing **Open with Notepad,** as shown in Figure 11.5.

FIGURE 11.5   Opening a .vmx file in Notepad.

With the *.vmx file open in Notepad, add the following line in the file: `gui.restricted="TRUE"` as shown in Figure 11.6. It is recommended that you give normal users read-only access to the file so that they can't modify the configuration. Finally, repeat this step and add all of the .vmx shortcuts to the desktop or appropriate place as shown in Figure 11.7.

About Limited Snapshot Control

You can give a user who has a restricted interface the ability to just power off, take a snapshot, or revert to snapshot. This is accomplished by opening the VMware Workstation Control Center (see Figure 11.8) and choosing **VM | Settings | Options | Snapshot | When Powering Off | Ask Me.** Now, when a user chooses **File | Exit,** he is given the choice of powering off, taking a snapshot, or reverting to a snapshot, as shown in Figure 11.9.

```
winXPPro.vmx - Notepad
File  Edit  Format  View  Help
config.version = "7"
virtualHW.version = "3"
scsi0.present = "TRUE"
memsize = "200"
ide0:0.present = "TRUE"
ide0:0.fileName = "Windows XP Professional.vmdk"
gui.restricted="TRUE"
ide1:0.present = "TRUE"
ide1:0.fileName = "Z:"
ide1:0.deviceType = "atapi-cdrom"
floppy0.present = "TRUE"
Ethernet0.present = "TRUE"
sound.present = "FALSE"
sound.fileName = "-1"
displayName = "WorkStation"
guestOS = "winXPPro"
priority.grabbed = "normal"
priority.ungrabbed = "normal"
powerType.powerOff = "default"
powerType.powerOn = "default"
powerType.suspend = "default"
powerType.reset = "default"
```

FIGURE 11.6 Adding the restricted user interface.

FIGURE 11.7 The .vmx shortcut to run restricted virtual machines.

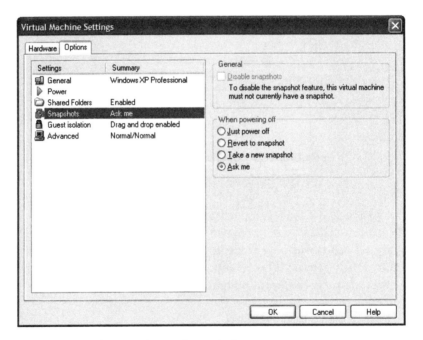

FIGURE 11.8 The snapshot options window.

Automatic Snapshot Return

In some cases you might want to have a restricted user interface combined with a snapshot that returns virtual machines to the same state as that in which they

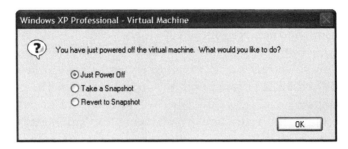

FIGURE 11.9   Power off options.

started. Let's configure this by turning the virtual machine on and preparing the operating system. Once you are finished configuring the operating system, take a snapshot and configure your virtual machine to return to the snapshot whenever it is powered off, as shown in Figure 11.10.

Remember to prepare your virtual machines before restricting the user interface. The previous example should be done before restricting the user interface.

NOTE

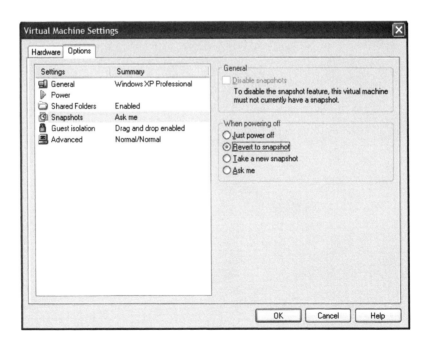

FIGURE 11.10   Choosing the revert to the snapshot option.

Now that you have configured the snapshot, it is time to lock down the interface again. Add `gui.restrictedTRUE"` to the *.vmx file and lock down the configuration file with NTFS permissions. Once the automatic snapshot return has been configured, whenever a user is finished working with the virtual machines, he would choose **File | Close** to exit the virtual machine. The next time he turns the virtual machine on, he is automatically returned to the snapshot. At any point, you can remove the restriction by changing the `gui.restricted="TRUE"` to `gui.restricted="FALSE"`.

This chapter has explained how to lock down your virtual machine with NTFS security. You also learned how to configure some of the advanced security features VMware Workstation has to offer. In the next chapter, we will teach you how to configure virtual networks with VMware Workstation.

12 Networking Virtual Machines

In This Chapter

- About VMware Workstation Networking
- Configuring a Bridged Network
- Configuring a Host-Only Network
- Configuring Network Address Translation
- About Vnetsniffer
- About Virtual MAC Addresses
- Configuring a Custom Virtual Network

One of the great features of VMware is its ability to set up advanced networking with virtual machines. With proper technique, you can access virtual machines from your local area network as well as configure routing between multiple virtual machines. Additionally, you can configure port forwarding to forward packets to a virtual machine Web server. In this chapter, we will discuss how to configure VMware to perform these advanced techniques by starting from the beginning and getting more complex as we dig deeper into the chapter. Let's start by defining VMware Workstation networking terminology.

ABOUT VMWARE WORKSTATION NETWORKING

First, let's go over some of the basic terminology that you will need to become familiar with in order to be successful with this chapter. Within VMware Workstation you have the ability to configure the following virtual networks:

- Bridged networking
- Host only
- Network address translation
- Custom
- Virtual switch
- Bridge
- Host virtual adapter
- DHCP server
- Virtual network adapter

Bridged Networking

When you use bridged networking, your virtual machine is connected to the LAN as if it were a physical PC connected to your network. It can be assigned a DHCP address or a static IP address. You can configure shares on your virtual machine and ping any machine on your LAN, including the host PC. In other words, when you use bridged networking, you are taking a physical network adapter on your host PC and allowing your virtual machines to communicate with the physical network.

Host Only

When you use a host-only network, your virtual machines can communicate with the host PC only. You cannot communicate with any other physical PC on the network. If you want to communicate with other physical computers on your LAN, you can use bridged networking. Host-only adapters are adapters that are visible in the network connections on your host PC but do not have any affiliation with the physical network adapters on your host PC. Figure 12.1 shows the VMware network adapters under the LAN or high-speed Internet category.

Network Address Translation

Any virtual machine that you create will share the IP and MAC address of the host. The host PC and the virtual machine appear as only one computer on your physical network.

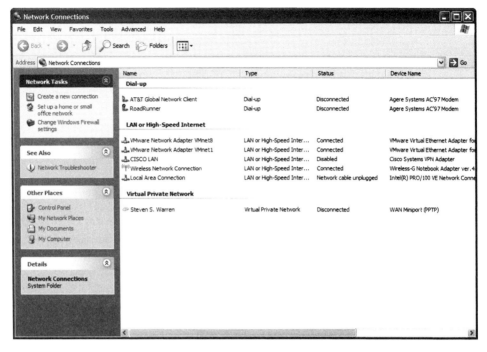

FIGURE 12.1 VMware host adapters.

Custom

A custom network allows you to customize your virtual network to suit your individual needs. This will be discussed in detail later in the chapter.

Virtual Switch

A virtual switch has the same definition and functionality as a physical switch. The virtual switch allows you to connect networking components to each other. In VMware Workstation, you can have up to nine virtual switches in your virtual environment, and you can connect one or more virtual machines to your virtual switch.

Bridge

In VMWare Workstation, the bridge allows you to connect your virtual machine to the host PC and to the local area network (LAN) that your host computer is configured to use.

Host Virtual Adapter

The host virtual adapter allows communication between your host computer and the virtual machine on the host in host-only and NAT configurations. Basically, a host-only adapter is displayed in your Network Connections on the host computer but has no ties or relationship to your physical adapter on the computer installed with VMware Workstation.

The default installation of VMware Workstation installs the host-only adapter on VMnet1.

DHCP Server

The virtual DHCP server provides you with IP addresses for your virtual machines in host-only and NAT environments. If your virtual machine is bridged to an external network, a DHCP server on the network will assign it an IP address, or the virtual machine can be assigned an IP address automatically.

Virtual Network Adapters

Whenever you configure a virtual machine from the wizard, it is automatically configured with one virtual network adapter. In VMware Workstation, you can have up to three virtual network adapters in each virtual machine.

CONFIGURING A BRIDGED NETWORK

A bridged network is the default configuration when you create new virtual machines (see Figure 12.2). It is also one of the easiest ways to configure a virtual machine with Internet access when you're first learning how to use VMware Workstation. It is easy because you are connecting the physical adapter of the host PC to the virtual machine, which allows the virtual machine to connect to the physical network or LAN. For example, if you connect your laptop to your physical network, your specific laptop will get an IP address and show up in Active Directory as a computer on the network. Now, if you install VMware Workstation 5 and create a virtual machine with bridged networking, it is as if you have two computers hooked up to the network. As long as it has a valid IP address on the network, it will also show up in Active Directory. For all intents and purposes, it will act exactly like a physical PC on the LAN. Let's dig a little deeper into what bridged networking looks like.

FIGURE 12.2 Assigning the network connection.

Once VMware Workstation is installed and configured, whatever physical network adapter you had enabled on your PC will be automatically bridged to VMnet0. The default installation of VMware Workstation installs three virtual switches by default: VMnet0, VMnet1, and VMnet8. Let's take a look at how VMware Workstation automatically bridges the physical adapters. Begin by opening VMware Workstation from the Start menu. Next, click **Edit | Virtual Network Settings** as shown in Figure 12.3. The Virtual Network Editor consists of six tabs. In this section we will explain the following tabs:

- Summary
- Automatic Bridging
- Host Virtual Network Mapping

Summary Tab

The Summary tab (see Figure 12.3) displays the active current virtual network switches available. You can view what switches are currently active, a summary of what the switch does, the subnet, and whether DHCP is enabled.

Automatic Bridging

The Automatic Bridging tab (see Figure 12.4) allows you to automatically bridge all network adapters that were enabled at the time of installation. On this tab you have the ability to **Enable Automatic Bridge**, which will automatically choose the available physical network adapter to bridge to VMnet0.

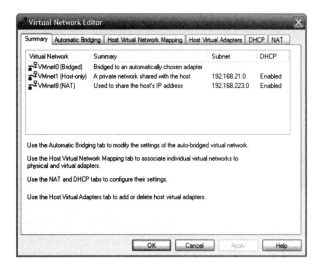

FIGURE 12.3 The Virtual Network Editor window.

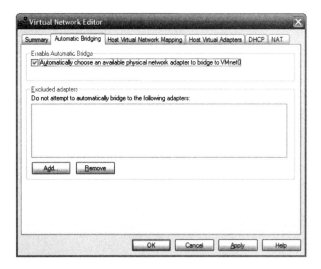

FIGURE 12.4 Enabling automatic bridging.

For example, assume your computer has two network connections: a Wireless G Network Adapter and an Intel PRO/100 VE. If you disable your wireless card, you are hooked up to a LAN, and if you create a virtual machine with bridged networking, it will automatically bridge to the Intel PRO/100 VE, when this option is selected. If you are not hooked into the LAN and you have your wireless network card enabled, it will automatically bridge to your wireless card if you have this option selected. If you have automatic bridging enabled and you want to see which network adapter is enabled, deselect **Enable Automatic Bridge** and click **Apply**. Next, click on the **Summary page** as shown in Figure 12.5, and view which VMnet0 is bridged to on the Summary tab. Additionally, if you want to exclude one of these network adapters from the automatic bridging process, click the **Add** button and choose the appropriate network adapter (see Figure 12.6) that you want to exclude from the automatic bridging process. Figure 12.7 illustrates how to exclude a network adapter.

If you do not have the Enable Automatic Bridge, you will not be able to modify the available network adapters.

NOTE

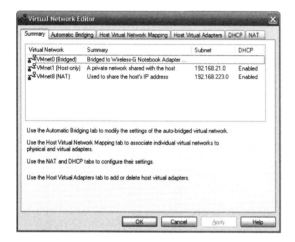

FIGURE 12.6 Choose the appropriate network adapter to exclude from automatic bridging.

FIGURE 12.5 Disable the Automatic Bridge to view which card is bridged to the physical adapter.

Host Virtual Network Mapping

On the Host Virtual Network Mapping tab (see Figure 12.8) you can define and configure the following actions:

■ Assign VMnet switches to an appropriate network adapter .
■ Assign physical network adapters to be configured with bridged networking.
■ Edit the subnet settings.
■ Edit the DHCP settings.

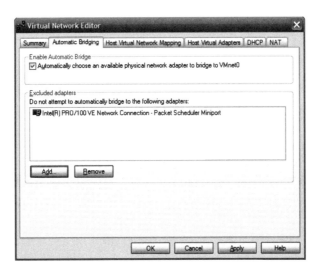

FIGURE 12.7 The Automatic Bridging tab with an excluded network adapter configured.

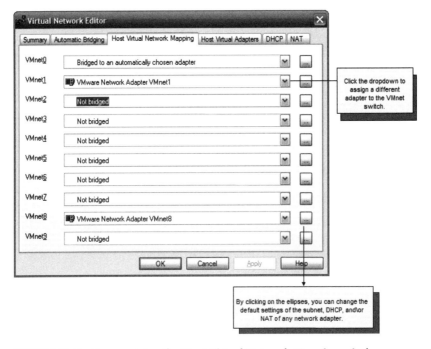

FIGURE 12.8 Summarizing the Host Virtual Network Mapping window.

CONFIGURING A HOST-ONLY NETWORK

In many cases, you might need to provide network connectivity between a virtual machine and the host computer only. If this is the case, you would configure a host-only network in VMware Workstation 5. When you choose this option in the New Virtual Machine wizard as shown in Figure 12.9, the virtual machine uses the VMnet1 host-only switch to communicate with the virtual network adapter that is visible to the host PC. When you install VMware Workstation, the virtual network adapter is installed automatically on the VMnet1 switch; it also assigns it the appropriate IP address so that the host-only network will work appropriately. Figure 12.10 illustrates a host-only network. When you configure virtual machines and use the **Host-Only** option in the New Virtual Machine wizard, the virtual and host machines are connected to a private network. IP addresses on this network are provided by VMware's DHCP server.

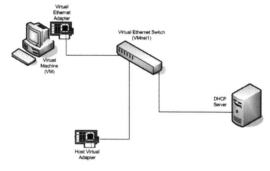

FIGURE 12.10   Host-only networking diagram.

FIGURE 12.9   Assigning host-only networking.

About the VMware DHCP Server

If you want to make changes to VMware's internal DHCP service, open VMware Workstation from the Start menu and choose **Edit | Virtual Network Settings | DHCP Tab**. Figure 12.11 illustrates the DHCP tab. On this window, the current configured virtual switches and DHCP ranges are displayed. Furthermore, you can **Start**, **Stop**, and **Restart** the DHCP service on any one of the virtual switches by highlighting the appropriate virtual network and choosing one of the three command buttons. When you highlight a virtual network, you have the ability to view the properties of the selected network, as shown in Figure 12.12, as well as to remove a virtual network. On the DHCP Setting window or when you view the properties of the DHCP highlighted virtual network adapter, you can modify the start and end address being used by your virtual machines. Additionally, you can set the lease duration for DHCP clients.

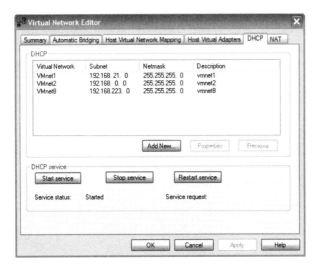

FIGURE 12.11 The DHCP tab displays the virtual network as well as the subnet and netmask.

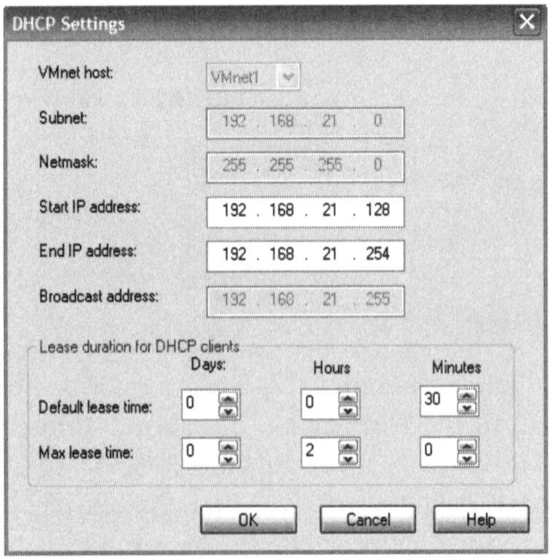

FIGURE 12.12 Editing the default lease time and max lease time.

Adding a new DHCP range requires you to click the **Add New** button and choose a VMnet switch. VMware Workstation has nine VMnet switches that you can choose from. Once you choose a VMnet from the dropdown, click **OK** and the new virtual network appears in the DHCP summary window as shown in Figure 12.13. Click **Apply** to have VMware Workstation automatically configure the appropriate DHCP range. Figure 12.14 illustrates a properly configured VMnet5 virtual network with a DHCP range.

The default installation of VMware Workstation installs a host-only network on VMnet1, a host-virtual network with network address translation (NAT) on VMnet8, and bridged networking on VMnet0. This leaves you seven virtual switches to choose from when creating DHCP ranges. The DHCP configuration you create is stored in a text file called vmnetdhcp.conf and the DHCP leases are stored in a file called vmnetdhcp.leases. These files are located in C:\Documents and Settings\All Users\Application Data\VMware. When you create a new DHCP range from the DHCP tab, it does not create the host virtual adapter. However, if you create a new host virtual adapter, it does create the appropriate DHCP range.

You will not be able to see these files unless you enable Show Hidden Files and Folders from the folder options.

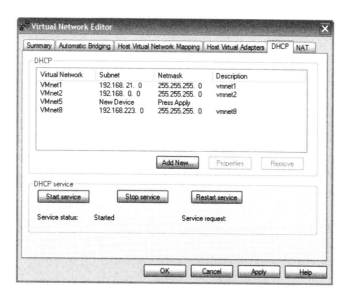

FIGURE 12.13 Adding/editing the DHCP settings.

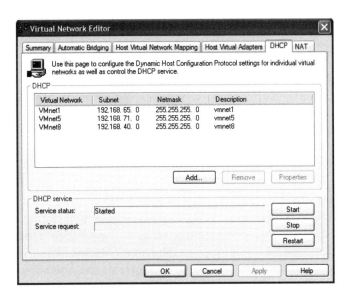

FIGURE 12.14   Creating the VMnet5 DHCP network.

About Host Virtual Adapters

The Host Virtual Adapters tab (see Figure 12.15) is where you will create additional host-only network adapters. In order to configure a new virtual adapter, click the **Add New Adapter** button and choose a VMnet network adapter as shown in Figure 12.16. Click **OK** and **Apply** to begin installing the host virtual network adapter. After you click **Apply**, you might receive a hardware installation message (see Figure 12.17). Click **Continue Anyway** to proceed and the network adapter appears on the Host Virtual Network Adapters summary window.

In addition to creating network adapters, you can enable, disable, and remove an adapter by selecting the applicable network adapter on the Host Virtual Adapters tab and choosing the appropriate command button.

When you create a new virtual network adapter, an appropriate DHCP range is also configured to ensure that your virtual machine receives the proper IP address from the DHCP server. If you are familiar with routing and networking, you can modify the DHCP range.

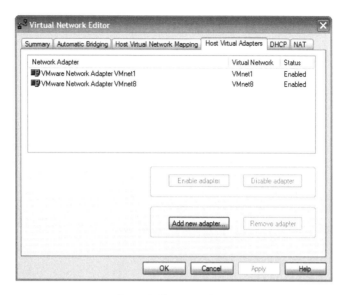

FIGURE 12.15 A view of all of your host virtual adapters.

FIGURE 12.16 Adding a new host adapter.

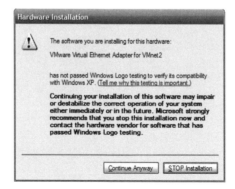

FIGURE 12.17 Hardware installation message.

CONFIGURING NETWORK ADDRESS TRANSLATION

Are you working with a limited number of IP addresses on your network? Does your organization have a security policy in place that does not allow you to connect virtual machines to the network? If so, the ability of VMware Workstation to configure NAT translation is right up your alley. When you configure virtual machines with NAT translation, your virtual machines obtain access to your LAN using the host's IP address. Behind the scenes, a private network is configured on the host computer and the virtual machine receives an IP address from the virtual DHCP server. Basically all traffic running on your virtual machines looks like traffic coming from the single IP address of your computer. Let's configure NAT now.

NAT also allows you to quickly obtain Internet access when using dial-up connections.

Configuring a Custom Network Address Translation

In order to configure NAT, start VMware Workstation 5 from the Start menu. Click the **Edit | Virtual Network Settings | NAT** tab as shown in Figure 12.18. Next, choose the **VMnet switch** from the drop-down menu and the Confirm NAT on a bridged VMNET window appears as shown in Figure 12.19. Click **Yes** to enable DHCP for the applicable VMnet network and click **Apply**. The default installation of VMware Workstation installs VMnet8 with the NAT service.

Unless you are a seasoned veteran with routing, you should let the virtual DHCP assign the IP addresses. A simple mistake in how you configure the DHCP server can give you a lot of grief.

FIGURE 12.18 The NAT tab.

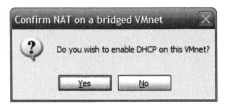

FIGURE 12.19 Confirmed NAT on a
bridged VMNET.

Next, you will edit the virtual machine settings in the Control Center by highlighting the virtual machine in the Favorites window and selecting **Edit virtual machine settings**. Highlight **Ethernet** and choose the appropriate (see Figure 12.20)
network connection:

NAT: Used to share the host's IP address. Choose this setting to take advantage of NAT on the default virtual network.

Custom Specific virtual network: Choose this option if you created a custom
virtual adapter on which you configured the NAT service.

*The NAT service configuration is stored in a text file called vmnetnat.conf; it is lo-
cated in c:\documents and settings\all users\application data\vmware. You can
open and view the file in Notepad or any text editor of your choice.*

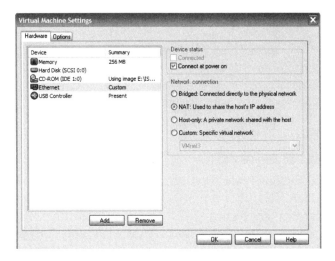

FIGURE 12.20 Choosing your network connection.

About Port Forwarding

When you configure NAT with your virtual machines in VMware Workstation, you can also configure port forwarding to allow physical computers to communicate with services running on your virtual machines. For example, if you had a physical computer and you wanted to contact a Web server on a virtual machine, this would be impossible because the physical computer can send traffic only to the host computer's IP address. If you configure a NAT configuration with port forwarding, then the VMware NAT service will convert and forward the IP address so that it can communicate with the Web server when a physical computer sends traffic to a Web server on a virtual machine. Figure 12.21 illustrates how this would work.

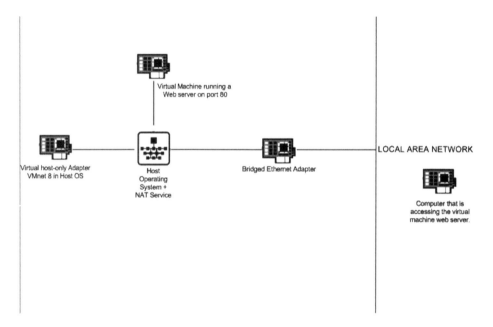

Virtual Machine running a
Web server on port 80

LOCAL AREA NETWORK

Virtual host-only Adapter
VMnet 8 in Host OS

Host
Operating
System +
NAT Service

Bridged Ethernet Adapter

Computer that is
accessing the virtual
machine web server.

FIGURE 12.21 Port forwarding diagram.

Configuring Port Forwarding

In order to configure port forwarding, click **Edit | Virtual Network Settings** from the menu bar. Next, click on the **NAT** tab and click the **Edit** button to configure port forwarding (see Figure 12.22). On the NAT Settings window, click the **Port forwarding** button and choose **Add** to enter a host port, forwarding IP address, and description (see Figure 12.23). Once you have entered the appropriate forwarding information, make sure the NAT service is running on VMnet8 or whatever virtual network you installed NAT on. Once you have verified that it is running, open a browser from another computer on the network and browse to the Web server. The traffic or packets will be routed to the virtual machine. If you were to stop the NAT service you would get a page not found error. For example, assume your host computer does not have a Web server installed on it, but if you open a browser and type *http://stevenw*, an Under Construction Web page appears (see Figure 12.24). This happens because you have port forwarding configured to let traffic flow to the Web server of a virtual machine on your host computer. Now if you were to stop the NAT service on the NAT tab, you would get the message shown in Figure 12.25 when you typed *http://stevenw* in a browser.

Keep in mind that if you are using port forwarding to access virtual machines, a static IP address is better than a DHCP address. If your DHCP lease ends and the virtual machine is assigned a different IP address, the port forwarding will no longer work.

NOTE

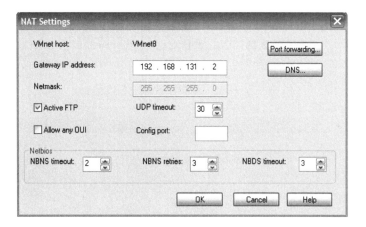

FIGURE 12.22   Configuring port forwarding.

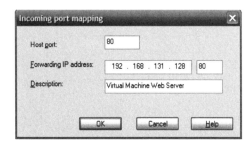

FIGURE 12.23   Add a host port and forwarding IP address to configure port forwarding.

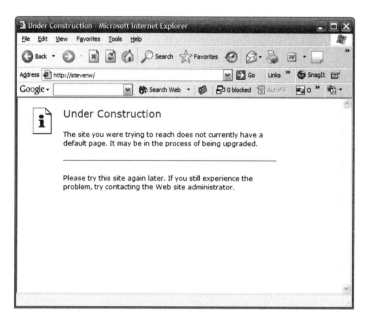

FIGURE 12.24 The under construction Web page is located on a virtual machine.

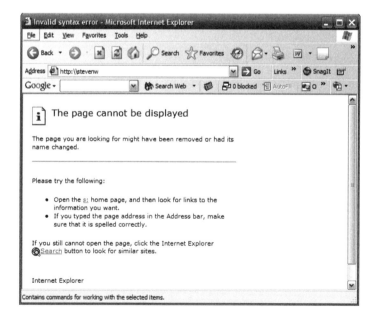

FIGURE 12.25 Stopping the NAT service causes the port forwarding to fail.

ABOUT VNETSNIFFER

A packet sniffer, network monitor, and/or network analyzer is used to troubleshoot network traffic. You can use the information trapped by the packet sniffer to identify problems such as bottlenecks or other transmission errors. VMware Workstation is packaged with a utility called Vnetsniffer. With this tool, you can display network traffic between virtual machines as well as between the host PC and the virtual machines. Furthermore, if you use this utility with the /e switch, the Vnetsniffer will log information such as packet size, source IP, ICMP message types, and MAC addresses. This utility is accessed via the command prompt. Let's show you how to work with this tool.

Working with Vnetsniffer

Let's begin by opening a command prompt (**Start | Programs | Accessories | Command Prompt**). With the command prompt open, browse to c:\program files\vmware\vmware workstation. Next type `vnetsniffer VMnet(#)` and choose a virtual network to monitor; you can monitor VMnet0 to VMnet8. We will monitor VMnet8, so your syntax is as follows: `vnetsniffer VMnet8` as shown in Figure 12.26. Now let's run Vnetsniffer again with the /e switch as shown in Figure 12.27. As you can see, this is a very simple tool to work with. Let's move on to a discussion about virtual MAC addresses.

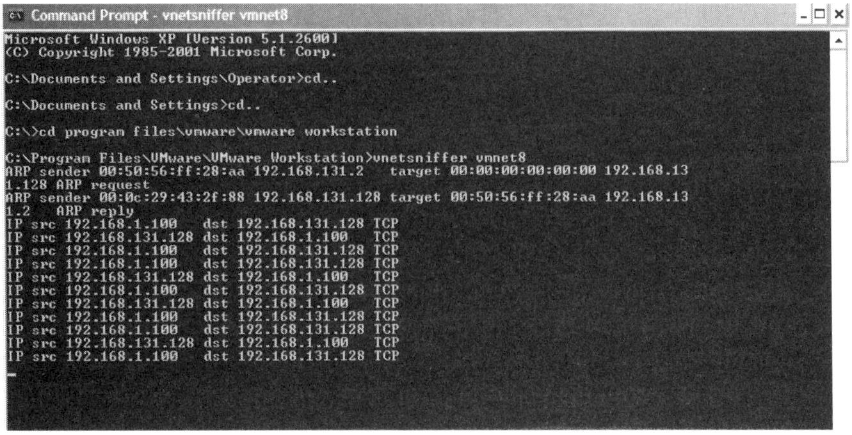

FIGURE 12.26   The Vnetsniffer syntax.

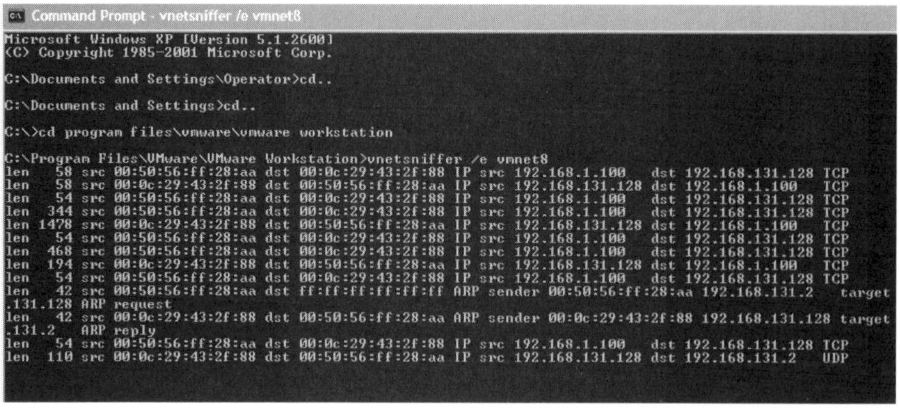

FIGURE 12.27 The Vnetsniffer gives you more routing information with the /e switch.

ABOUT VIRTUAL MAC ADDRESSES

A MAC address is a unique identifier associated with a network adapter. Typically MAC addresses are 48 bits in length and a 12 digit hexadecimal such as xx:xx:xx:ss:ss:ss. The first half of a MAC address is the ID of the adapter manufacturer. You can browse to *http://standards.ieee.org/regauth/oui/index.shtml* and input the first half of the MAC address. It will query the database and return the manufacturer. For example, if you input 00-12-17 it returns the following, as shown in Figure 12.28. The second half of the MAC address contains the serial number that is assigned to the adapter by the manufacturer. Let's take what we have learned now and apply it to VMware Workstation 5.

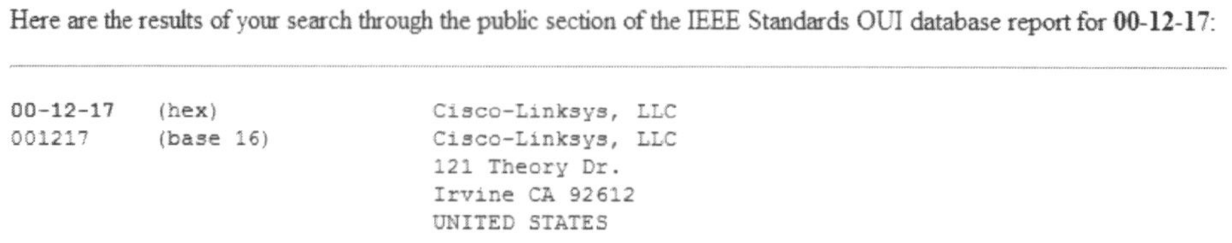

Here are the results of your search through the public section of the IEEE Standards OUI database report for **00-12-17**:

```
00-12-17   (hex)        Cisco-Linksys, LLC
001217     (base 16)    Cisco-Linksys, LLC
                        121 Theory Dr.
                        Irvine CA 92612
                        UNITED STATES
```

FIGURE 12.28 Cisco-Linksys is the adapter manufacturer.

Just as a physical adapter has a unique identifier associated with a network adapter, so does a virtual adapter. For example, on the computer that has VMware Workstation installed, open a command prompt and type `ipconfig /all`. It will display your VMware Workstation host virtual adapters and their unique MAC addresses, as shown in Figure 12.29. If we take the first half of the MAC address (00-50-56) and search the IEEE Standards, information is returned as shown in Figure 12.30. This is one of the prefixes for the VMware adapters. Finally, the second half is used as a unique identifier, but the last octet represents the host virtual adapter installed on the host computer. For example, VMnet1 has a 01 for the last octet of the MAC address and VMnet2 has a 02 for the last octet in the MAC address.

VMware can also use 00-0C-29 and 00-05-69 as a prefix for network adapters.

NOTE

```
Ethernet adapter VMware Network Adapter VMnet8:

        Connection-specific DNS Suffix  . :
        Description . . . . . . . . . . . : VMware Virtual Ethernet Adapter for VMnet8
        Physical Address. . . . . . . . . : 00-50-56-C0-00-08
        Dhcp Enabled. . . . . . . . . . . : No
        IP Address. . . . . . . . . . . . : 192.168.131.1
        Subnet Mask . . . . . . . . . . . : 255.255.255.0
        Default Gateway . . . . . . . . . :

Ethernet adapter VMware Network Adapter VMnet1:

        Connection-specific DNS Suffix  . :
        Description . . . . . . . . . . . : VMware Virtual Ethernet Adapter for VMnet1
        Physical Address. . . . . . . . . : 00-50-56-C0-00-01
        Dhcp Enabled. . . . . . . . . . . : No
        IP Address. . . . . . . . . . . . : 192.168.52.1
        Subnet Mask . . . . . . . . . . . : 255.255.255.0
        Default Gateway . . . . . . . . . :
```

FIGURE 12.29   The MAC address that is assigned to the adapter.

```
00-50-56    (hex)            VMWare, Inc.
005056      (base 16)        VMWare, Inc.
                             44 ENCINA AVENUE
                             PALO ALTO CA 94301
                             UNITED STATES
```

FIGURE 12.30   VMware is the adapter manufacturer.

About UUID

The UUID is the unique identifier that all virtual machines receive; it is a 16-digit number. The uuid.location is a number that is generated on the basis of the host computer's UUID and the path to the virtual machine's configuration file. The uuid.bios is simply the uuid.location when the virtual server is first booted. You can open up the *.vmx file to view the uuid.location and uuid.bios as shown in Figure 12.31. The *.vmx file is located in the default directory where each of your virtual machines is created. Now if you view the last three digits of the uuid.bios and then run an `ipconfig /all` to see the MAC address of your virtual network card, the last three digits will be the serial number of the virtual network card. For example, if the uuid.bios is 56 4d a1 1f e5 fa a0 f9-ed e2 76 1e 0e 43 2f 88 then the MAC address of the virtual adapter within the virtual machine will be 00-0C-29-43-2F-88.

```
win2000pro.vmx - Notepad
File Edit Format View Help
config.version = "8"
virtualHW.version = "4"
scsi0.present = "TRUE"
memsize = "256"
scsi0:0.present = "TRUE"
scsi0:0.fileName = "windows 2000 Professional.vmdk"
ide1:0.present = "TRUE"
ide1:0.fileName = "E:\ISO\EN_WIN2000_PRO_SP4_.ISO"
ide1:0.deviceType = "cdrom-image"
floppy0.present = "FALSE"
ethernet0.present = "TRUE"
usb.present = "TRUE"
sound.present = "FALSE"
sound.fileName = "-1"
displayName = "Windows 2000 Professional"
guestOS = "win2000pro"
priority.grabbed = "normal"
priority.ungrabbed = "normal"

scsi0:0.redo = ""
ethernet0.addressType = "generated"
uuid.location = "56 4d a1 1f e5 fa a0 f9-ed e2 76 1e 0e 43 2f 88"
uuid.bios = "56 4d a1 1f e5 fa a0 f9-ed e2 76 1e 0e 43 2f 88"
```

FIGURE 12.31 The UUID configuration.

The UUID will not change unless you move the virtual machine to a different location or workstation. If you do this and you open and power on the virtual machine, you will be presented with a dialog box asking you how you want to configure your UUID. Figure 12.32 illustrates the dialog box that you will receive when you move the location of your virtual machine. If you create a new identifier, the uuid.location and uuid.bios are given a new MAC address. Keeping the existing identifier keeps the existing uuid.location and uuid.bios. If you keep the existing uuid.location and uuid.bios and you have another copy of the virtual machine out on the network or on your workstation, you take the risk of having duplicate MAC addresses.

If this dialog box is bothersome and you no longer want to receive this message when you move the location of your virtual machines, you can perform the following: add uuid.action="keep" to the .vmx file. By adding this line to the .vmx file of the virtual machine in question, you ensure that the UUID will always remain the same.

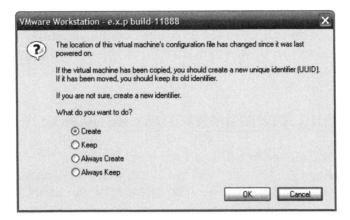

FIGURE 12.32   When you move the location of a virtual machine, you must either keep or create a UUID.

Manually Assigning a MAC Address

In order to guarantee that each virtual machine will receive a unique MAC address, you can manually set this configuration. In order to accomplish this task, browse to the default directory where VMware Workstation is installed and open the applicable virtual machine. Inside the folder for the applicable virtual machine, you will find the VMware configuration file (.vmx file). Open this file with Notepad and remove the following lines:

- Ethernet[N].generatedAddress
- Ethernet[N].addressType
- Ethernet[N].generatedAddressOffset

NOTE

The [N] stands for the number of the network card. VMware Workstation supports up to three virtual network adapters per virtual machine. If you had two network adapters installed in your virtual machine, then you would have to remove six lines. One set would have N=0 and another set would have N=1.

Now that you have removed the appropriate lines from the VMware Workstation configuration file, you are ready to add the following line:

- Ethernet[N].address = 00:50:56:XX:YY:ZZ

The first half of the MAC address needs to be the identifier of VMware; 00:50:56 is this identifier. On last half of the MAC address, XX must be a valid hexadecimal number between 00h and 3Fh, and YY and ZZ must be valid hexadecimal numbers between 00h and FFh.

CONFIGURING A CUSTOM VIRTUAL NETWORK

At this point, you should be very comfortable working with the networking features of VMware Workstation. With this in mind, let's take it a step forward and create a custom network configuration that consists of a Web server, firewall, and workstation PC. The Web server and the workstation will be separated by the firewall. The physical network adapter on the computer will not have access to this configuration.
The configuration will consist of the following:

- 192.168.1/24
- 10.0.0.1/24
- 172.16.0/16

In this example, we are using private IP addresses. With your configuration, IP address structure will be different based on your needs.

Let's start by creating three virtual machines in VMware Workstation. When creating these virtual machines with the New Virtual Machine wizard, choose **Do not use a network connection** on the Network Type window (see Figure 12.33). Now we are going to add our first virtual adapter by choosing the **Edit | Virtual Network Settings | Host Virtual Adapters** tab, and click **Add new Adapter**. Select VMnet2 from the drop-down menu and click **OK**. This will create the first virtual adapter on your custom network. Go ahead and repeat this process to create the second virtual adapter. In this example, we created the second virtual adapter on VMnet3. At this point, we have the following three virtual adapters configured:

- VMnet0
- VMnet2
- VMnet3

Now let's configure the firewall virtual machine to have two Ethernet adapters. To accomplish this task, we will highlight the firewall server in the Favorites window and **Edit virtual machine settings**. On the Virtual Machine Settings windows, click **Add** on the Hardware tab and add an Ethernet adapter in the Add Hardware wizard. Now repeat this process to add a second Ethernet adapter. Figure 12.34 illustrates the current configuration in the VMware Control Center. On the workstation computer and Web server, repeat the above process and add one Ethernet adapter to each virtual machine. You now have the following configured:

- VMnet0 switch
- VMnet2 switch
- VMnet3 switch
- Firewall virtual machine with two Ethernet network adapters
- Web server virtual machine with one Ethernet network adapter
- Workstation PC virtual machine with one Ethernet network adapter

You can now load the operating system on each virtual machine. For the purposes of this example, we have each virtual machine loaded with Windows Server 2003. Once you have finished loading the OS on each virtual machine, you can configure the switches and IP addresses appropriately.

Now let's highlight the Web server in the Favorites window and choose **Edit virtual machine settings**. On the Hardware tab of the Virtual Machine Settings window, highlight **Ethernet** and choose the **Custom: Specific** virtual network radio button. Choose **VMnet2** from the drop-down menu as shown in Figure 12.35. This will connect the Web server's virtual network adapter to VMnet2 switch.

Now let's highlight the firewall virtual machine in the Favorites window and choose **Edit virtual machine settings**. On the Hardware tab of the Virtual Machine Settings window, highlight **Ethernet** and choose the **Custom: Specific** virtual network radio button. Choose **VMnet2** from the drop-down menu. Next, highlight **Ethernet 2** and choose the **Custom: Specific virtual network** radio button and choose **VMnet3** from the dropdown menu. This will connect the firewall's virtual Ethernet adapter to the VMnet2 switch and the Ethernet2 adapter to the VMnet3 switch.

Now let's highlight the workstation PC in the Favorites window and choose **Edit virtual machine settings**. On the Hardware tab of the Virtual Machine Settings window, highlight **Ethernet** and choose the **Custom: Specific virtual network** radio button. Choose **VMnet3** from the dropdown; this will connect the workstation PC virtual network adapter to the VMnet3 switch. We have now completed the infrastructure and are ready to assign the appropriate IP addresses and default gateways to our virtual machines.

FIGURE 12.33 Do not use a network connection when configuring a virtual machine on a custom network.

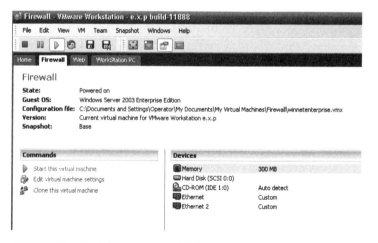

FIGURE 12.34 Adding a second Ethernet adapter in the Control Center.

Working through this chapter might seem a little intimidating at first, but the more time you spend in this area of the product, the more you will come to appreciate all that it has to offer. Now that you have a good understanding of virtual networks and you have installed quite a few virtual machines, it is time to find out how to monitor and enhance your experience when working with virtual machines. In our next chapter we will go over performance tuning and optimization of your virtual machines.

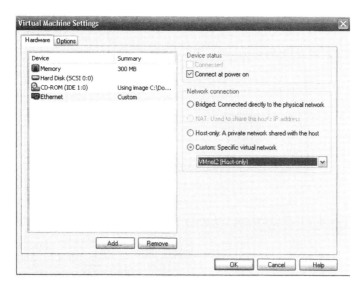

FIGURE 12.35   Choosing a custom virtual switch on your custom network.

13 Performance Tuning and Optimization of Virtual Machines

In This Chapter

- VMware Workstation Optimization Settings
- Monitoring Virtual Machines
- Monitoring VMware Workstation Performance Settings

erformance tuning and optimizing are very important if you want to keep your virtual machines running at their peak capacity. Here is an analogy: you would not buy a new car and not maintain it; you would balance the tires, check the tire pressure, and change the oil. With VMware Workstation there are certain things that you can do to maintain and even optimize the virtual environment. This chapter is dedicated to helping you maximize your configuration settings and to showing how you can monitor the performance and behavior of your virtual machine environment.

VMWARE WORKSTATION OPTIMIZATION SETTINGS

This section contains tips on how to get the most out of your newly installed software. Let's begin by discussing the working directory of VMware Workstation 5.

About the Working Directory or Default Location

The working directory is the default location where all of your virtual machines are installed. If you do not change this location, it defaults to the My Documents\My Virtual Machines folder of the profile you used to install VMware Workstation. For maximum performance take advantage of a second hard drive on your host system. By having two drives, you can increase performance by keeping VMware Workstation from accessing data on the same physical disk. By keeping the host operating system on one disk and all virtual machines on another disk, disk-intensive applications will not compete with each other. Figure 13.1 shows how you can change the default location.

FIGURE 13.1 Changing the default location of where your virtual machines are created.

Memory Optimization

The virtual machines in VMware Workstation use physical memory to run. With that being said, you can see that the amount of memory you have on your physical computer can be a limitation on how many concurrent virtual machines you run at a single time. It can also be a limitation on running one virtual machine effectively. For example, if you have a Windows XP computer with 128 MB of RAM, you won't be able to run VMware Workstation. If you have a Windows XP machine with 256 MB of RAM, you should be able to run one or two virtual machines maximum, but performance would be very slow. A computer with, say, 2 GB of RAM would allow you to run many virtual machines concurrently or one virtual machine with plenty of memory.

To make the most out of your memory, highlight the applicable virtual machine and edit the virtual machine settings. On the Hardware tab, highlight **Memory** and tweak this setting until you get the right amount of memory for your individual virtual machine. On a global level, you can configure memory by going to the **Edit | Preferences | Memory** tab (see Figure 13.2). You have the following options:

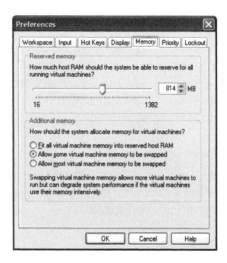

FIGURE 13.2 Configuring your memory settings on a global level.

Reserved Memory

A Windows system doesn't do very well when you don't give it the memory it needs. When the operating system needs more memory, it begins to swap between memory and the page file. To prevent this, you can set the reserved memory accordingly. For example, if your host computer has roughly 1.5 GB of RAM and you always want to have 512 MB of RAM for your operating system, you would set the slider to roughly 841 MB.

How should the system allocate memory for virtual machines?

After specifying the reserved memory, you can choose one of the following options. Let's go over them in detail.

Fit all virtual machine memory in reserved host RAM.

This setting gives you the best performance possible because it runs only the amount of memory you specify in the Reserved memory box. For example, if you allocate 841 MB of RAM to reserved memory, your virtual machines will use only memory that is reserved. At this level, no swapping will take place. Now do you understand why this setting allows for great performance? If you have plenty of memory and are running only a few virtual machines, this setting is perfect for you. If your operating system is running only 256 MB of memory, this setting is less desirable because you will not have much memory to create virtual machines.

Allow some virtual machine memory to be swapped.

This setting is great if you want to get more out of your memory. It allows some swapping to take place but gives you the benefit of having more virtual machines to work with. This setting can cause performance degradation, so monitor it until you find that spot where your operating system is happy and the virtual machine performance is sufficient.

Allow most virtual machine memory.

This setting allows you to swap as much host operating system memory as necessary. With this setting you can run many virtual machines, but you can hit a plateau and see a severe performance degradation.

Host Disk Defragmentation

Just as fragmentation of the disk takes place on a physical computer, it also happens within virtual machines and within the working directory that holds your virtual machines. If you notice performance degradation with any aspect of your virtual machines, run the Disk Defragmenter (see Figure 13.3) on the drive that contains the working directory.

Shrinking and Defragmenting Virtual Disks

Over a period of time, your virtual disk will grow and performance will degrade. To prevent this, you can defragment the virtual disk. Prior to performing this task, the virtual machine in question must be powered off. Next, highlight the virtual machine you want to defragment and Edit the virtual machine settings.

On the Hardware tab, highlight the virtual **Hard Disk** and click the **Defragment** button (see Figure 13.4). Figure 13.5 displays a progress bar as the virtual hard drive is defragmented. A disk defragmentation complete message appears when the process is complete. Now we'll move on to shrinking a virtual disk drive.

Defragmenting a disk is a time-consuming process, depending on the size of your virtual disk. It is best to do it when you are not working with other virtual machines.

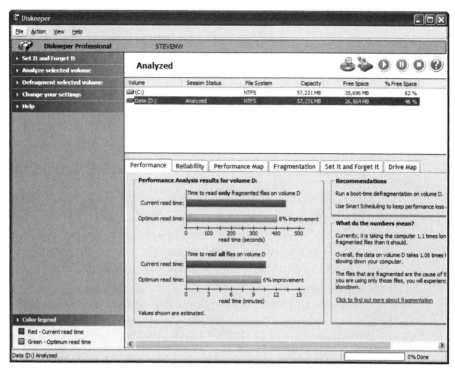

FIGURE 13.3   Defragmenting the hard drive on the host system.

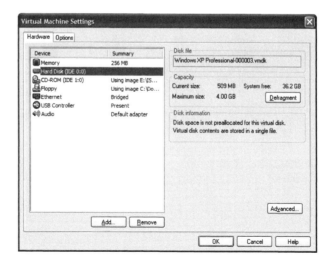

FIGURE 13.4   Defragmenting a virtual disk.

FIGURE 13.5 A progress bar indicating the percentage of the virtual drive that is complete.

Shrinking a virtual disk requires all snapshots for that disk to be removed. Prior to shrinking the disk, make a backup copy of the virtual drive and archive for safe-keeping. For more information on archiving a virtual machine, see Chapter 16. You can delete your snapshots by highlighting the applicable virtual machine and selecting **VM | Snapshot | Snapshot Manager** and deleting all snapshots. For more information on how to delete snapshots, see Chapter 8.

Next, double-click the **VMware Tools** icon in the system tray as shown in Figure 13.6. On the VMware Tools Properties window, select the **Shrink** tab and select which partition you want to shrink as shown in Figure 13.7. Click the **Prepare to shrink** button and a progress bar shows preparation of the disk (see Figure 13.8). At the end of this process, you are asked whether to shrink (see Figure 13.9) the disk now. Click **Yes** to shrink the disk. A progress bar shows when the process is complete. Click **OK.**

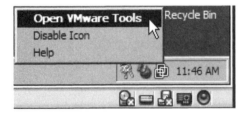

FIGURE 13.6 Opening the VMware Tools from the system taskbar.

FIGURE 13.7 Select the virtual partition you want to shrink.

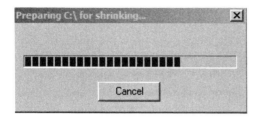

FIGURE 13.8   Preparing the virtual partition for a virtual disk shrink.

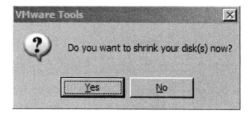

FIGURE 13.9   Shrinking the disk.

Guest Operating System Selection

For optimum performance, it is important that you choose the correct guest operating system when creating your virtual machines. This is necessary because VMware Workstation optimizes certain configurations using these selection criteria. You can double check this setting by highlighting each virtual machine in the VMware Control Center and choosing **VM | Settings | Options** and then **General setting,** as shown in Figure 13.10.

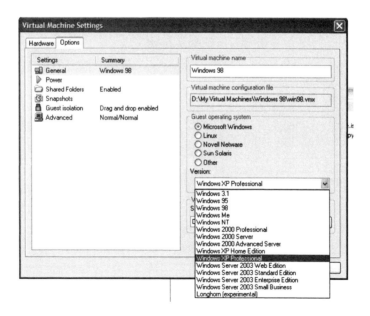

FIGURE 13.10   Choosing the correct guest operating system.

Debugging Mode

When running VMware Workstation 5, you can be in one of two modes: normal or debugging. Running a virtual machine in debugging mode is slower than in normal mode but is helpful with troubleshooting problems. When you are in debugging mode, a log file is written to the directory where your virtual machine resides. You can change from normal mode to debugging mode by highlighting the applicable virtual machine in the VMware Control Center and choosing **VM | Settings | Options Tab |** and selecting **Advanced Settings**. If the **Run with debugging information** checkbox is checked, you are in debug mode. If it is unchecked, you are in normal mode. For better performance of your virtual machines, make sure the **Run with debugging information** checkbox is deselected. Figure 13.11 shows the Virtual Machine Settings window where the run with debugging information resides.

More than debug information is written to the log file. A log file is also created in normal mode with less information.

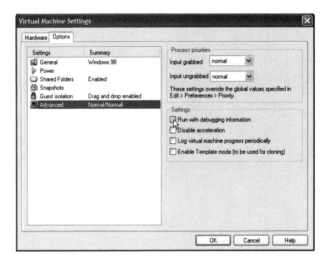

FIGURE 13.11 You can run a virtual machine with debugging information.

Remove Unnecessary Virtual Hardware

You can increase performance by removing any unnecessary virtual hardware. For example, if you are not using USB device or have no need for audio, you can remove this hardware by selecting the applicable virtual machine and choosing **VM | Settings | Hardware.** Next, highlight the applicable device and click **Remove.**

Running Virtual Machines from the Network

In general, you should steer clear of running virtual machines over the network. Please read about linked clones in Chapter 9 for more information on how to run virtual machines over the network using this method.

Snapshots

If you do not have a need to use snapshots, you will get better performance out of your virtual machines by disabling them. You can disable snapshots by choosing **VM | Settings | Options | Snapshots | Disable Snapshots**. For more information on snapshots, see Chapter 8.

CD-ROM Drive Polling

In order to get the best performance from your virtual machines, you should disconnect the CD-ROM device. You can reconnect it whenever you want to access or install software from a CD-ROM. To disconnect the device, highlight the applicable virtual machine in the VMware Control Center and choose the **VM | Settings | Hardware** tab and select **CD-ROM** from the menu bar. Next, deselect **Connect at power on** and make sure **Connected** is deselected as well. If **Connected** is dimmed out, it is because the applicable virtual machine is powered off. Figure 13.12 provides an example of how to deselect the device status.

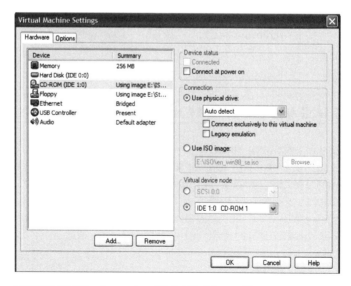

FIGURE 13.12 Removing CD-ROM drive polling.

Disable Effects

In order to get better performance from Windows virtual machines, you can disable effects. Effects give Windows XP a great look and feel, but if you are more concerned with performance, you can disable them by going to the **Start | Control Panel | Display | Appearance** tab. Next, click the **Effect** button and deselect all of the checkboxes as shown in Figure 13.13.

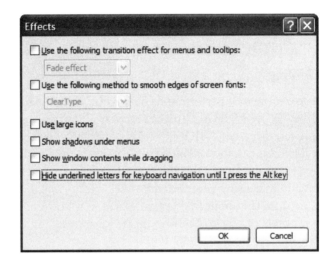

FIGURE 13.13   Gain performance in Windows XP by removing effects.

MONITORING VIRTUAL MACHINES

Have you ever been running virtual machines concurrently and felt one of them was causing a problem to your host system? You might just want to do some performance testing or see how much utilization a specific virtual machine is creating. It is easy to begin monitoring virtual machines with the VMware Workstation Performance Monitor. Let's go over the counters that are installed with VMware Workstation 5 before we dig into performance monitoring. Counters are described in Table 13.1.

TABLE 13.1   Counters

Counter Name	Description
Guest Locked Memory Bytes	The number of bytes of simulated physical memory that are locked by the guest operating system.
Guest Virtual Physical Memory Bytes	The number of bytes of simulated physical memory in the virtual machine.
Network Bytes Received/sec	The number of bytes received by the guest operating system over the network.
Network Bytes Sent/sec	The number of bytes sent by the guest operating system over the network.
Network Bytes Transferred/sec	The number of bytes sent or received by the guest operating system over the network.
Network Packets Received/sec	The number of network packets received by the guest operating system.
Network Packets Sent/sec	The number of network packets sent by the guest operating system.
Network Receive Errors/sec	The number of network errors from receiving packets by the guest operating system.
Network Send Errors/sec	The number of network errors from sending packets by the guest operating system.
Network Transfer Errors/sec	The number of network errors from sending or receiving packets by the guest operating system.
Network Transfers /sec	The number of network operations performed by the guest operating system.
Percent Guest Physical Memory Touched	The percentage of simulated physical memory recently used by the guest operating system.
Virtual Disk Bytes Read/sec	The number of bytes transferred for disk read operations performed by the guest operating system.
Virtual Disk Bytes Transferred/sec	The number of bytes transferred to disk operations performed by the guest operating system.
Virtual Disk Bytes Written/sec	The number of bytes transferred to disk write operations performed by the guest operating system.
Virtual Disk Reads/ sec	The number of disk read operations performed by the guest operating system.

$\rightarrow$

Counter Name	Description
Virtual Disk Transfers/sec	The number of disk operations performed by the guest operating system.
Virtual Disk Writes/sec	The number of disk write operations performed by the guest operating system.

MONITORING VMWARE WORKSTATION PERFORMANCE SETTINGS

On many occasions, we need to monitor running virtual machines. It might be because we are running multiple virtual machines or there might be some performance issues. In any event, VMware Workstation 5 comes packaged with a set of performance counters that are interwoven within Microsoft's Performance mmc. Let's begin by opening the performance management console from the Start menu. Click **Start | Control Panel | Administrative Tools | Performance** and the performance management console appears as shown in Figure 13.14.

You cannot monitor virtual machines installed on a Linux host, but you can monitor all Linux virtual machines installed on a Windows host.

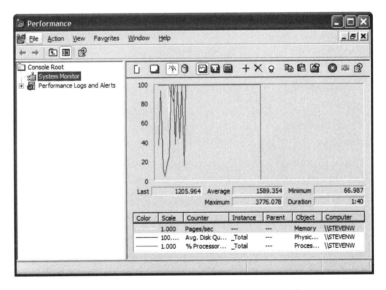

FIGURE 13.14 The performance management console.

Next, click the + sign from the toolbar and the Add Counters window appears. From the Performance object drop-down list, choose **VMware**, as shown in Figure 13.15. Once you choose **VMware**, a list of running virtual machines will appear and you can select to monitor **All Instances** or a specific instance by choosing from the list. You can also click the **Explain** button to have each highlighted counter explained in detail. Once you have selected the applicable counters, click **Add** and **Close** to view your counters, as shown in Figure 13.16.

You can select multiple counters from the list by holding down the Ctrl key and choosing all of the applicable counters for the tasks you are monitoring

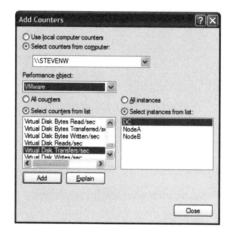

FIGURE 13.15 Adding a counter to the performance console.

You should now be able to optimize your virtual machines for your specific environment. If you run into problems, you now have the ability to monitor virtual machines for performance. We are now ready to move on to working with converting a PC virtual disk to a VMware Workstation virtual disk.

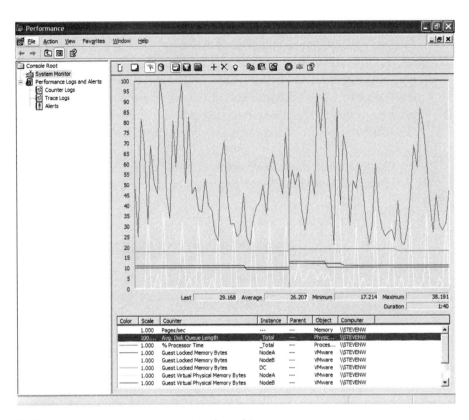

FIGURE 13.16 Monitoring your virtual machines.

14 Virtual to Virtual (V2V) Conversion

In This Chapter

- What Is the Virtual Machine Importer?
- Virtual Machine Importer Requirements
- Installing the Virtual Machine Importer
- Uninstalling the VMware Virtual Machine Importer
- Converting Virtual PC to VMware Workstation 5

WHAT IS THE VMWARE VIRTUAL MACHINE IMPORTER?

The VMware Virtual Machine Importer is a VMware utility that allows you to migrate virtual machines from Microsoft Virtual PC to one of the following VMware Workstation releases:

- VMware Workstation 5
- VMware Workstation 4.x

VMware has created a simple wizard that allows you to search for any Virtual PC (VPC) virtual machine and transform it into a standalone VMware Workstation virtual machine. When the VMware Workstation virtual machine is created, it keeps all of the configuration settings of the original VPC configuration. Additionally, migrating VPC settings to VMware Workstation does not destroy the VPC virtual machine. You can continue to use this virtual machine as well, but remember not to run both the converted virtual machine and original VPC virtual machine at the same time on the same network unless you run Sysprep on one of the computers.

Once a Virtual PC virtual machine is transformed, there will be some hardware difference, but that is to be expected considering that VMware Workstation and Virtual PC use different hardware drivers in their configurations. Additionally, once a virtual machine is migrated from VPC to VMware Workstation, the following will be identical:

- All data and software
- Computer name
- SID
- Profiles

VIRTUAL MACHINE IMPORTER REQUIREMENTS

In order to use the Virtual Machine Importer successfully, you need to be running one of the following operating systems:

- Windows 2003
- Windows XP Professional
- Windows 2000
- Windows NT

Once the migration process is finished, you can migrate the new virtual machine to any one of the VMware Workstation supported platforms.

VPC Requirements

In order to convert a VPC virtual machine, it must meet the following requirements:

- The virtual machine to be converted must be from Version 7 or later.
- Macintosh virtual machines are not supported.
- The operating system you are converting must be a VMware Workstation supported platform.
- All virtual machines must be turned off during the migration process.

Now that we have provided you with a general overview, let's install the product.

INSTALLING THE VIRTUAL MACHINE IMPORTER

The Virtual Machine Importer has the versatility of being installed on either a virtual machine or a physical machine. In order to install the Virtual Machine Importer, you must first download the latest version of the software from VMware. Once you have obtained the software from *www.vmware.com/download,* run the executable or the installer locally on either the virtual machine or the physical machine and you are presented with the Welcome window as shown in Figure 14.1.

According to VMware, you should not run this installer via Terminal Service.

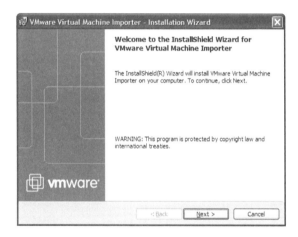

FIGURE 14.1   The VMware Virtual Machine Importer.

Next, accept the license agreement and add the customer information as shown in Figure 14.2. On the Setup Type window, select **Complete** or **Custom** installation. If you choose a custom installation, you can specify the drive where you want the installation files. The installation requires 14 MB of disk space. Click **Install** to begin the installation and you will be notified when the Virtual Machine Importer has been successfully installed to your hard drive (see Figure 14.3). The Virtual Machine Importer can be accessed from **Start | All Program | VMware | VMware Virtual Machine Importer**. At this point, we are ready to convert our first virtual PC to VMware Workstation 5.

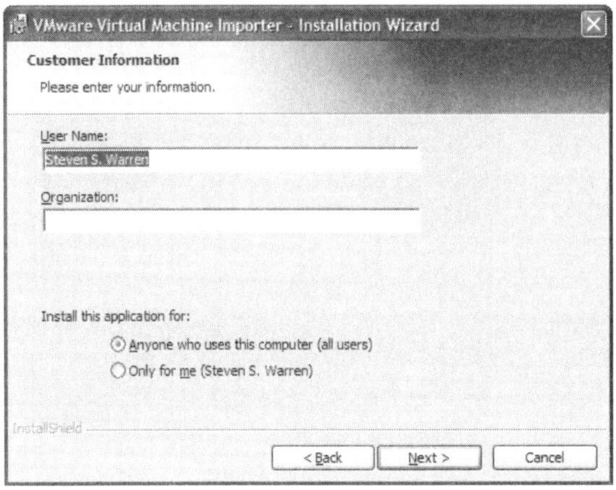

FIGURE 14.2 Entering your customer information.

FIGURE 14.3 The installation is completed.

UNINSTALLING THE VMWARE VIRTUAL MACHINE IMPORTER

Uninstalling Virtual Machine Importer can be done by going to **Start | Control Panel | Add/Remove Programs | VMware Virtual Machine Importer** and selecting **Change**. You have the following options:

- **Modify:** Changes which program features are being installed.
- **Remove:** Removes the Virtual Machine Importer.

CONVERTING VIRTUAL PC TO VMWARE WORKSTATION 5

The conversion process is very intuitive, but it is very important that you have the Virtual PC virtual machine powered off prior to converting. Do not confuse powering off with just saving the state of the virtual machine. To simplify, shut down your virtual machine as if you were powering off a physical computer. At this point, launch the Virtual Machine Importer from the Start menu, and the Welcome to VMware Virtual Machine Importer window appears (see Figure 14.4). The default path is **Start | Programs | VMware | VMware Virtual Machine Importer**.

FIGURE 14.4 The Welcome window for the VMware Virtual Machine Importer.

On the Select the Appropriate Configuration window, you have the choice of a typical or custom option. Choosing a **Typical** option converts the Virtual PC virtual machine to a VMware virtual machine. The virtual machine is a complete copy and the source goes untouched. Choosing a **Custom** installation allows you to create a virtual machine for a specific version of VMware Workstation or allows you to link to the hard disk of the source machine. Refer to the next section if you perform a custom installation. Let's begin by choosing a **Typical** installation by clicking **Next** and browsing to the virtual PC source files. These are *.vmc files. Figure 14.5 shows you an example of a virtual PC source file. Once you have browsed to the proper location, click **Next** as shown in Figure 14.6. The Virtual Machine Importer inspects the VPC virtual machine and then asks you to specify the Virtual Machine name and location of the new VMware Workstation virtual machine (see Figure 14.7).

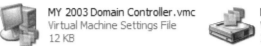
MY 2003 Domain Controller.vmc
Virtual Machine Settings File
12 KB

MyHard Disk.vhd
Virtual Machine Hard Drive Im...
2,636,430 KB

FIGURE 14.5 TheVirtual PC source file.

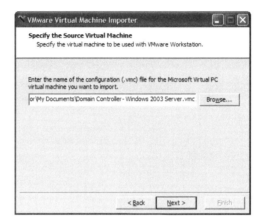

FIGURE 14.6 Specify the source file's location.

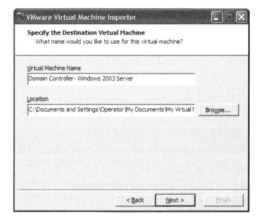

FIGURE 14.7 Enter a name and location for the converted virtual machine.

On the Ready to Start Importing window (see Figure 14.8), a summary of the conversion process is described in detail. If you agree, click **Next** and the conversion process starts as shown in Figure 14.9.

Once the conversion is complete, the Virtual Machine Importer displays a completion window. You can select the **Start my new virtual machine now** and click **Finish** or open the newly created virtual machine from within the VMware Control Center (see Figure 14.10). This can be done by choosing **File | Open** and browsing to the *.vmx file of the converted virtual machine.

Remember to install the VMware Tools after the conversion to get all of the functionality VMware Workstation 5 has to offer.

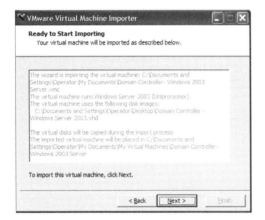

FIGURE 14.8 The Summary window.

FIGURE 14.9 The conversion from virtual PC to VMware Workstation 5 is in progress.

Virtual Machine Conversion Options

After specifying the location and name of the new VMware Workstation virtual machine, you have to make some decisions about how you want to configure the new virtual machine. There are two ways that Virtual Machine Importer can configure virtual machines:

- **Make a complete copy of the source virtual machine:** This option makes a completely separate copy that is identical to the source in VMware Workstation 5.
- **Link to the existing virtual machine:** Using this method is faster, but using the linked virtual machine with the virtual PC will invalidate the converted virtual machine. Additionally, you must be using VMware Workstation 5 or later to use this method.

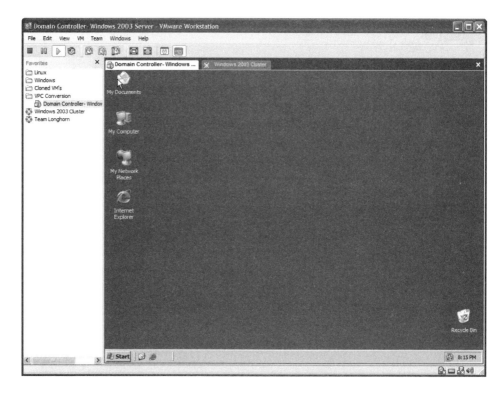

FIGURE 14.10   Starting the converted virtual machine in VMware Workstation 5.

We have already provided you with an example of how to make a complete copy of a virtual machine. Now let's show you how to link up to a virtual PC machine. First, run the **Virtual Machine Importer** from the Start menu. Next, choose **Custom** for the configuration as shown in Figure 14.11. On **Specify Source Virtual Machine**, browse to the .vmc file on your local machine. Click **Next** and Virtual Machine Importer validates that no errors exist and allows you to enter the destination of the linked virtual PC. Figure 14.12 shows a naming convention.

On the Select a Virtual Machine Format (see Figure 14.13) window, choose whether you want this virtual machine to have all the bells and whistles of a new Workstation 5 virtual machine or a legacy virtual machine compatible with the following platforms:

- VMware ESX Server 2.x
- VMware GSX Server 3.x
- VMware Workstation 4.x
- VMware ACE 1.x

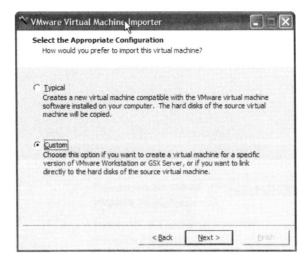

FIGURE 14.11   Choose custom to link to a virtual PC virtual disk.

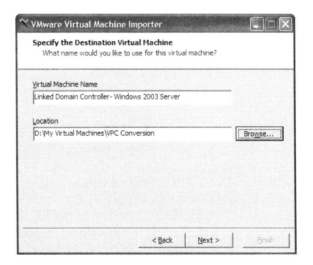

FIGURE 14.12   Creating a naming convention and folder for all virtual PC conversions.

Let's create a virtual machine with all the latest bells and whistles and proceed. On the Virtual Machine Import Options, we can:

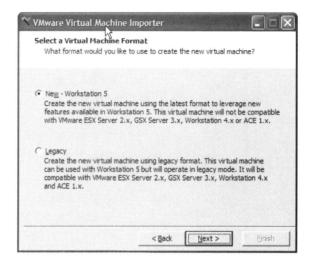

FIGURE 14.13 Choose the format of your virtual machine.

- Make a complete copy of the source virtual machine.
- Link to the existing virtual machine. Do not continue to use the source virtual machine after importing. If you try to run the virtual PC source machine, you will break the imported virtual machine.

Select **Link to an existing virtual machine** and click Next as shown in Figure 14.14. Review the summary information on the Ready to Start Importing page and click **Next** to start the process. A progress bar indicates the reconfiguration process,

FIGURE 14.14 Linking to an existing virtual machine.

and ends on the Virtual Machine Import is Complete window. Check the **Start my new virtual machine now** box and click **Finish**. The linked VMware Workstation boots to the applicable operating system as shown in Figure 14.15.

Now that we have gone over how to convert your Virtual PC virtual machine to VMware Workstation virtual machines, let's take it a step further and go over how to perform physical to virtual conversions (P2V).

FIGURE 14.15 Windows 2003 linked virtual machine.

15

Physical to Virtual Conversion

In This Chapter

- Physical to Virtual (P2V) Conversion Tools
- Using VMware P2V Assistant 2.0
- About Leostream P>V
- Norton Ghost 2003

In the past, if you had a major upgrade on the horizon, it might have been necessary for you to procure a QA test environment to test the upgrade prior to implementing it on your production environment. Virtual machines introduced a way to test environments without having to buy new hardware. Physical to virtual conversion (P2V) allows you to make an exact replica of your production environment for testing. Instead of having to manually re-create the environment, you can now use several P2V tools to create a mirror image of your production servers. In this chapter we will introduce you to some P2V tools that you can utilize to mirror your environment in VMware Workstation.

PHYSICAL TO VIRTUAL (P2V) CONVERSION TOOLS

Three ways to perform a P2V conversion will be discussed. They are:

■ VMware P2V Assistant 2.0
■ Leostream
■ Norton Ghost

Of the three methods, both P2V Assistant 2.0 and Leostream are packaged versions; Norton Ghost is a manual solution to P2V.

USING VMWARE P2V ASSISTANT 2.0

VMware P2V Assistant allows you to migrate a physical machine to a target virtual machine without making any changes to the source machine. Unlike Norton Ghost, this is fully supported by VMware and takes a lot of the guesswork out of performing a P2V migration. The conversion that takes place is identical in every aspect except that now you have the server or workstation running in a virtual machine for testing purposes.

P2V Requirements

The P2V Assistant software can be loaded on the following hardware:

■ A Workstation, laptop, or virtual machine running VMware Workstation, GSX Server, and/or ESX Server
■ A minimum of 10 MB of free space for the application and 200 MB free for temporary files, in addition to free space for your new virtual disks

You can visit *http://www.vmware.com/support/P2V2/doc/reqscomponents. html#1013277* for a complete list of the requirements necessary prior to installation of the product.

Installing VMware P2V Assistant

Your first step is to execute the installer that you received either by download or by the delivery of a CD-ROM. You must be logged on as an administrator to perform the installation. Figure 15.1 displays the Welcome window.

After you accept the end user license agreement, enter the user name and organization followed by the setup type. A custom installation allows you to change the default installation path. When you have made your choice, click **Install** to

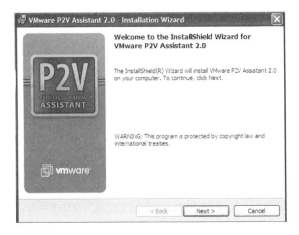

FIGURE 15.1 The VMware P2V Assistant Installation Wizard.

install the VMware P2V Assistant. Click **Finish** when the installation is complete. You might be prompted to reboot your computer.

Installing the P2V Source Machine Boot CD-ROM

Your second step is to either download the ISO image of the bootable CD-ROM used in the physical system you wish to migrate, or place the delivered CD-ROM in the source machine CD-ROM. Start your server or workstation and it will boot to the Welcome to P2V Assistant 2.0 Boot CD Wizard window (see Figure 15.2). Click **OK** and you will be prompted with a message, as shown in Figure 15.3, that describes how to get support if your hardware isn't detected.

FIGURE 15.2 The P2V Assistant 2.0 Boot CD Wizard.

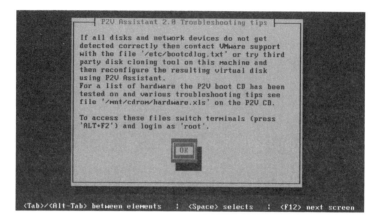

FIGURE 15.3 P2V Troubleshooting tips.

On the Disk and Network Devices Detected window (see Figure 15.4), all of your detected drives that you might want to convert are listed. Choose **Continue** and **No** if all of your disks and network cards have been detected as shown in Figure 15.5.

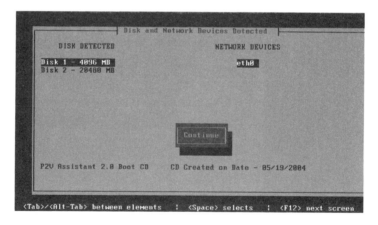

FIGURE 15.4 Viewing your detected network devices.

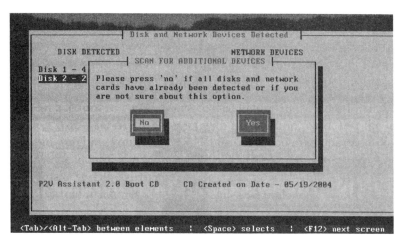

FIGURE 15.5   Scanning for additional devices.

The next window allows you either to use DHCP (see Figure 15.6) to obtain an IP address or to input one manually. Once this step is completed, you are shown a window with the following settings: Mac Address, Network Speed, Duplex, IP Address, Netmask, Gateway, Name Server, and the P2V Server Port that the P2V Assistant uses to connect to the source machine. See Figure 15.7 for a graphical representation of the settings.

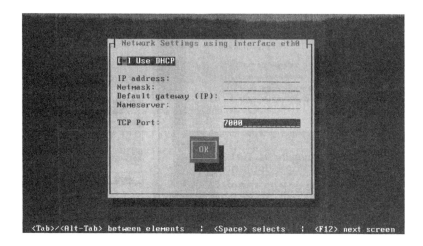

FIGURE 15.6   Choose the IP address method.

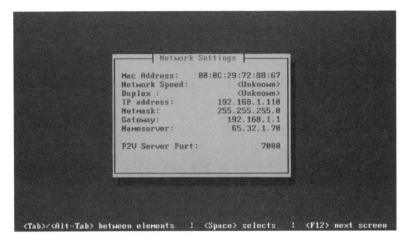

FIGURE 15.7 The Network Settings window.

At this point you should have the VMware P2V Assistant running and the source machine waiting for a connection on port 7000. In our next section, we will walk you through the P2V Assistant.

The P2V Assistant Wizard

On the helper machine, from the Start menu click **Start | VMware | VMware P2V Assistant 2.0**, and the license information is displayed. You have the option to view that license information if necessary by clicking the **License Info** button. Next, select your cloning option (see Figure 15.8) as follows:

Perform a system reconfiguration on an existing disk that contains an operating system: You would select this option if you have a disk that you restored an operating system image to and you want this disk to serve as the primary boot system disk in a new virtual machine. An example would be using a third-party imaging tool to restore an image to a virtual disk. Once the restore is complete, you would use this option to reconfigure the disk to become the primary bootable system disk in a new virtual machine.

Clone a source computer's physical disk to a virtual disk and optionally perform a system reconfiguration on the virtual disk: You would select this option if you want to use the VMware P2V Assistant to clone the disk and reconfigure it to work as a bootable virtual disk. After you choose this option, you must identify the source disk waiting for the connection as shown in Figure 15.9.

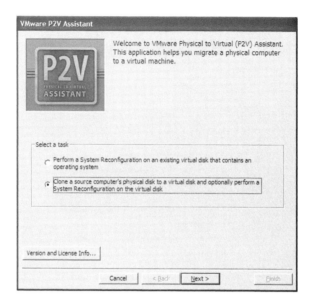

FIGURE 15.8 Choose the P2V migration.

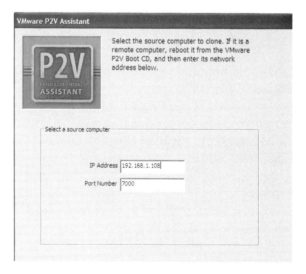

FIGURE 15.9 Enter the appropriate IP address to connect to the source computer.

Simply enter the IP address of the source machine and the port it is listening on. At this point, the P2V Assistant connects to the source computer and prompts you to select the source disk for migration (see Figure 15.10).

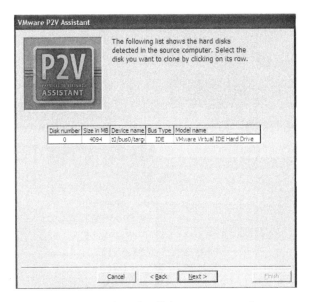

FIGURE 15.10 Select the disk you want to clone.

P2V Assistant 2.0 allows you to migrate only one physical disk at a time.

On the Disk Volume and Operating System Information window, verify that the information displayed is correct and proceed to the next window. Now you have a choice as to whether you want to clone the disk and reconfigure, or clone the disk and reconfigure later if necessary. If you are cloning a data disk, system reconfiguration is not necessary. If you are cloning a disk that contains the operating system, reconfiguration is necessary to get the disk to boot properly.

On the Disk Cloning Options window, you can choose to copy the temporary system files (pagefile.sys and hiberfil.sys) and the temporary Internet files. After accepting the defaults, it is time to create your new virtual disk. Browse to any location on your computer or network designated for disk creation.

If you create your disk files over the network, remember to map a network drive to that location on the machine that has the P2V Assistant installed. If you do not do this, you will not be able to create the .vmdk file.

Once you input the path and the size of the virtual hard drive, you have the option of splitting your virtual disks in 2 GB files or allocating the disk space at creation. It is recommended that you split your disk in 2 GB files so that if you ever have to archive or move them, they will fit comfortably on multiple DVDs. Next, by selecting to resize your disk partitions, you can see how much of your partition is being used and size it accordingly. For example, if you have a 20 GB partition but are only using 6 GB of it, you can resize the partition to 10 GB.

On the Reconfigure Options windows you can choose the following:

- Target VMware Product / Virtual Hardware
- System Reconfiguration Options

For the purposes of this book, we will be choosing Workstation 4.5.2 or higher (see Figure 15.11) as our virtual hardware. By default, the reconfiguration chooses to preinstall a temporary VMware SVGA driver to improve mouse and graphics on the first boot of the new virtual machine. This driver is replaced once you install VMware Tools. The reconfiguration also preserves the drive letter to volume mappings. At this point the wizard is finished and the system begins the clone and reconfiguration. Once the process is complete, you are presented with a completion window.

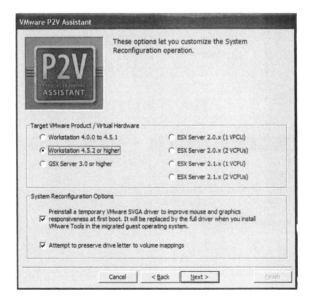

FIGURE 15.11   Choosing your system reconfiguration options.

ABOUT LEOSTREAM P>V

Leostream is a third-party utility that performs a simple automated physical to virtual conversion of the Windows platform. This includes the following operating systems: NT4, 2000, XP, and 2003 operating systems.

How Does It Work?

Leostream P>V consists of a P2V wizard and a Windows Host Agent. The P2V wizard is installed on the workstation or server that you want migrated. The Windows Host Agent is installed on a machine that has VMware Workstation installed. Leostream supports many virtual platforms but for the purpose of this book, we will be using VMware Workstation 5. During this process the P2V wizard and the Host Agent profile the source or origin machine and create an identical virtual machine on the computer that has the Windows Host Agent installed. Once this process completes, the second process uses a conversion program to copy the source disk to the virtual disk. Let's go over the install of the P2V wizard and Host Agent followed by a detailed walk-through of this program in action.

Installing the Leostream Host Agent Wizard

In order to install the agent, you must first download it from *http://www.leostream. com/support.* Once it is downloaded, double-click the executable and the Welcome window appears as shown in Figure 15.12. On the next window, accept the license agreement or click **Cancel** to exit the application. Finally, click **Install** to install the application as shown in Figure 15.13.

FIGURE 15.12 Leostream Host Agent Setup Wizard.

FIGURE 15.13 Click Install to begin installing the Host Agent.

Prior to the installation completing, you will be prompted to enter the Leostream Controller address. You can enter the IP address or DNS name of the controller. Basically, you are entering the IP address of the machine on which you are currently installing the Leostream Host Agent. Figure 15.14 displays the window that requires the Leostream controller address. Finally click **Finish** to start the Leostream Host Agent.

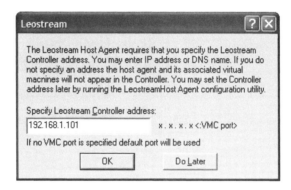

FIGURE 15.14   Specifying the controller address.

Configuring the Host Agent

The Windows Host Agent has the following tabs for configuration: Status, Options, Virtual Machines, Advanced, Logging, and About.

Status

The Status tab displays the status of the service as shown in Figure 15.15. You can start and stop the service if necessary.

Options

The Options tab (see Figure 15.16) enables you to edit the default options for startup, port numbers, and the Leostream controller address. All of this information is part of the default installation except for the Leostream controller address.

Virtual Machines

The Virtual Machines tab (see Figure 15.17) allows you to specify the location where your VMware Workstation 5 virtual machines are stored when they are converted from a physical machine.

FIGURE 15.15 Viewing the Status page.

FIGURE 15.16 Viewing the Options page.

Advanced

The Advanced tab (see Figure 15.18) allows you to enable SSL and guest agent support. This tab allows you to encrypt the communication between Host Agent and controller. This enables the controller to securely manage remote servers in addition to managing the optional guest agent, which runs Windows Machine Name, joins domains, etc. It is similar to Sysprep but works on a running system.

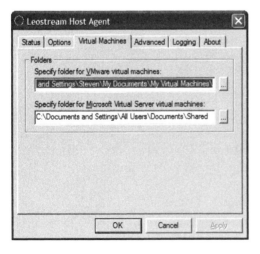

FIGURE 15.17 Specify the destination of your virtual machines.

FIGURE 15.18 Enabling advanced options.

Logging

The Logging tab (see Figure 15.19) gives you the ability to set logging options. By selecting the **Use NT Event Viewer**, you can see errors, warnings, and information in the event viewer as it pertains to the Windows Host Agent. Simply click the **Settings** button and select the NT events that apply.

Additionally, you have the option of having information written to the trace log. When you click on the **Trace Log Settings** button, you can set the location of the Leostream log (see Figure 15.20) and set the following events by choosing the **Set Events** button: errors, warnings, information, Winsock, trace, diagnostic, and dump.

On the Backup tab, as shown in Figure 15.21, you can set the frequency and schedule of your log file. It is recommended that you perform a daily backup and set the file size limit to 10 MB. The Backup Archive tab (see Figure 15.22) allows you to determine how many backup files are kept. You can choose an unlimited number or set the number of backups to retain.

FIGURE 15.19 Configuring the logging options.

FIGURE 15.20 Specify the location of the Leostream Host Agent log.

About

The About window (see Figure 15.23) displays The Windows Host Agent version number, copyright, and links to the Leostream home page, customer service, and product suggestions.

FIGURE 15.21 Configuring the backup frequency and schedule.

FIGURE 15.22 Choosing the backup archive options.

FIGURE 15.23 Company information.

Installing the Leostream P>V Wizard

To install the Leostream P>V Wizard, you must first download it from *http://www.leostream.com/support*. Once it is downloaded, double-click the executable and the Welcome window appears as shown in Figure 15.24. On the next window, accept the license agreement or click **Cancel** to exit the application. Click the **Install** button to install the application and the **Finish** button when it is complete. The Leostream P>V Wizard installs the software to \program files\ LeostreamP2V. It also adds the application to your desktop and Start menu.

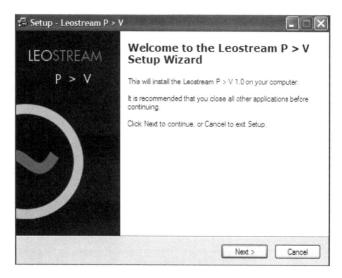

FIGURE 15.24   The P>V Setup Wizard.

Performing a Physical to Virtual Conversion via Leostream

In order to perform the conversion, make sure that you have the Windows Host Agent started and that VMware Workstation 5 is installed on the Windows Host Agent machine. Next, click **Start | Programs | Leostream P2V | Leostream P2V** and the Leostream Welcome window appears. To continue, click **Next** and you are prompted to enter your license key (see Figure 15.25).

In order to get a license, select the **Click here** to get license key link. This link takes you to *http://www.leostream.com/support*. Once you log in to the Web site (see Figure 15.26), click on the **Licenses** link and choose **Create** to create a new license. Enter the machine name, serial number and any applicable notes, as shown in Figure 15.27.

Once you click **Save** you are given a key (see Figure 15.28) to unlock the P2V wizard.Enter that key, as shown in Figure 15.29, in the P2V wizard and click **Next.**

FIGURE 15.25   Obtain a license key.

FIGURE 15.26   Log in to the support site.

On the Virtual Machine Destination window (see Figure 15.30) specify the IP address or DNS name of the Windows Host Agent that is running on a destination or target server. At this point, the P2V wizard contacts the target machine and you

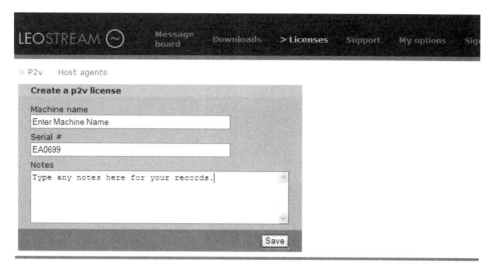

FIGURE 15.27   Creating a P2V license.

FIGURE 15.28   The P2V license key.

are given the Virtual Machine Options window as shown in Figure 15.31. The virtual machine options allow you to set the memory of the new virtual machine as well as change the size of the hard disk.

If the P2V wizard cannot locate the destination or target machine, then the Windows Host Agent is not running.

FIGURE 15.29 Unlock the P2V wizard.

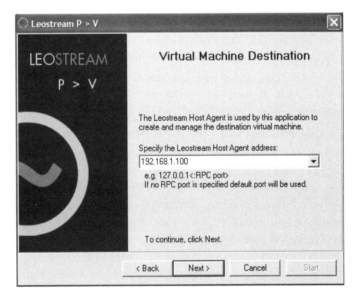

FIGURE 15.30 Specify the IP address or DNS name of the Host Agent.

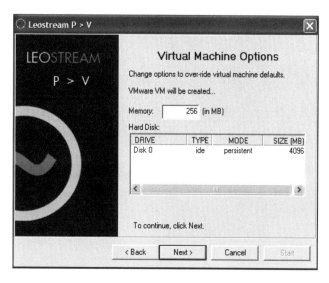

FIGURE 15.31 Configure the memory and virtual disk space of the virtual machine.

About Disk Transport Options

The Disk Transport Options window (see Figure 15.32) is where you create the boot disk that the operating system boots to in order to copy the source hard drive over to the destination server. You can choose from the following:

Acronis: Use this option to prepare the machine for an Acronis True Image.

Leostream: Use this option to create a single floppy Leostream disk.

Leostream Plus: Use this option to create three floppies. This disk transport option supports a larger set of disk and network adapters.

Leostream Advanced: Use this option to manually select your disk and network adapters. When you choose this option, you can select from a list of NIC and SCSI adapters.

Symantec Ghost: Use this option to use Symantec Ghost as your disk transport option.

Other: This method copies the contents of any floppy to the destination virtual floppy.

FIGURE 15.32 Choose the Disk Transport provider.

Leostream Converter

Now that you have created your boot disk, click the **Start** button, as shown in Figure 15.33, to create the virtual machine on the destination server. A virtual machine identical to the source machine is created and automatically booted to the Leostream Converter program as shown in Figure 15.34.

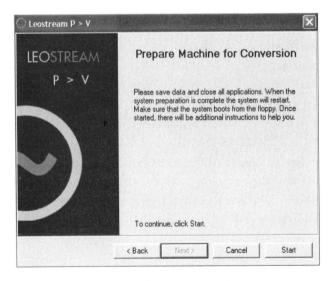

FIGURE 15.33 Starting the P2V conversion process

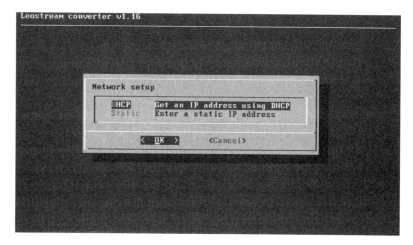

FIGURE 15.34   The Leostream converter network setup.

You have the option of getting an IP address from DHCP or entering a static IP address. Next, specify that the drive will be inserted into this machine (see Figure 15.35) and click **OK**. The destination virtual machine is now waiting to receive the source data as shown in Figure 15.36.

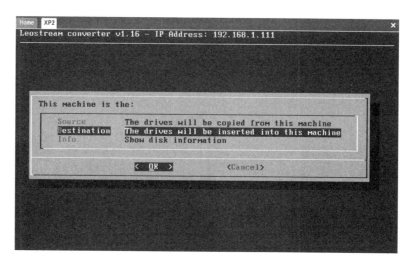

FIGURE 15.35   Leostream converter options.

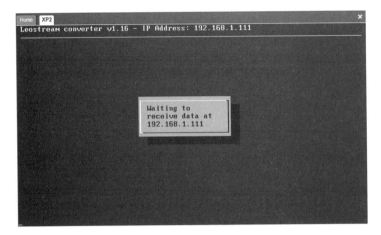

FIGURE 15.36 The Leostream converter is waiting to receive data.

After the virtual machine is prompted to reboot, the source machine also has to reboot and start up with the floppy disk to run the converter program. Upon reboot, you have the option of obtaining an IP address via DHCP or manually entering one.

Next, choose **The drives will be copied from this machine** (see Figure 15.37) and click **OK**. You now can choose the disk or partition you want to copy as shown in Figure 15.38. At this point, the data is being transferred to the virtual machine and you are told when the transfer is complete, as shown in Figure 15.39. As you can see, this is a very powerful but simple tool to use. You can access a free trial at *http://leostream.com*. On the home page, click the **Free Trial** button and see for yourself.

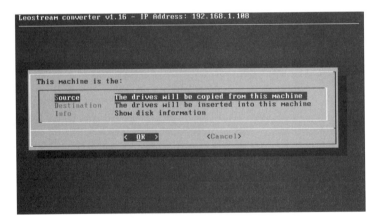

FIGURE 15.37 Copying the drives.

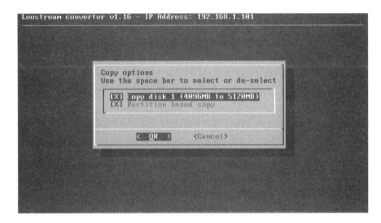

FIGURE 15.38   Choose the copy option for the P2V conversion.

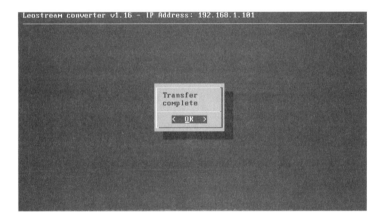

FIGURE 15.39   The transfer complete message.

NORTON GHOST 2003

If cost is a factor when it comes to performing a P2V, you can use Norton Ghost to meet some of your needs. There are certain limitations to using Norton Ghost with VMware Workstation. It is recommended that you restrict this method to P2V source computers including the following:

- Windows 95
- Windows 98
- Windows Me
- Windows 2000
- Windows XP

Furthermore, this method assumes that the image you are converting to a virtual machine has been created with an IDE drive. Converting SCSI drives with Norton Ghost is complicated and outside the scope of this book.

With Norton Ghost, you have the following ways to create a physical to virtual (P2V) conversion:

- Network P2V
- P2V via an image

Performing Network P2V Conversion

Using this method, one computer acts as the master and another computer acts as the slave. The end result is that one computer sends its data or image directly to the other computer (usually a virtual machine) via a TCP/IP connection. It is recommended that you do not use this method on production environments. This method works well with development environments on Windows XP/2000 computers. Let's go over it in detail.

Creating Your Peer to Peer Boot Disk

Your first step is to start the target virtual machine and boot it to the Ghost boot disk. The easiest method of creating the boot disk is by using a virtual floppy. Creating virtual floppies is very easy if you use a product called WinImage. It can be downloaded at *http://www.winimage.com*. Once you have installed WinImage, click **Start | Programs | WinImage | WinImage**. Next, Click **File | New** and choose **1.44 MB** as shown in Figure 15.40. Click **OK** and save as an *.ima file as shown in Figure 15.41.

Because you are restoring the image inside a virtual machine, the process can be arduous. Please be patient with the conversion as it is slightly slower than working with a physical PC.

Now that you have created your virtual floppy, start your target virtual machine and open Ghost from **Start | Programs | Norton Ghost 2003 | Norton Ghost** or double-click the Ghost icon in the system tray. Next, click **Ghost Utilities | Norton**

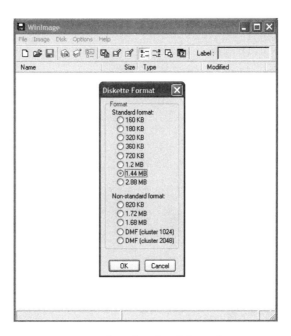

FIGURE 15.40 Choosing the diskette format.

FIGURE 15.41 Select the image file (IMA) extension.

Ghost Boot Wizard (see Figure 15.42) and select **Peer to Peer Network Boot Disk** (see Figure 15.43).

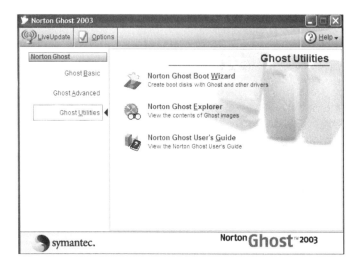

FIGURE 15.42 Norton Ghost Boot Wizard.

FIGURE 15.43 Peer to Peer Network Boot Disk.

To create the Ghost boot disk, you must choose the **AMC PCNET family network interface card** as shown in Figure 15.44. On both the DOS version window and the Ghost executable locations, accept the defaults. Next, assign a manual IP address or have a DHCP server assign your IP address. You are now ready to choose your destination floppy drive (see Figure 15.45).

FIGURE 15.44   Select the appropriate network interface card.

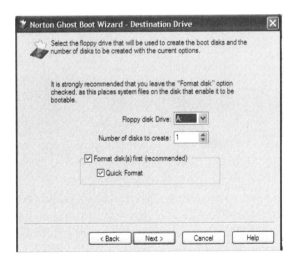

FIGURE 15.45   Formatting and creating your Norton boot disk.

In the VMware control center, choose **VM | Settings** and highlight your **Floppy 1** setting on the Hardware tab (see Figure 15.46). Under the Use floppy image, make sure the path is pointing to the blank floppy image you created. Once you have verified the floppy is correct, click the **Connected** checkbox under Device status and click **OK** (see Figure 15.47).

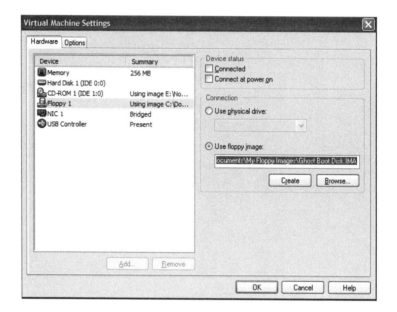

FIGURE 15.46 Create a floppy image.

FIGURE 15.47 Connecting the floppy image device.

Now that your virtual floppy is connected, click **Next** on the Destination Drive window (see Figure 15.45) and review your settings on the Summary window. Click **Next** and you will be prompted to format your virtual floppy; then the virtual floppy is configured with the Ghost boot disk. Restart your virtual machine using your boot disk and upon reboot, choose **Peer to peer | TCP/IP | Slave**. The next step is to prepare the source computer that connects to the target computer.

Configuring the Source Computer

The master computer is the computer that holds the image or data that you want to migrate to the source machine. The easiest way to begin the transfer is to choose **Ghost Advanced | Peer-to-Peer** from the operating system you want to migrate as shown in Figure 15.48.

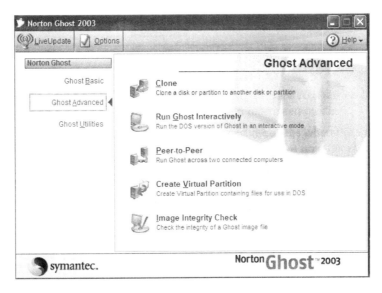

FIGURE 15.48   The Norton Ghost Peer-to-Peer option.

Next, choose **TCP peer-to-peer** and click **TCP/IP driver settings** on the Advanced Settings window. On the TCP/IP driver settings window, browse to your network driver and click **Finish** and **OK**. Click **Run Now** and Norton Ghost will restart your computer and ask for additional options. When the computer boots, choose **Peer to peer | TCP/IP | Master** and type in the IP address of the target computer (see Figure 15.49). Now choose **Disk | Disk** and Norton Ghost will display the partition information. Choose the appropriate partition information and then the clone will begin as shown in Figure 15.50.

Once you have finished cloning, it is recommended that you Sysprep your machine using Microsoft's Sysprep utility. You can download the utility at *http://www. microsoft.com/windows2000/downloads/tools/sysprep/default.asp.*

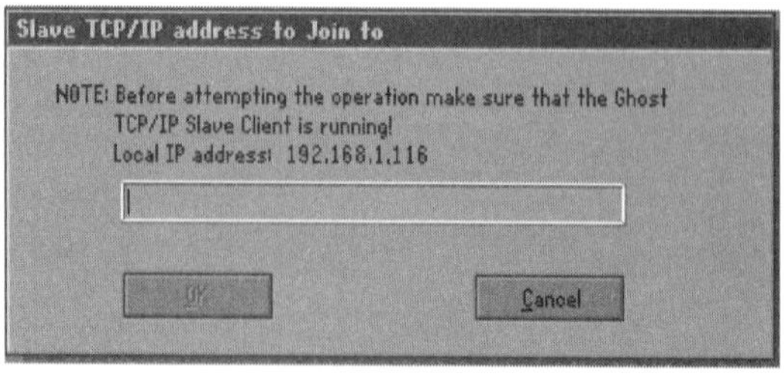

FIGURE 15.49 Enter the IP address of the slave computer.

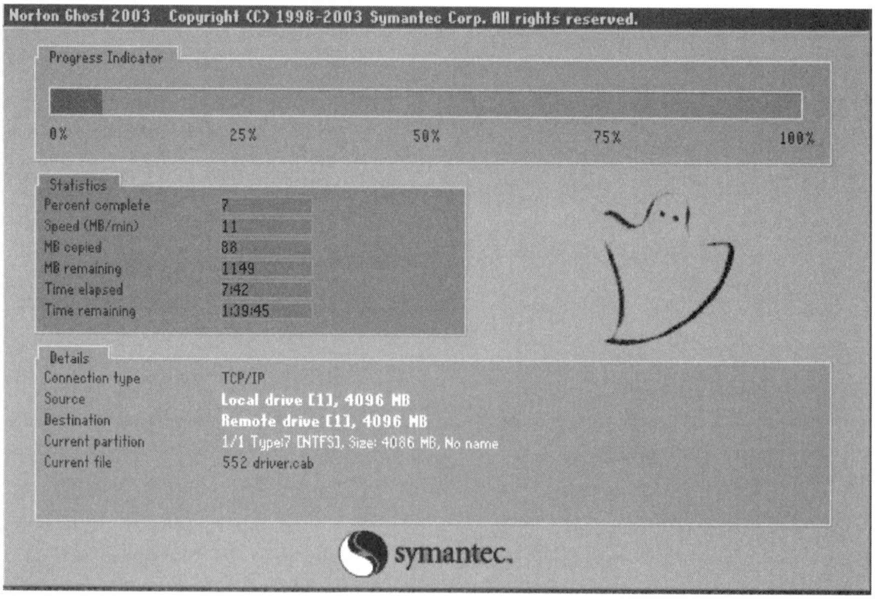

FIGURE 15.50 Copy the data.

Note that in some instances, you might have to copy the hal.dll from a similar operating system in VMware. For example, if you P2V a Windows XP machine, you can take the hal.dll from an already existing and working installation of Windows XP within the virtual machine. Simply browse to the Windows\System32 directory and copy the hal.dll to a safe location. Once it is in that safe location, open a new virtual machine that is already configured with VMware Workstation and the identical operating system and service pack and add that imaged disk to the configuration.

Once you have added the disk, boot the virtual machine and copy the hall.dl to the appropriate place.

P2V via an Image

With this method, you first take an image of the computer you want to P2V. Once you have the image, you can map a drive to it on your network and restore it to a virtual machine. You can also copy the image to an additional drive on the virtual machine and restore the image from within the virtual machine or locally. This method requires you to have a huge amount of disk space but is successful if you have the real estate.

Taking advantage of P2V technology can allow you to take your infrastructure to the next level. Imagine you are about to upgrade your Exchange server but you first want to test how the upgrade or service pack will affect your system. Simply bring the server into a virtual machine via P2V and test away with no downtime to your end users. In our next chapter, we will show you some of the tips and tricks that VMware Workstation has to offer.

16 Tips and Tricks

In This Chapter

- Installing VMware Workstation as a Service
- Disabling the Shutdown Event Tracker on a Windows Server 2003
- Creating a Screen Shot or a Movie of a Virtual Machine
- Using BgInfo with Your Virtual Machines
- Creating Virtual Floppies with WinImage
- Working with the Virtual Floppy Driver
- Working with the Virtual Disk Manager
- Using the DiskMount Utility
- Archiving Virtual Machines
- Using RAW Disk Partitions in VMware Workstation
- Using WinISO
- Working with VMware Workstation from the Command Line
- Working with the VMrun Command Line
- Modifying the Tip of the Day
- Working with Shared Folders
- Keyboard Shortcuts

The tips and tricks chapter describes many of VMware Workstation's hidden treasures as well as some third-party utilities that will help your productivity with VMware Workstation.

INSTALLING VMWARE WORKSTATION AS A SERVICE

Currently, VMware Workstation does not support the ability to run virtual machines as a service.

As soon as you log off your computer, the running virtual machines are shut down or powered off. If you can install virtual machines as a service, you can perform the following:

■ Enable your host system to logon to a virtual domain controller.
■ Save time booting your virtual machines.

Here is how you can install VMware Workstation 5 as a service.

Requirements

In order to run virtual machines as a service, you must have the following Windows Resource Kit Tools:

■ Instsrv.exe
■ Srvany.exe

You can download the Windows 2003 Resource Kit tools (rktools.exe) at *http://www.microsoft.com/downloads/details.aspx?FamilyID=9d467a69-57ff-4ae7-96ee-b18c4790cffd&DisplayLang=en*. After you install the tools, copy the instsrv.exe and srvany.exe to the windows\system32 directory. It is then recommended that you reboot your computer.

Configuring VMware Workstation as a Service

The first step to configuring VMware Workstation as a service is to locate the VMware Workstation executable. The default location of the VMware Workstation executable is c:\program files\vmware\vmware workstation\vmware.exe. Once you have located VMware.exe, the crucial step in the process is to locate the path of the configuration file of the virtual machine that you want to turn into a service. In a virtual machine the .vmx file is the file that stores the configuration for a virtual machine. In order for VMware Workstation to run as a service, you have to be able to locate the path to the .vmx file. For example, if your virtual machines are all saved to D:, the path would be as follows: D:\My Virtual Machines\Workstation\winXPPRO.vmx. Once you have the path to the executable and the path to the configuration file, you are ready to create the service.

Creating the Service

First it is recommended that you create a name standard for all of your virtual machines. For example, if you are creating a domain controller to run as a service, you might call it vmware_dc. Once you have the standard, click **Start | Programs| Accessories | Command Prompt** and type the command shown in Figure 16.1.

```
C:\WINDOWS\system32\cmd.exe                                          _□×

Microsoft Windows XP [Version 5.1.2600]
(C) Copyright 1985-2001 Microsoft Corp.

C:\Documents and Settings\Steven>Instsrv VMWARE_SUSE C:\windows\system32\srvany.exe

The service was successfuly added!

Make sure that you go into the Control Panel and use
the Services applet to change the Account Name and
Password that this newly installed service will use
for its Security Context.

C:\Documents and Settings\Steven>
```

FIGURE 16.1   Creating a service via a DOS prompt.

Listing 16.1 will create a service that will automatically run the SuSE 9.1 operating system.

LISTING 16.1   Creating the Virtual Machine Service

```
Instsrv VMWARE_SUSE C:\windows\system32\srvany.exe
```

Next, open the registry by clicking **Start | Run |**. Then type regedit and expand HKEY_LOCAL_MACHINE\SYSTEM\CurrentControlSet\Services\"name of your VMware Service subkey". In this example, the name of the service is VMWARE_SUSE. Right-click on the **VMWARE_SUSE** name key and choose **New | Key** and call the subkey Parameters as shown in Figure 16.2.

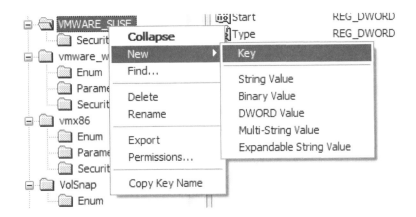

FIGURE 16.2   Adding a new parameter key.

Next, right-click on the **Parameters** subkey and choose **New | String Value** and call the key Application, as shown in Figure 16.3. Double-click the **Application key value** and enter the path to the vmware.exe and the virtual machine's .vmx file as shown in Figure 16.4.

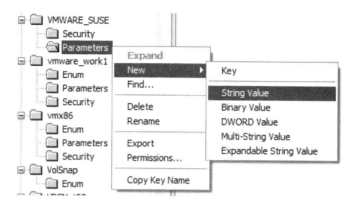

FIGURE 16.3 Creating a string value.

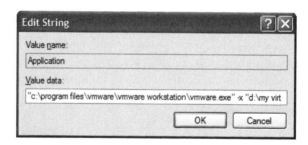

FIGURE 16.4 Enter the path to the .vmx configuration file.

The default path is C:\program files\vmware\VMware Workstation\VMware. exe followed by the path to the virtual machine's .vmx file. Remember to put this path in double quotation marks. Listing 16.2 displays the configuration path needed to run virtual machines as a service.

LISTING 16.2 Application Value

```
"c:\program files\vmware\vmware workstation\vmware.exe" —x "d:\my
virtual machines\vm\suse linux 9.1\suse.vmx"
```

Now that you have added the path, you need to set the start-up options for the newly created service. Click **Start | Run |** and type services.msc and browse to the service you just created for your VMware Workstation virtual machine (see Figure 16.5). Double-click on the service and select the **Log On** tab. On the General tab choose **Automatic** as the startup type and then select the **Log On** tab and select the **Local System account** to run the service (see Figure 16.6). Additionally, you also need to select **Allow service** to interact with the desktop. Next, test the service by starting it and watching your virtual machine start. You might be prompted to create a new unique identifier as shown in Figure 16.7. The final test is to reboot your machine to make sure the virtual machine starts as well. You can repeat these steps for as many virtual machines as your system can handle.

VMware Virtual Mou...	Part of the...	Manual	Local System
VMWARE_SUSE		Automatic	Local System
vmware_work1		Manual	Local System
Volume Shadow Copy	Manages a	Manual	Local System

FIGURE 16.5 The virtual machine service.

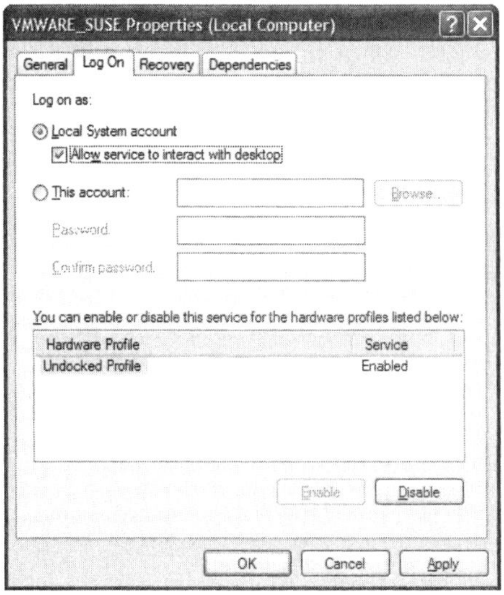

FIGURE 16.6 Configuring the service.

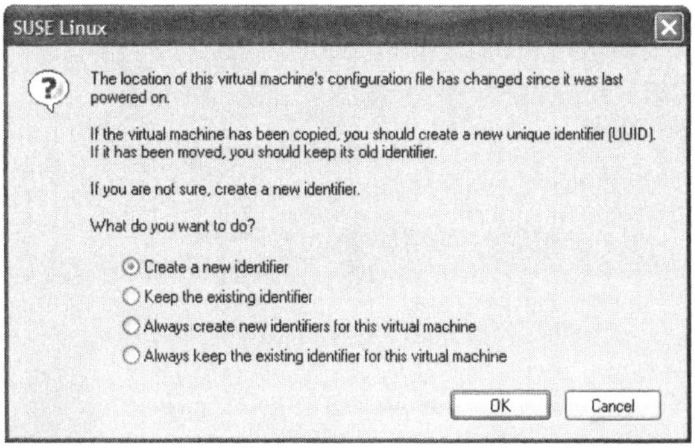

FIGURE 16.7 Configuring your unique identifier (UUID).

When running virtual machines as a service, make sure all floppy drives, CD-ROM, and other devices are disconnected. It is also recommended that you disable VMware Hints by adding the following line to your *.VMX file, as shown in Figure 16.8: Hints.hideall="TRUE".

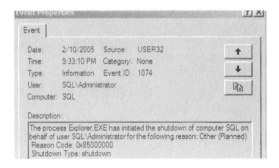

FIGURE 16.8   The virtual machine .vmx file.

DISABLING THE SHUTDOWN EVENT TRACKER ON WINDOWS SERVER 2003

In Windows Server 2003, the shutdown event tracker provides IT professionals the ability to track restarts and shutdowns of Windows Server 2003. At any given point, you can view the shutdown event tracker log by searching for the User 32 event in the event viewer mmc console, as shown in Figure 16.9.

FIGURE 16.9   The shutdown event tracker.

When you work with your virtual machines, using the shutdown tracker can become cumbersome. By default, the shutdown tracker is enabled on all Windows Server 2003 machines, but it can be disabled. In order to disable the shutdown event tracker, open **Group policy** from the Run menu. Next, click **Start | Run** and type `gpedit.msc`; click **OK**. Expand **Computer Configuration | Administrative Templates | System** and double-click the **Shutdown event tracker** as shown in Figure 16.10 and choose **Disabled**. You have now successfully disabled the shutdown event tracker.

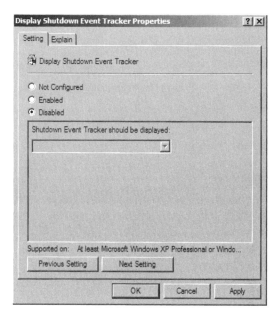

FIGURE 16.10 Disabling the shutdown tracker.

CREATING A SCREENSHOT OR A MOVIE OF A VIRTUAL MACHINE

With VMware Workstation, you can perform the following:

- Take a screenshot
- Take a movie of a virtual machine

About Screenshots

At any point in time, you can take a screenshot of a virtual machine by selecting **VM | Capture Screen** as shown in Figure 16.11.

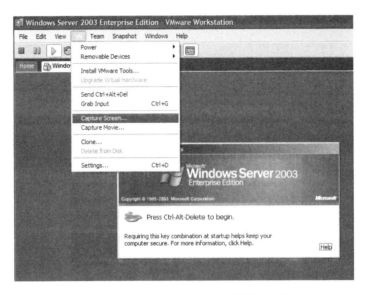

FIGURE 16.11   Capturing a screenshot in VMware Workstation.

About Movies

Not only can you take a screenshot of your virtual machines but you can also capture a movie. This is very helpful if you want a movie for training. In order to capture a movie, click **VM | Capture Movie** from the menu bar (see Figure 16.12).

Next, select a directory location. The default is the name of the active virtual machine. Once you have chosen your directory location, enter a file name for the movie and choose the movie quality. Select the **Omit frames** in which nothing occurs if you want to keep the file size low. Click **Save** to begin recording the movie and a red circle appears in the status bar as shown in Figure 16.13.

You can play back your video using any compatible movie player. If you distribute the movie to someone who doesn't have VMware Workstation 5 installed, you must install the VMware codec available on the VMware Web site.

FIGURE 16.12   Capturing a movie.

FIGURE 16.13   The red circle appears
when you start recording a movie.

USING BGINFO WITH YOUR VIRTUAL MACHINES

With BgInfo you have the ability to display information about your computer such
as computer name, IP address, service pack, etc. This tool is very handy with your
virtual machines as it lets you keep track when you have multiple virtual machines
running on your desktop.

You can download BgInfo from *http://www.sysinternals.com/ntw2k/freeware/
bginfo.shtml.* Once it is downloaded, place the BgInfo.exe in your startup folder to
ensure that your system information is updated each time you boot your computer.
Figure 16.14 displays BgInfo in action.

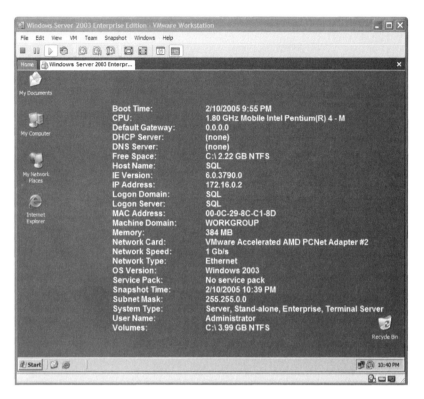

FIGURE 16.14 BgInfo.

CREATING VIRTUAL FLOPPIES WITH WINIMAGE

With VMware Workstation, you can use virtual floppies. Using virtual floppies is extremely helpful when you have to install guest operating systems such as Windows 95 or Windows 98. You can download WinImage from *http://www.winimage.com/*. With WinImage, you can create virtual floppy files and manage existing virtual floppy disks. Let's walk through how to create a virtual floppy disk in WinImage.

Creating a Virtual Floppy Disk

After downloading a trial version of WinImage, double-click **winimage.exe** and choose **File New** as shown in Figure 16.15. Select the **1.44 MB Standard Format** and click **OK**. You can now inject or add files to the image by drag and drop or click **Image | Inject** from the menu bar as shown in Figure 16.16. Once you have added your files, click **File | Save As** and select **IMA** as the **Save as** type, and enter a file name such as floppy. Click **Save** and your virtual floppy drive has been created. You can also just create a blank floppy image and add files to it once you connect it in VMware as shown in Figure 16.17.

FIGURE 16.15   Choosing the floppy drive format.

FIGURE 16.16   Adding files to the virtual floppy drive.

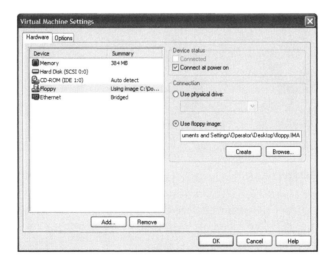

FIGURE 16.17   Connecting the virtual floppy drive to a VMware virtual disk.

WORKING WITH THE VIRTUAL FLOPPY DRIVER

Another tool that you can enjoy is the Virtual Floppy Driver. With this tool, you can mount a floppy image file as a virtual floppy drive on your host computer. It will assign the floppy image to a drive letter and allow you to edit the drive as you see fit. This can become very handy as you get more into virtual machines. You can catalog a whole list of virtual floppies for all of your needs. You can download the tool at *http://chitchat.at.infoseek.co.jp/vmware/vfd.html*.

After you download the tool and extract the files to a directory on your hard drive, double-click the **vfdwin.exe** and the Virtual Floppy Drive Control Panel appears (see Figure 16.18). On the Driver tab click **Start** to mount Drive0 and Drive1 with virtual floppy drives (see Figure 16.19). When you click **Start**, it assigns the drives and you can change the drive letter by clicking on **Drive0** or **Drive 1** and clicking **Change**. Simply select the drive letter as shown in Figure 16.20.

FIGURE 16.18   The VFD control panel.

FIGURE 16.19   The virtual drives are mounted to Y: and Z:.

At this point, any image created with WinImage can be mounted to either drive by highlighting **Drive0** or **Drive 1** and selecting **Open**. Next, browse to your image and click **Open** as shown in Figure 16.21. Now that you have mounted the file, you can browse the virtual drive (see Figure 16.22) and edit the files.

To obtain bootdisks to use with VMware Workstation 5, visit www.bootdisk.com. This Web site has a variety of bootdisks that you can experiment with.

FIGURE 16.20 Selecting the drive letter.

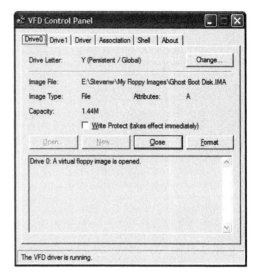

FIGURE 16.21 You can change the mounted drive letter.

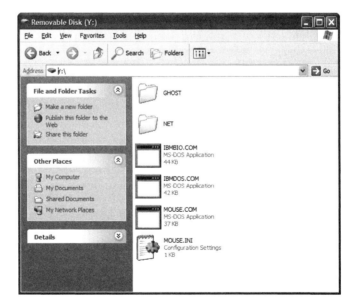

FIGURE 16.22 Editing the Virtual Floppy Driver files.

Creating Virtual Floppy Disks

With this tool, it is a snap to create new virtual floppy disks. Simply click the **Drive0** or **Drive1** tab and click **New**. Next, give the floppy a file name such as floppy.flp, select the capacity, and click **OK** (see Figure 16.23). The floppy is now mounted to the virtual drive letter and ready for you to add files.

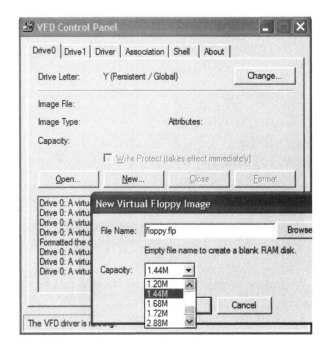

FIGURE 16.23   Choosing the size of the new floppy image.

Once you have added files, click **Close** to unmount the disk and connect the floppy disk to the virtual floppy drive in the VMware Control Center (see Figure 16.24). In this example, we uploaded a picture to the virtual floppy as shown in Figure 16.25.

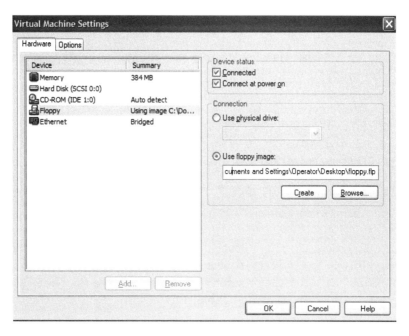

FIGURE 16.24   Connecting the floppy drive to a VMware Workstation.

FIGURE 16.25   Opening a picture inside the virtual floppy drive.

WORKING WITH THE VIRTUAL DISK MANAGER

The Virtual Disk Manager is a tool that allows you to perform the following with VMware Workstation 5:

- Create virtual disk files.
- Edit virtual disk files.
- Manage virtual disk files with scripts.
- Defragment virtual disk files.
- Expand virtual disk files.
- Create disk templates.
- Shrink virtual disks.

In order to run the Virtual Disk Manager, you must open a command prompt and browse to the directory where you installed VMware Workstation (see Figure 16.26). To execute the program type `vmware-vdiskmanager.exe`. The parameters to run this utility are shown in Table 16.1.

TABLE 16.1   Virtual Disk Manager Options

Options	Description
-c	Create disk; need to specify other create options.
-d	Defragment the specified virtual disk.
-k	Shrink the specified virtual disk.
-n <source-disk>	Rename the specified virtual disk; need to specify destination disk name.
-p	Prepare the mounted virtual disk specified by the drive letter for shrinking.
-q	Do not log message.
-r <source-disk>	Convert the specified disk; need to specify destination disk type.
-x <new-capacity>	Expand the disk to the specified capacity.
-a <adapter>	Adapter type (ide, buslogic, or lsilogic).
-s <size>	Capacity of the virtual disk.
-t <disk-type>	Disk type id.
Disk Type: 0	Single growable virtual disk.
Disk Type: 1	Growable virtual disk split in 2 GB files.
Disk Type: 2	Preallocated virtual disk.
Disk Type: 3	Preallocated virtual disk split in 2 GB files.

```
C:\Program Files\VMware\VMware Workstation>VMware-vdiskmanager.exe
VMware Virtual Disk Manager - build 12206.
Usage: vmware-vdiskmanager.exe OPTIONS diskName | drive-letter:
Offline disk manipulation utility
  Options:
     -c                       : create disk; need to specify other create options
     -d                       : defragment the specified virtual disk
     -k                       : shrink the specified virtual disk
     -n <source-disk>         : rename the specified virtual disk; need to
                                specify destination disk-name
     -p                       : prepare the mounted virtual disk specified by
                                the drive-letter for shrinking
     -q                       : do not log messages
     -r <source-disk>         : convert the specified disk; need to specify
                                destination disk-type
     -x <new-capacity>        : expand the disk to the specified capacity

  Additional options for create and convert:
     -a <adapter>             : adapter type (ide, buslogic or lsilogic)
     -s <size>                : capacity of the virtual disk
     -t <disk-type>           : disk type id

  Disk types:
     0                        : single growable virtual disk
     1                        : growable virtual disk split in 2Gb files
     2                        : preallocated virtual disk
     3                        : preallocated virtual disk split in 2Gb files

  The capacity can be specified in sectors, Kb, Mb or Gb.
  The acceptable ranges:
                        ide adapter : [100.0Mb, 950.0Gb]
                        scsi adapter: [100.0Mb, 950.0Gb]
        ex 1: vmware-vdiskmanager.exe -c -s 850Mb -a ide -t 0 myIdeDisk.vmdk
        ex 2: vmware-vdiskmanager.exe -d myDisk.vmdk
        ex 3: vmware-vdiskmanager.exe -r sourceDisk.vmdk -t 0 destinationDisk.vmdk
        ex 4: vmware-vdiskmanager.exe -x 36Gb myDisk.vmdk
        ex 5: vmware-vdiskmanager.exe -n sourceName.vmdk destinationName.vmdk
        ex 6: vmware-vdiskmanager.exe -k myDisk.vmdk
        ex 7: vmware-vdiskmanager.exe -p m:
              (A virtual disk first needs to be mounted at m:
              using the VMware Diskmount Utility.)
```

FIGURE 16.26   The Vdiskmanager command line.

The default installation of VMware Workstation is c:\program files\VMware
VMware Workstation.

Virtual Disk Tasks

We'll begin by using this utility to create a new virtual disk. In this example, let's create a 5 GB IDE fixed virtual disk (see Figure 16.27) with the following command:

```
Vmware-vdiskmanager —c —s 5GB —a ide —t 2 ssw.vmdk
```

Virtual disks are created in the directory where VMware Workstation has been installed unless otherwise specified (see Figure 16.28). If you want to create your virtual disk in a different directory use the following syntax, which specifies a location:

```
Vmware-vdiskmanager —c —s 5GB —a ide —t 2 "d:\my virtual
machines\test.vmdk"
```

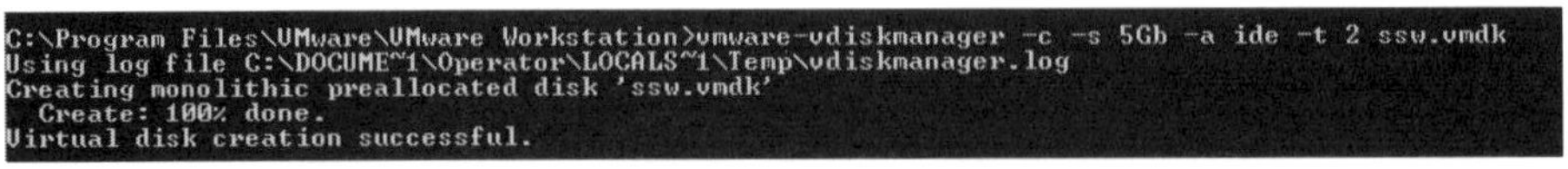

FIGURE 16.27   Command line to create a new IDE fixed virtual disk.

netadapter.inf   netbridge.inf   netware.iso   ntwrap.dll

sigc.dll   ssleay32.dll   ssw.vmdk   ssw-flat.vmdk

FIGURE 16.28   The virtual disk is created in the default directory unless otherwise specified.

The interface for creating virtual disks is very intuitive. Using the command line, you can create disks that are growable and/or preallocated. You can be as creative as you like using this interface to create disks. Let's move forward now and defrag a virtual disk. The command line for defragging a virtual disk is as follows:

```
VMware-vdiskmanager.exe –d "D:\My Virtual Machines\windows 2000
Advanced Server.vmdk"
```

In this example, we defragged a Windows 2000 Advanced server disk located in a different directory other than the default (see Figure 16.29). Let's continue by changing the ssw.vmdk disk above from a preallocated disk to a dynamic growing disk (see Figure 16.30). The syntax is as follows:

```
VMware-vdiskmanager.exe -r ssw.vmdk -t 0 sswgrowable.vmdk
```

Once you have attached the new disk within the VMware Control Center and tested the new disk with the applicable operating system, you can delete the old disk or vmdk file. At this point you should be feeling pretty comfortable and confident using this tool. Let's keep going and expand the preallocated 500 MB disk to 1 GB with the following syntax:

```
C:\Program Files\VMware\VMware Workstation>vmware-vdiskmanager -x 1gb
"d:\my virtual machines\Windows_XP.vmdk"
```

```
C:\Program Files\VMware\VMware Workstation>vmware-vdiskmanager.exe -d "D:\My Virtual Machines\windows 2000 Ad
anced Server.vmdk"
Using log file C:\DOCUME~1\Operator\LOCALS~1\Temp\vdiskmanager.log
  Defragment: 100% done.
Defragmentation completed successfully.
```

FIGURE 16.29   Defragmenting a virtual disk from the command line.

```
C:\Program Files\VMware\VMware Workstation>VMware-vdiskmanager.exe -r ssw.vmdk -t 0 sswgrowable.vmdk
Using log file C:\DOCUME~1\Operator\LOCALS~1\Temp\vdiskmanager.log
Creating a monolithic growable disk 'sswgrowable.vmdk'
  Convert: 100% done.
Virtual disk conversion successful.
```

FIGURE 16.30   Changing from a preallocated disk to a dynamic growing disk.

Once you have added disk space, it must be partitioned and formatted with the guest operating system or third-party tools.

Let's say at some point you want to shrink a virtual disk. This can be done by using the following syntax:

```
vmware-vdiskmanager.exe -k "d:\my virtual machines\windows 2000
advanced server.vmdk"
```

These examples should provide you with the basics to use this powerful utility. Let's move on now and discuss the VMware DiskMount utility.

USING THE DISKMOUNT UTILITY

In order to use the DiskMount utility, you must first download and install the product from the VMware Web site. Once it is installed, you can access the program from the command prompt by browsing to the `c:\program files\ vmware\vmware diskmount utility` (see Figure 16.31).

```
C:\Program Files\VMware\VMware DiskMount Utility>vmware-mount.exe /?
VMware-mount [driveletter:] [path-to-virtual-disk] [options]
VMware DiskMount Utility version 5.0.0 build-12206
Copyright (c) 1998-2003 VMware, Inc. All rights reserved.

This utility mounts VMware virtual disks under Microsoft Windows.
Use "VMware-mount" without arguments to list the currently-mounted volumes.

   /d    deletes the mapping to a virtual drive volume
   /f    forcibly deletes the mapping to a virtual drive volume
   /v:N  mounts volume N of a virtual disk
   /p    displays the partitions (volumes) on a virtual disk
   /y    open the virtual disk whether or not a snapshot is in effect
   /n    do not open the virtual disk if a snapshot is in effect
   /?    displays this usage information
```

FIGURE 16.31   The DiskMount syntax.

With this utility you can mount a virtual drive without having to open it in VMware Workstation. This can save you valuable time; instead of powering on a virtual machine and using drag and drop or mapping a drive and copying, this utility will mount your virtual drive to a drive letter and you can browse the drive and copy and paste whatever information you desire. The syntax is as follows:

```
Vmware-mount [options] [drive letter:] [\\path\to\virtual disk]
```

Your options are shown in Table 16.2.

TABLE 16.2 DiskMount Options

Option	Description
/d	Deletes the mapping to a virtual drive volume.
/f	Forcibly deletes the mapping to a virtual drive volume.
/v:N	Mounts volume N of a virtual disk.
/p	Displays the partitions (volumes) on a virtual disk.
/y	Opens the virtual disk whether or not a snapshot is in effect.
/n	Does not open the virtual disk if a snapshot is in effect.
/?	Displays usage and syntax information.

Now that you understand the syntax of this command line, let's go over some examples. In our first example, we will mount the following:

- Windows 2000 Advanced Server virtual disk
- Windows XP Professional virtual disk
- Windows 2000 Professional virtual disk

The syntax is as follows (see Figure 16.32):

```
Vmware-mount.exe w: "d:\my virtual machines\Windows 2000 advanced
server.vmdk"

Vmware-mount.exe u: "D:\My Virtual Machines\Windows XP.vmdk"

Vmware-mount.exe v: "D:\My Virtual Machines\Windows 2000 Prof.vmdk"
```

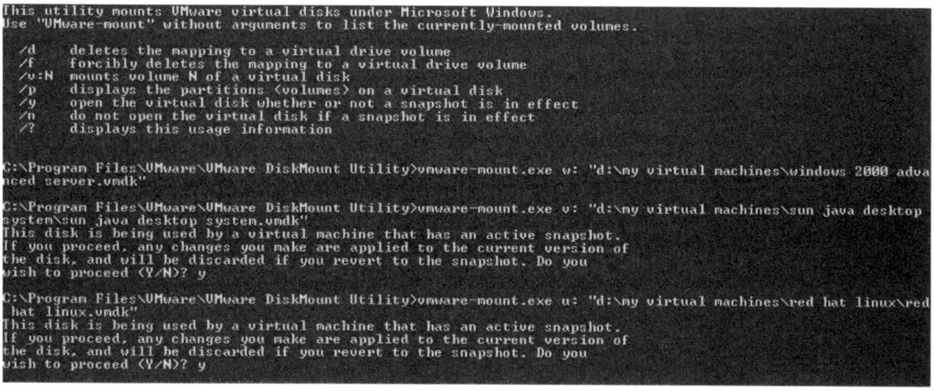

FIGURE 16.32   Mounting operating systems syntax.

Once you mount the virtual drives, they will show up on your computer as shown in Figure 16.33.

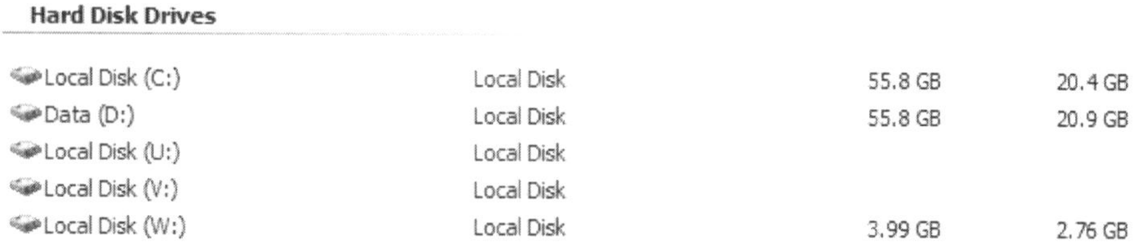

Hard Disk Drives

Local Disk (C:)	Local Disk	55.8 GB	20.4 GB
Data (D:)	Local Disk	55.8 GB	20.9 GB
Local Disk (U:)	Local Disk		
Local Disk (V:)	Local Disk		
Local Disk (W:)	Local Disk	3.99 GB	2.76 GB

FIGURE 16.33   Viewing the mounted virtual hard drive in Explorer.

If you need to display the currently mounted virtual disk via the DiskMount utility, use the syntax shown in Figure 16.34.

FIGURE 16.34   Syntax that lists all mounted virtual machines.

When you are finished working with a virtual disk, you can dismount the virtual disk by using the following syntax:

```
Vmware-mount.exe w: /d
Vmware-mount.exe u: /d
Vmware-mount.exe v: /d
```

If for some reason that syntax doesn't work, you can forcibly delete the mapping to the virtual drive by using the following syntax:

```
Vmware-mount.exe w: /f
Vmware-mount.exe u: /f
Vmware-mount.exe v: /f
```

About DiskMount Limitations

When working with the DiskMount utility, here are some factors to consider:

- You can mount only disks formatted with FAT (12/16/32) and NTFS file system.
- You can mount a virtual disk that has a snapshot, but if you revert to the snapshot, you will lose all changes made to the disk while it is mounted.
- You can't mount a virtual disk if the vmdk file is compressed or read only.

If you try to use this utility when a virtual machine is already running, you will receive the error shown in Figure 16.35.

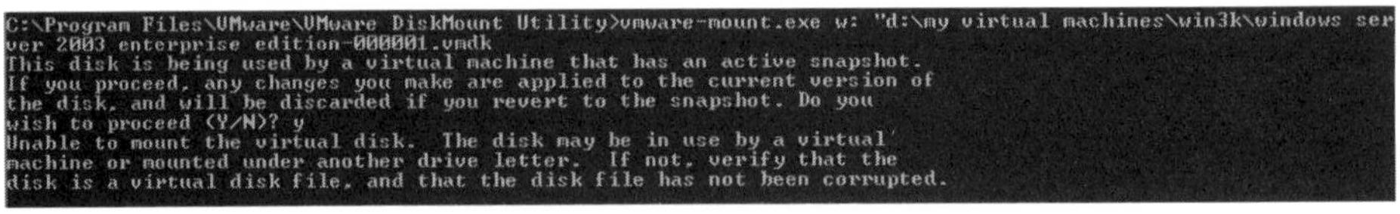

FIGURE 16.35 You cannot mount a drive with an active snapshot.

ARCHIVING VIRTUAL MACHINES

In many situations, it is helpful to back up and archive your virtual machines. You have spent a great deal of care creating these virtual machines and you never know when they might be useful again. The easiest way to archive your virtual machines is to use a product called winrar to accomplish this task. You can download winrar at *http://www.rarlab.com/*.

In this example, we will archive Sun Java Desktop System. We will begin by browsing to the folder that contains the Sun Java Desktop System virtual machine files. Next, right-click on the folder that contains the files and choose **Add to Archive** as shown in Figure 16.36.

On the Compression Method dropdown choose a compression method and on the split to volume bytes choose **650** if you are planning to burn to CD-ROM or **3,500,000,000** if you plan to burn to DVD. By choosing to split your files, you are able to archive to CD-ROM and DVD-ROM. Once you have chosen your options, choose **OK**. Figure 16.37 shows the archiving process in action.

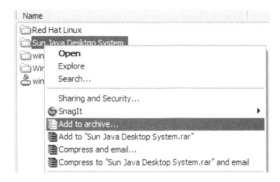

FIGURE 16.36   Adding the virtual machine to a winrar archive.

FIGURE 16.37   Compressing the virtual machine's data.

Once winrar finishes creating the archive, you can burn it to CD-ROM or DVD-ROM and store for safekeeping.

USING RAW DISK PARTITIONS IN VMWARE WORKSTATION

If you want to experiment with using Raw Disk partitions, you can create virtual machines to access partitions on the physical disk. If you create a virtual machine in this manner, you might see a performance boost because data is not stored in a single file but written and read from the physical disk. In order to make this less complicated, we recommend that you do not try to install a virtual machine to your system partition. Use a second hard drive and partition according to your needs. For example, you might partition your second hard drive into three:

■ One partition to install Windows 2003 Server
■ One partition to install Windows XP Professional
■ One partition to install Red Hat Linux

Figure 16.38 illustrates the partitions in Disk Management.

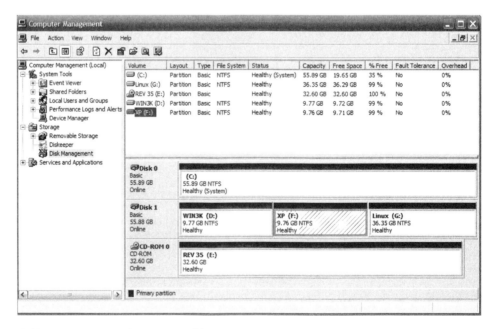

FIGURE 16.38 Creating your partitions.

Once you have partitioned your drive, you can create a new virtual machine via the New Virtual Machine Wizard. When you get to the Select a Disk window, choose **Use a physical disk** (for advanced users; see Figure 16.39). A warning message will appear about the limited support and will take you to an updated link for information (see Figure 16.40). Click **OK** and select **Use individual partitions**. Next, select the appropriate device from the dropdown and click **Next** (see Figure 16.41)

FIGURE 16.39 Selecting a physical disk.

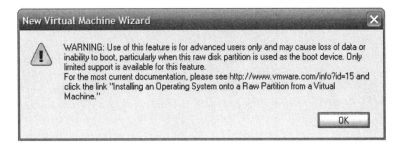

FIGURE 16.40 Warning message.

FIGURE 16.41 Choosing the appropriate drive for installation.

On the Select Physical Disk Partitions (see Figure 16.42), choose the partition where you want the operating system installed. Click **Finish** and begin installing your operating system.

VMware does not recommend running virtual machines in this manner. Be very careful when experimenting with this as you can render your operating system unusable.

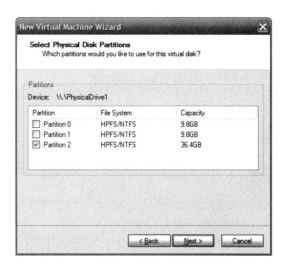

FIGURE 16.42 Choosing the appropriate partition for installation.

USING WINISO

As you start getting into virtual machines, you will want to rid yourself of CD-ROMs and DVD-ROMs to install operating systems and software. Because VMware Workstation supports ISO images, you can create a whole library of ISO images and never have to carry around any drums. For example, you might have an entire library of ISO images on an Iomega Rev Disk. The disk could hold 35 GB of ISO images and run super fast on USB 2.0.

In order to transform a library to ISO images, you can use WinISO, which can be downloaded at *http://www.winiso.com/*. It is a very simple utility to use. Let's go over how to convert an installation to an ISO file. Open WinISO from the Start menu by clicking **Start | All Programs | WinISO | WinISO**. The screen appears as shown in Figure 16.43.

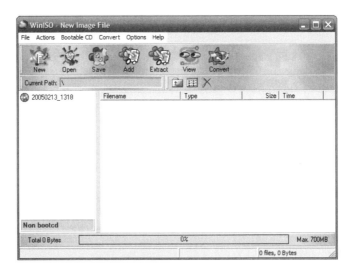

FIGURE 16.43   Starting WinISO.

Next, click on the **Add** button and add a source file or files that you want to convert to ISO. In this example, assume you just recently purchased Ad-Aware and want to convert the downloaded aawseplus.exe to an ISO image. Simply click **Add** and browse to the file, or you can drag and drop the file on the WinISO console. Once you have added your files, click **Save** and provide a file name. The **Save as** type defaults to the Standard ISO9660 format. At this point, you have successfully created an ISO image.

You can also quickly create an ISO image from a CD-ROM by putting your CD-ROM in the tray and clicking **F6** or **Actions | Make ISO from CDROM**. In this example, we are converting NortonGhost9.00 CD-ROM to an ISO image. Figure 16.44 and Figure 16.45 illustrate the process of converting a CD-ROM to ISO.

In order to keep the identical file structure of the CD-ROM, accept the default option of ASPI. In this mode, you keep the ISO file structure of the original CD-ROM.

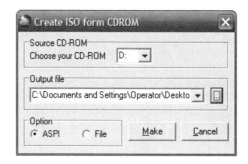

FIGURE 16.44 Creating the ISO image from CD-ROM.

FIGURE 16.45 Progress complete indicator.

WORKING WITH VMWARE WORKSTATION FROM THE COMMAND LINE

Included with VMware Workstation is a command line with switches that will enable you to do a host of things. The syntax for using VMware Workstation from the command line is as follows:

```
Vmware [-x] [-X] [-q] [-s <variablename>=<value>]
[-m] [-v] [/<path_to_config>/<config>.virtual machine]
[X toolkit options]
```

Table 16.3 shows and describes the command-line switches.

TABLE 16.3   Command-Line Switches

Switch	Description
-x	Powers on the virtual machine automatically when VMware Workstation starts.
-X	Automatically turns on VMware Workstation and puts the virtual machine in full-screen mode.
-q	Closes the virtual machine's tabs when the virtual machine powers off. If there are no other machines open, it exits the program as well.
-s	Sets the specified variable to the specified value. Any variable names and values that are valid in the configuration file may be specified on the command line with the -s switch.
-m	On a Linux host, starts the program in Quick Switch mode.
-v	Displays the product name, version, and build number.
/<path_to_config>/ <config>.virtual machine	Launches a virtual machine using the specified configuration file.
X toolkit options	Can be passed as arguments, although some of them (most notably the size and title of the VMware Workstation window) cannot be overridden.

For example, you can create a batch file that automatically opens VMware and runs a particular virtual machine. The syntax is as follows:

```
"c:\program files\vmware\vmware workstation\vmware.exe" -x "D:\My
Virtual Machines\Windows Server 2003 Enterprise
Edition\winnetenterprise.vmx"
```

Figure 16.46 illustrates the command line in action. You can continue playing around with the command line until you create the applicable configurations for your environment.

FIGURE 16.46 The VMware Workstation command line.

WORKING WITH THE VMRUN COMMAND LINE

With the release of VMware Workstation 5, a separate command line application is available as well to run teams. The syntax is as follows:

```
Vmrun COMMAND [option]
```

Table 16.4 shows the VMrun commands and options.

TABLE 16.4 VMrun Commands and Options

Command	Description	Option
List	Lists running virtual machines.	
Start	Starts a virtual machine.	Path to VM
Stop	Stops a virtual machine or team.	Path to VM or Path to Team
Reset	Resets a virtual machine or team.	Path to VM or Path to Team
Suspend	Suspends a virtual machine or team.	Path to VM or Path to Team
Upgradevm	Upgrades virtual machine to current version. Remember to install VMware Tools inside guest operating system after upgrade.	Path to virtual machine

MODIFYING THE TIP OF THE DAY

The Tip of the Day feature located at Help | Tip of the Day is a very good resource for a beginner. As a user you have the ability to create your own tips of the day by browsing to the C:\Program Files\VMware\VMware Workstation\messages\en folder and opening the tip_list.vmsg file in Notepad (see Figure 16.47).

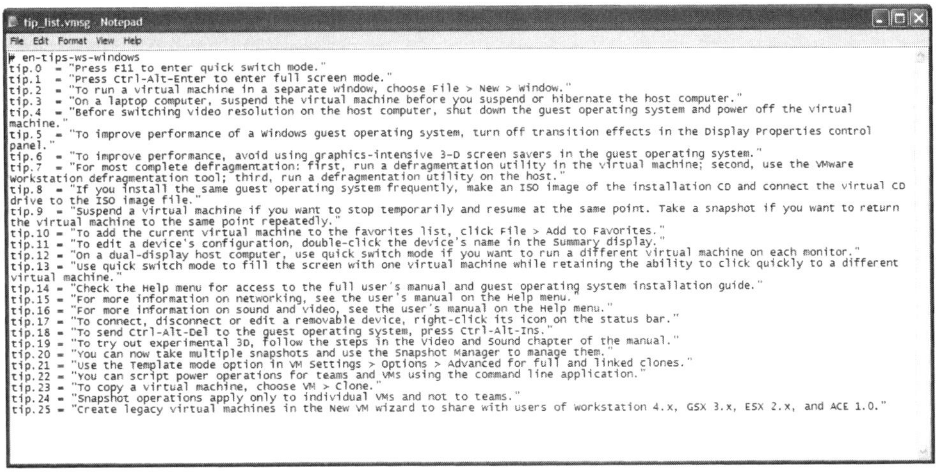

FIGURE 16.47 Customizing the Tip of the Day.

Next, at the end of the file add the next sequential number and create a tip. For example, we will add the following line:

```
Tip.21 = "You can configure VMware Workstation 5 to work with
clustering by configuring a shared disk and adding the correct
parameters to the .vmx configuration file."
```

Figure 16.48 displays the tip in the Tip of the Day format.

FIGURE 16.48 A customized Tip of the Day appears.

WORKING WITH SHARED FOLDERS

Normally when you want to transfer files from computer to computer, you copy them over the network to a shared folder. VMware has taken this concept and has come up with its own way to share folders. Before we show you how to do this, you must make sure you have VMware Tools loaded or the feature will not be available.

Creating a Shared Folder

To create a shared folder, click **VM | Settings** on any applicable virtual machine. You can even create a shared folder while a virtual machine is running. Next, click the **Options** tab and highlight **Shared folders** as shown in Figure 16.49.

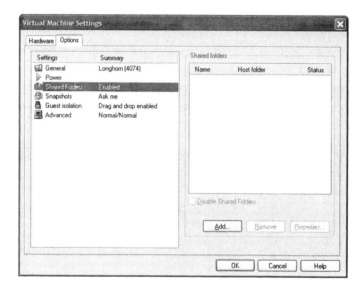

FIGURE 16.49 Accessing the Shared Folders window.

In the Shared Folders box, click **Add** and the Welcome to the Add Shared Folder Wizard appears. The wizard walks you through creating a folder or drive to share out as shown in Figure 16.50.

After you choose the folder you have the following options that you can specify on the folder's attributes:

- Enable this share.
- Read-only.
- Disable after this session. Disable the share the next time the virtual machine is powered off or suspended.

FIGURE 16.50   Add Shared Folder Wizard.

VMware Workstation shared folders are accessed in the same way a network share (see Figure 16.51) is accessed. The syntax is as follows:

```
\\.host\shared folders\<name of share>
```

FIGURE 16.51   Viewing the contents of the shared folder within a virtual machine.

KEYBOARD SHORTCUTS

If you like to keep your hand off the mouse, knowing the shortcuts for working with virtual machines will be valuable. Table 16.5 shows the keyboard shortcuts.

TABLE 16.5 Keyboard Shortcuts

Shortcut	Action
Ctrl-B	Power on.
Ctrl–E	Power off.
Ctrl-R	Reset the power.
Ctrl-Z	Suspend.
Ctrl-N	Create a new virtual machine.
Ctrl-O	Open a virtual machine.
Ctrl-F4	Close the current virtual machine.
Ctrl-D	Edit the virtual machine's configuration.
Ctrl-G	Grab input from keyboard and mouse.
Ctrl-P	Edit preferences.
Ctrl-Alt-Enter	Full screen mode.
Ctrl-Alt	Leave full screen mode and return to normal.
Ctrl-Alt-Tab	Switch among open virtual machines while mouse and keyboard input are not grabbed. VMware Workstation must be the active application.
Ctrl-Tab	Switch among open virtual machines while mouse and keyboard input are not grabbed. VMware Workstation must be the active application.
Ctrl-Shift-Tab	Switch among open virtual machines while mouse and keyboard input are not grabbed. VMware Workstation must be the active application.

The tips and tricks in this chapter should enhance your overall experience with using VMware Workstation. As you gain more experience with this product, you will find that these tools will become more and more handy. In our next chapter we'll take it one step further by showing you how to simulate Microsoft clustering in a Windows 2003 environment.

17 High Availability with VMware Workstation

In This Chapter

- Creating the Virtual Environment
- Adding Network Cards
- Configuring Shared Disks in VMware Workstation
- Configuring the Cluster Service on a Windows 2003 Server
- Installing SQL Server 2005
- Installing SQL Server 2005 on the Second Instance

Is your company considering a high-availability solution for Exchange, SQL Server, Internet Information Services (IIS), or for a particular third party? Are you a developer who just wants to test the application you are writing in a clustered environment? If you are currently working on a disaster recovery plan which includes a high-availability solution, the preparation, planning, and testing of a disaster recovery plan can become very costly. Suppose you could configure and test a high-availability plan on a desktop or laptop computer running VMware Workstation. Would saving your company thousands of dollars on a test system make a difference? In this chapter we are going to teach you how to configure VMware Workstation to run a Windows 2003 cluster. As a bonus we are going to show you how to install SQL Server 2005 on your cluster. Let's begin by creating the environment in VMware Workstation.

CREATING THE VIRTUAL ENVIRONMENT

We will begin by explaining how to prepare the virtual environment to work with clustering. In order to create a clustering solution, you will need to do the following:

- Create, install, and configure a virtual Windows 2000 or Windows 2003 domain controller with DNS installed and configured. When creating Windows 2003 virtual machines, accept the default of **LSI Logic Adapter** in the New Virtual Machine wizard.
- Create, install, and configure two virtual machines with Windows 2000 Advanced Server or Windows 2003 Server Enterprise Edition.
- Ensure that any virtual machine participating in the cluster has a public and private network configuration. Basically, each node will need two network cards, each with a public IP address and a private IP address.
- Ensure that all of these virtual servers have static IP addresses.
- Ensure that the virtual machines that are going to represent the nodes of the cluster are joined to the domain.
- Have access to the Windows 2000 Advanced Server CD-ROM or copy the I386 directory to the virtual machine.
- Have access to the Windows 2003 Enterprise Edition CD-ROM or copy the I386 directory to the virtual machine.
- Create a Domain User account on the domain controller such as Cluster_Service; this account will be used to run the cluster service.
- Create a Domain User account on the domain controller such as SQL_Service; this account will be used to run the MSSQL service and the SQLServerAgent service.

Once you have the environment configured, you will add the additional network cards to the nodes that will participate in the cluster.

ADDING NETWORK CARDS

Now that you have created the disks, you also need to run the Hardware wizard and add a second Ethernet adapter to each virtual machine that will be participating in the cluster. Simply highlight the applicable virtual machine and **Edit** the virtual machine settings. Click **Add** on the hardware tab and select **Ethernet Adapter**. Click **Finish** to add the adapter. The VMware Control Center now displays the additional network card as shown in Figure 17.1.

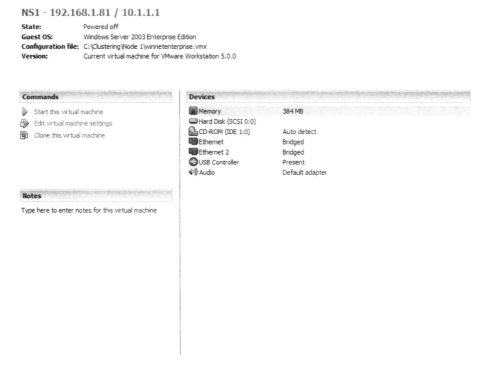

NS1 - 192.168.1.81 / 10.1.1.1

State:	Powered off
Guest OS:	Windows Server 2003 Enterprise Edition
Configuration file:	C:\Clustering\Node 1\winnetenterprise.vmx
Version:	Current virtual machine for VMware Workstation 5.0.0

Commands
- Start this virtual machine
- Edit virtual machine settings
- Clone this virtual machine

Notes
Type here to enter notes for this virtual machine

Devices

Memory	384 MB
Hard Disk (SCSI 0:0)	
CD-ROM (IDE 1:0)	Auto detect
Ethernet	Bridged
Ethernet 2	Bridged
USB Controller	Present
Audio	Default adapter

FIGURE 17.1 Adding network cards to each node or virtual machine in the cluster.

For the purpose of this example, we are going to use a bridged network connection for all of our Ethernet Adapters. For more information on the other types of network configurations you can use, see Chapter 12.

Private Network Configuration

For clustering to work properly, you must configure two network cards on each VMware Workstation virtual server. The private network allows for communication between each of the nodes, which is commonly known as the heartbeat. To add a network card, open **VMware Workstation** from the Start menu. Next, choose **Settings** from the VM menu. Now, choose **Add** and select **Network Adapter**. Click **Next** and select **Bridged Connection**. Finally, click **Finish**. The next time you power on the virtual server, it will have an additional network card. Repeat these steps on each virtual machine that will be part of the cluster.

For example, assume that you have two virtual machines (swcluster1 and sw-cluster2). After you add the additional network cards, you must configure them for the heartbeat connection. You might configure your heartbeat on node 1 (swcluster1) with the IP address 10.1.1.2, and on node 2 (swcluster2) with the IP address 10.1.1.3. When you set up the static IP address, it is important that you click the **Advanced** tab in the TCP/IP Properties dialog box and choose **Disable NetBIOS Over TCP/IP**, as shown in Figure 17.2. All cluster nodes communicate via TCP/IP only. If you do not choose this option, you might have problems with your node-to-node communication.

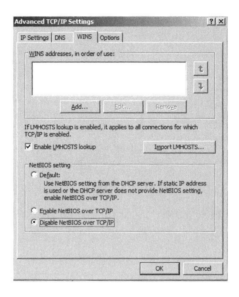

FIGURE 17.2   Disable NetBIOS over TCP/IP.

Public Network Configuration

To configure your public network connection, right-click on your second network card and assign the appropriate IP address, DNS, and WINS settings. Next, verify connectivity by opening a command prompt and typing `ipconfig /all` (as shown in Figure 17.3) on each node in the cluster to verify the configurations. When each node is properly configured with a private and a public network address and you have tested connectivity, it is time to make sure that each node is connected to the domain. To do this, simply right-click on **My Computer**, click the **Network Identification** tab (on both clustered machines), and verify that you are connected to the desired Active Directory domain. Next, power down both nodes but leave the domain controller running. Before you begin to install clustering, you must know your virtual server name and the IP address you are assigning to the cluster.

```
C:\WINDOWS\system32\cmd.exe                                        _ |□| x|

Ethernet adapter Heartbeat:

    Connection-specific DNS Suffix  . :
    Description . . . . . . . . . . . : VMware Accelerated AMD PCNet Adapter
    Physical Address. . . . . . . . . : 00-0C-29-90-5B-77
    DHCP Enabled. . . . . . . . . . . : No
    IP Address. . . . . . . . . . . . : 10.1.1.2
    Subnet Mask . . . . . . . . . . . : 255.255.255.0
    Default Gateway . . . . . . . . . :
    NetBIOS over Tcpip. . . . . . . . : Disabled

Ethernet adapter LAN:

    Connection-specific DNS Suffix  . :
    Description . . . . . . . . . . . : VMware Accelerated AMD PCNet Adapter #2
    Physical Address. . . . . . . . . : 00-0C-29-90-5B-81
    DHCP Enabled. . . . . . . . . . . : No
    IP Address. . . . . . . . . . . . : 192.168.1.52
    Subnet Mask . . . . . . . . . . . : 255.255.255.0
    Default Gateway . . . . . . . . . : 192.168.1.1
    DNS Servers . . . . . . . . . . . : 192.168.1.50
                                        65.32.1.65

C:\Documents and Settings\Administrator>
```

FIGURE 17.3   Testing connectivity between nodes.

CONFIGURING SHARED DISKS IN VMWARE WORKSTATION

Before you can create a clustered solution in VMware Workstation, you must configure your shared disks. In order to do this, create a folder on your hard drive and label it accordingly. For this example, we will call it Cluster_Disks as shown in Figure 17.4

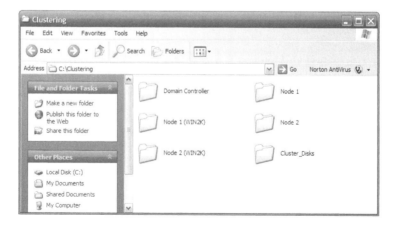

FIGURE 17.4   Creating the folder where your shared disks will reside.

Next, highlight any one of the three virtual machines you created in the Favorites window and **Edit** the virtual machine settings. On the Virtual Machine Settings window, click the **Add** button to start the Add Hardware Wizard. Choose **Hard Disk** on the Hardware Type window and click **Next**. On the Select a Disk window, choose **Create a new virtual disk** and click **Next**. On the Select a Disk Type window, accept the default of **SCSI** (Recommended) and click **Next**. The Specify Disk Capacity is where you will size the virtual disk. Make sure to size this according to your needs. When you have finished sizing it accordingly, select the **Allocate all disk space now** checkbox as shown in Figure 17.5.

FIGURE 17.5   Creating the virtual disk.

Click **Next** and browse to the folder (see Figure 17.6) where your shared disks will be stored. Click **Finish** to have the shared disk created. This can take a good amount of time to create; it all depends on the size of the disk (see Figure 17.7).

When the disk is created, highlight the disk on the Hardware tab and click **Re-move** as shown in Figure 17.8. The first disk we created was the quorum disk, and now we will create two more shared disks. This will allow us to configure an active/passive cluster or an active/active cluster. Repeat the process to create two additional shared disks.

It is very important to remove the disk from the Hardware tab after it is configured. Do not forget. Highlight each disk you created and click the Remove button.

NOTE

FIGURE 17.6 Creating a shared disk such as a quorum drive.

FIGURE 17.7 The progress bar.

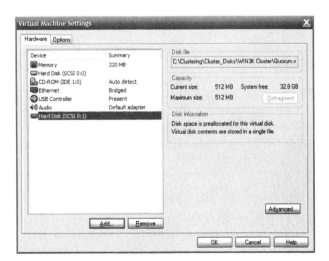

FIGURE 17.8 Removing the disk after creation.

When you have finished creating your disks, the disk configuration (see Figure 17.9) is displayed in the Cluster_Disks folder.

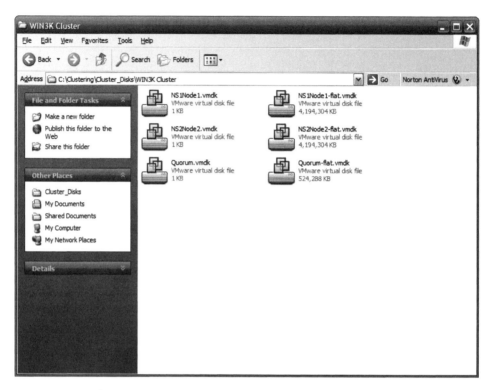

FIGURE 17.9 The shared disk configuration.

Editing the VMX File

Now that we have created our shared disks, we need to modify the VMX or VMware Configuration file for each node that will participate in the cluster. In order to edit the *.vmx file, browse to the location of your virtual machines and open the file (.vmx) in Notepad. Figure 17.10 illustrates how to open a *.vmx file in Notepad.

Do not attempt this step if your virtual machines are running. Please make sure they are powered off and that you have EXITED from the VMware Workstation program. Once you have exited the program, follow these steps. If you do not exit VMware Workstation, the shared disks will not boot properly and you will have to boot into the BIOS to correct the problem.

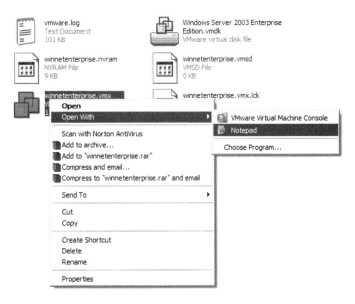

FIGURE 17.10   Opening the .vmx file in Notepad.

After opening the *.vmx file in Notepad for the applicable virtual machine, you will need to add the following lines to the VMware Configuration file.

```
disk.locking="false"
scsi1:0.present="TRUE"
scsi1:0.filename="path to vmdk file"
scsi1:0.mode="independent-persistent"
scsi1:1.present="TRUE"
scsi1:1.filename="path to vmdk file"
scsi1:1.mode="independent-persistent"
```

By adding the `disk.locking="false"`, you are allowing the disk to be shared. Scsi1:0.filename is the location of your shared disk. Setting the disk to independent-persistent safeguards the shared disk, because information is permanently written to disk and is not affected by snapshots. For every disk you use, you must increase the number.

For example, SCSI1:0 will be the Quorum drive, SCSI1:1 will be another disk, and SCSI1:2 will be another disk. With the above example, you would add the following to your configuration:

```
disk.locking="false"
scsi1:0.fileName = "C:\Clustering\Cluster_Disks\WIN3K
Cluster\Quorum.vmdk"
scsi1:0.mode = "independent-persistent"

scsi1:1.present = "TRUE"
scsi1:1.fileName = "C:\Clustering\Cluster_Disks\WIN3K
Cluster\NS1Node1.vmdk"
scsi1:1.mode = "independent-persistent"

scsi1:2.present = "TRUE"
scsi1:2.fileName = "C:\Clustering\Cluster_Disks\WIN3K
Cluster\NS2Node2.vmdk"
scsi1:2.mode = "independent-persistent"
```

Now that you understand what needs to be added, make sure both virtual machines have their *.vmx file updated with the appropriate syntax. Figure 17.11 and Figure 17.12 illustrate the *.vmx file on both virtual machines.

FIGURE 17.11 Editing the .vmx file.

FIGURE 17.12 Editing the .vmx file on the other virtual machine.

After you add the information to the virtual machine configuration files, the VMware Control Center will show you the new disk configuration and you will see the disks in the lower righthand corner. Figure 17.13 and Figure 17.14 illustrate the disk configuration and the virtual disks in action, respectively.

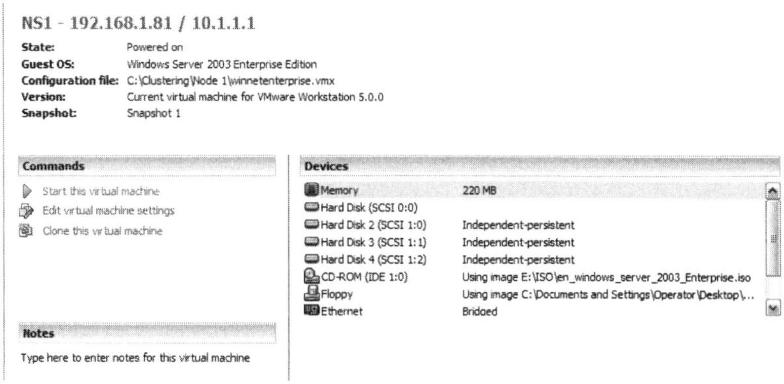

FIGURE 17.13 Updated shared disk configuration.

FIGURE 17.14 Status bar shows the updated disks.

You are now ready to power on the first virtual machine that will participate in the cluster. Do not power on both virtual machines at the same time. Power on the first virtual machine, configure the disks, and install the cluster service before powering on the second virtual machine.

Booting into the BIOS

If you power on your virtual machine for the first time and it tries to boot from a shared disk, you must power on each node to the BIOS to make sure the disks will load in the appropriate order. Power on the first computer and choose **F2** to enter the BIOS. Use the arrow keys to move to the Boot menu. On the boot menu, move the arrows until the focus is on the +Hard Drive. Next, click **Enter** and make sure Disk (0:0) is at the beginning of the boot order. When you configure a cluster, the boot disk goes last, so if you do not perform these steps, you will not be able to boot your operating system after adding the shared disks. Once you have Disk (0:0) at the beginning of the boot order, save your changes and repeat the process on the second node.

Configuring the Drives

Once you've successfully added the shared disks, you can power up the first virtual machine. In order to configure your drives, right-click on **My Computer** and select **Manage**. You can also access this via Administrative Tools. Under Storage, select **Disk Management** and the Computer Management Console opens. When you go into Disk Management for the first time, you will be prompted to write the disk signature and upgrade the disk to a dynamic disk. Choose **Yes** to write the disk signature. Choose **No** to the option to upgrade the disk to a dynamic disk.

*If you accidentally upgrade the disks to dynamic disks, don't sweat it because you can just right-click on the **Disk** box and choose **Revert To Basic**.*

Clustering needs to have basic disks to work properly.Verify that you can see the unformatted shared disks (see Figure 17.15) via Disk Management. Once you've verified that you can see the shared disk, you can partition the disk accordingly. In this example, we are preparing our nodes for an active/active cluster of SQL Server 2000 and 2005. The following will be our disk configuration:

Disk 1 will be our Quorum drive.

Disk 2 will be our First Instance Data and Log drive.

Disk 3 will be our Second Instance Data and Log drive.

Figure 17.16 shows our disk configuration when it is complete.

We could have added two more drives as well to separate SQL Server's data and log drives.

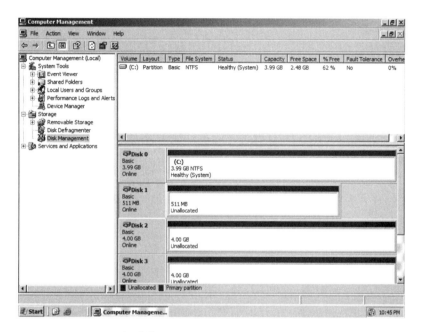

FIGURE 17.15   Basic disks.

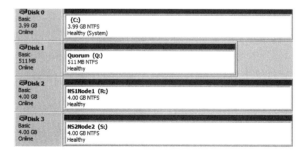

FIGURE 17.16   Disk configuration.

CONFIGURING THE CLUSTER SERVICE ON A WINDOWS 2003 SERVER

We are finally at the moment of truth where all of our work will be tested. This is the easy part now. We will start by clicking **Start | All Programs | Administrative Tools | Cluster Administrator**. The Cluster Administrator window appears with an Open Connection to Cluster dialog. Click the dropdown and choose **Create a new cluster** as shown in Figure 17.17.

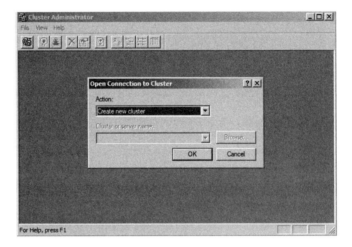

FIGURE 17.17   Creating the cluster.

On the New Server Cluster Wizard, choose a valid cluster name and click **Next** to continue, as shown in Figure 17.18. After you enter a valid cluster name, the computer name of the node participating in the cluster is populated (see Figure 17.19).

On the Analyzing Configuration window (see Figure 17.20), the wizard does the following:

- Checks for existing cluster
- Establishes node connection(s)
- Checks node feasibility
- Finds common resources on nodes
- Checks cluster feasibility

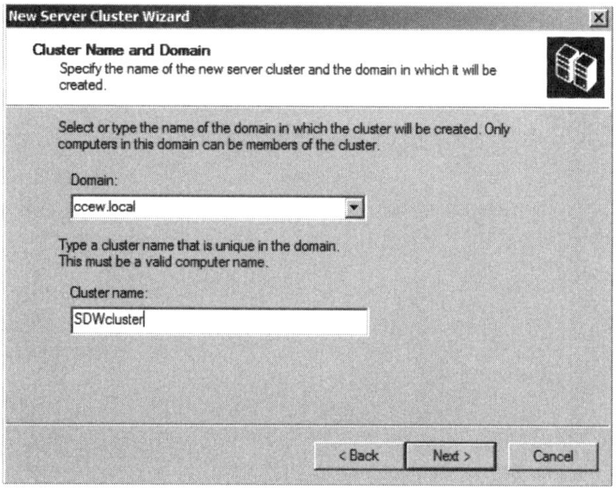

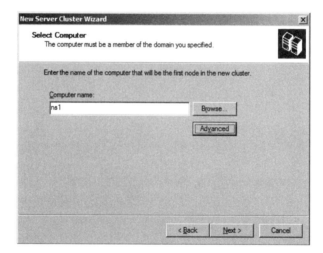

FIGURE 17.18   Create a cluster name.

FIGURE 17.19   The name of the node that participates
in the cluster.

You can expand the + signs to make sure everything looks good in your cluster, as shown in Figure 17.21. Additionally, you can view the log and the detail by selecting the appropriate button. If your cluster has problems, you can fix the problems as defined in the configuration and reanalyze.

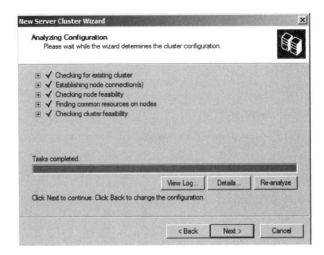

FIGURE 17.20   Analyzing the cluster configuration.

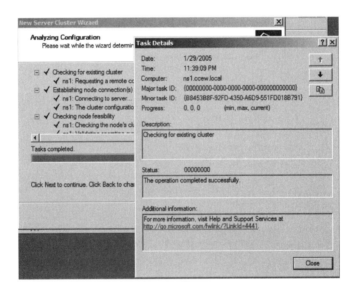

FIGURE 17.21   Viewing the details of the cluster configuration.

On the IP address window, input the cluster IP address as shown in Figure 17.22. This will be the IP address to manage the cluster. On the Cluster Service Account window (see Figure 17.23), enter a valid domain user account that the cluster service will utilize. This account will be added to the local administrator group on all nodes of the cluster.

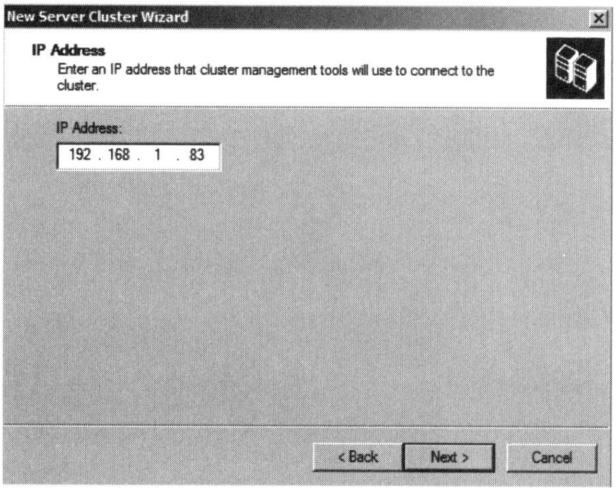

FIGURE 17.22   IP address of the cluster.

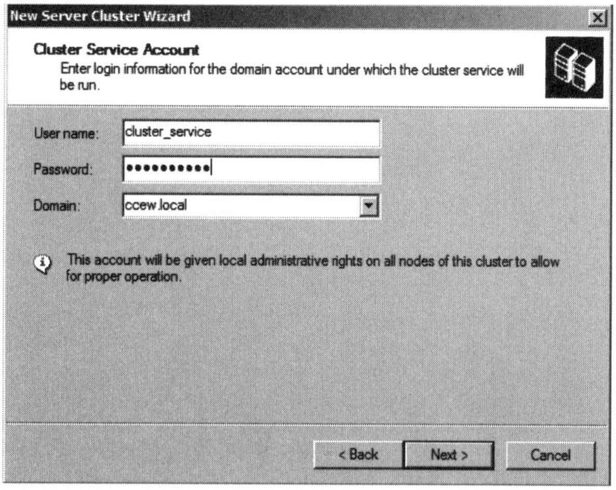

FIGURE 17.23   Account that runs cluster services.

The Proposed Cluster Configuration window (see Figure 17.24) allows you to review your configuration and make changes if necessary. You click on the **Quorum** button to make sure you have the right disk assigned (see Figure 17.25) to the quorum. Click **Next** to create the cluster configuration.

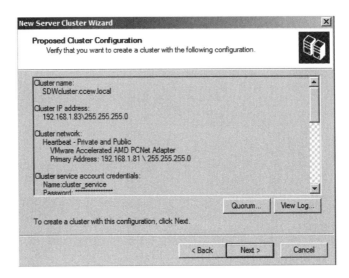

FIGURE 17.24 Review the configuration of the cluster.

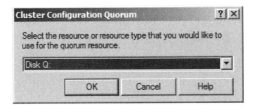

FIGURE 17.25 Selecting the quorum drive.

Once the cluster is completed, you can review the details by expanding the + signs. Figure 17.26 illustrates a completed cluster configuration. Click **Next** and **Finish**. You have successfully configured your first virtual node with a Windows 2003 cluster. Let's move on and power on the second node now.

We will begin again by clicking **Start | All Programs | Administrative Tools | Cluster Administrator**. The Cluster Administrator window appears with an Open Connection to Cluster dialog. Click the dropdown and choose **Add nodes to cluster** and the cluster name as shown in Figure 17.27. Click **OK** and the Welcome to the Add Nodes Wizard appears.

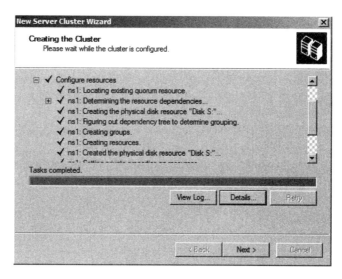

FIGURE 17.26   A completed cluster configuration.

FIGURE 17.27   Adding the second virtual
node to the cluster.

On the Select Computer window, the computer name is automatically populated in the Computer Name text box. Click **Add** to add the computer to the selected computers as shown in Figure 17.28. The configuration is analyzed and, as long as there are no problems, you are able to move forward in the wizard and enter the Cluster Service Account window as shown in Figure 17.29.

You are now asked to review the configuration. Click **Next** and the node will be added to the cluster. Click **Finish**. You have now successfully created a virtual Windows 2003 cluster. For more information on clustering a Windows 2003 server, see *http://www.microsoft.com/windowsserver2003/techinfo/overview/clustering.mspx.*

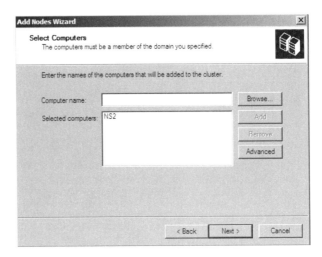

FIGURE 17.28 Adding the computer name to the selected computers on the node.

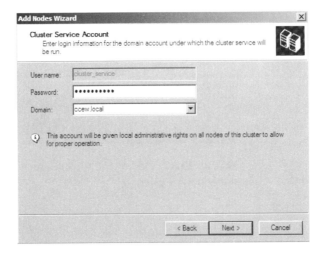

FIGURE 17.29 Populate the password of the cluster account.

Testing the Windows 2003 Cluster

You can test the failover process by right-clicking on any group and choosing **Move group** (see Figure 17.30). If everything is configured properly, you will see the group move from its current node to the available node. Another test would be to move all of the groups to a particular node and then power off the virtual machine that is currently active. You can actually see the failover occur. This would simulate a total shutdown or failure of a node. You can also simulate a failover by expanding the **Groups** folder, highlighting a group in the details pane, right-clicking on the disk, and choosing **Initiate Failure** (see Figure 17.31). You will see some minor activity and then the status will return to normal. This happens because the cluster will try to correct itself three times before failing over. You must initiate a failure four times in a row to have the disk move nodes.

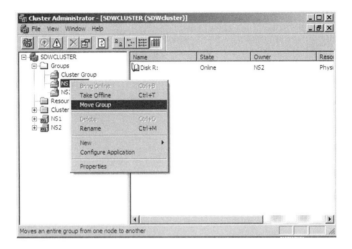

FIGURE 17.30   Testing the failover of a cluster node.

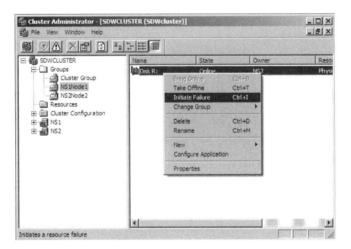

FIGURE 17.31   Initiating a manual failover.

INSTALLING SQL SERVER 2005

Now that we have properly configured our cluster, let's move forward and install an active/active configuration of SQL Server 2005. We will begin by moving all disks to NS1 in preparation for our installation. Next, we will need to create the MS DTC resource prior to installing SQL Server 2005. Right-click on **Cluster_Group** and choose **New | Resource**. On the New Resource window, input MSDTC in the Name field and choose **DTC** as the Resource type (see Figure 17.32). The Possible Owners should be populated with all nodes as shown in Figure 17.33. The Dependencies for MSDTC are Network Name and Physical Disk as shown in 17.34. Click **Finish** and the MSDTC resource is created. Finally, right-click on the resource and bring it online.

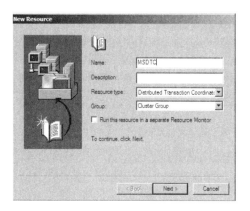

FIGURE 17.32 Creating a MSDTC resource.

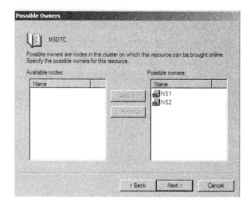

FIGURE 17.33 Adding the nodes to the MSDTC resource.

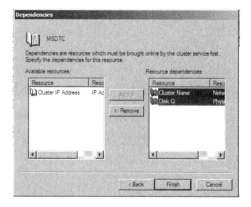

FIGURE 17.34 Assigning the proper dependencies to the MSDTC resource.

*Before you can bring the MSDTC resource online, you must enable DTC access from Add/Remove Components. Simply highlight **Application Server** and click **Details**. Next, select **Enable network DTC access** and click **OK** to install.*

You can also create a separate group and add the MSDTC resource as opposed to adding it to the Cluster Group. For simplicity we are adding it to the Cluster Group, but in the real world, you would want to create a separate group.

Now that we have MSDTC configured with all of our resources on node NS1, let's install our first instance of SQL Server 2005. Place the CD-ROM in the tray or use an ISO image to install. If you choose **VM | Settings**, you have the option of using either the physical CD-ROM drive or an ISO image.

On the SQL Server 2005 Welcome window, choose **Run the SQL Server Installation Wizard** as shown in Figure 17.35. Next, accept the end user license agreement and SQL Server will install the following components (see Figure 17.36):

■ .NET Framework 2.0
■ Microsoft SQL Native Client
■ Microsoft SQL Server Beta 2 Support Files

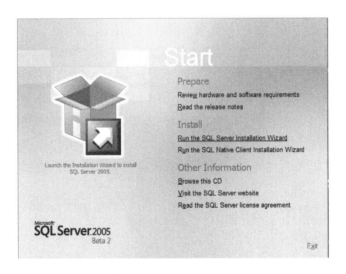

FIGURE 17.35   Microsoft SQL Server 2005 Beta 2 Splash Screen.

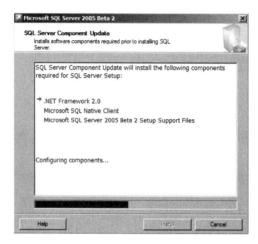

FIGURE 17.36 Installing the required components.

Once the required components are installed successfully, the SQL Server 2005 Welcome to the Microsoft SQL Server Installation Wizard window appears as shown in Figure 17.37. Click **Next** and a system configuration check takes place to validate that you have everything necessary to complete the upgrade. Figure 17.38 depicts the system configuration check in action.

FIGURE 17.37 Microsoft SQL Server Installation Wizard Welcome page.

FIGURE 17.38   The installation wizard checks
to make sure you have a system that can
properly handle the installation.

On the Registration Information window, enter your name and 25-character
product key. Click **Next** and choose the components (see Figure 17.39) you wish to
install. You might have noticed that the **Install as virtual server** checkbox is enabled, because the installation is cluster aware. In the Instance Name window
choose **Named Instance** (see Figure 17.40), as we are going to install an active/
active configuration and a virtual server name as shown in Figure 17.41.

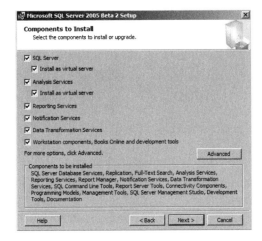

FIGURE 17.39   Choosing your installation
components.

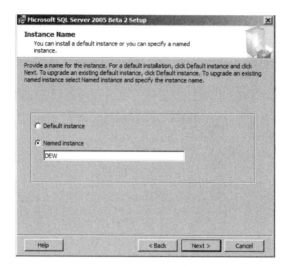

FIGURE 17.40 Creating a named instance.

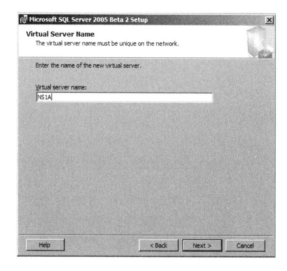

FIGURE 17.41 Creating a virtual server name.

On the Virtual Server Configuration window enter the applicable (see Figure 17.42) IP address and select the cluster group where you want the SQL Server data files installed (see Figure 17.43). On the Cluster Node Configuration, accept the defaults (see Figure 17.44) and enter a valid administrator account for all nodes in the cluster. On the Service Account window, enter a Domain user account as shown in Figure 17.45. On the Authentication Mode window, choose either **Windows Authentication Mode** or **Mixed Mode**. If you choose **Mixed Mode**, specify an SA login password. On the Collation Setting window, accept the defaults for the Report Server Directories.

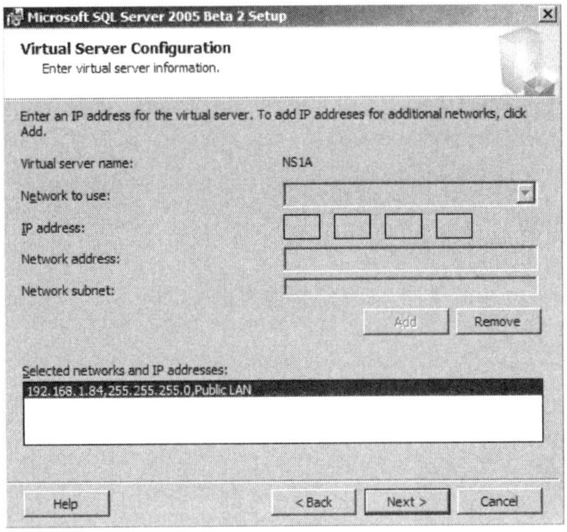

FIGURE 17.42   Entering a valid IP address for your virtual server.

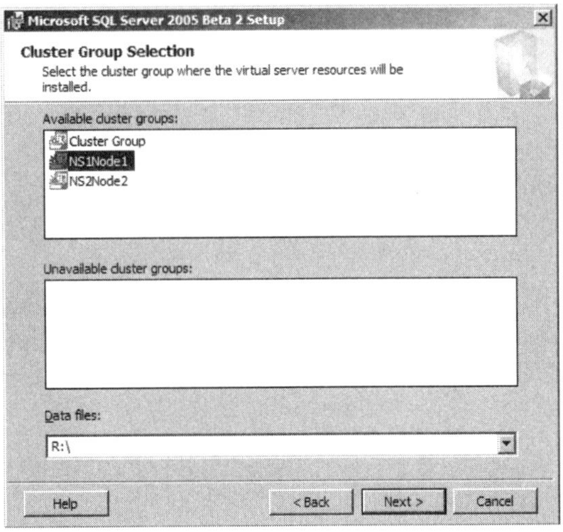

FIGURE 17.43   Selecting the cluster group that houses the SQL Server data files.

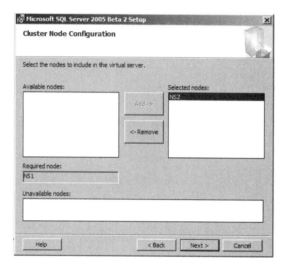

FIGURE 17.44 Adding the applicable nodes to the cluster.

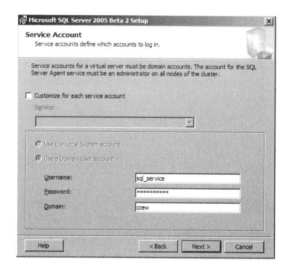

FIGURE 17.45 Assigning a domain user account to the SQL services.

On the Report Server Database Setup window, accept the defaults as shown in Figure 17.46 and specify the report server delivery settings by entering an SMTP server address and the email address of the sender. Next, decide whether you want to send Fatal error reports to Microsoft and choose **Next**. Finally, review the summary window (see Figure 17.47) and choose **Install**. Sit back and relax, as this is going to take a while.

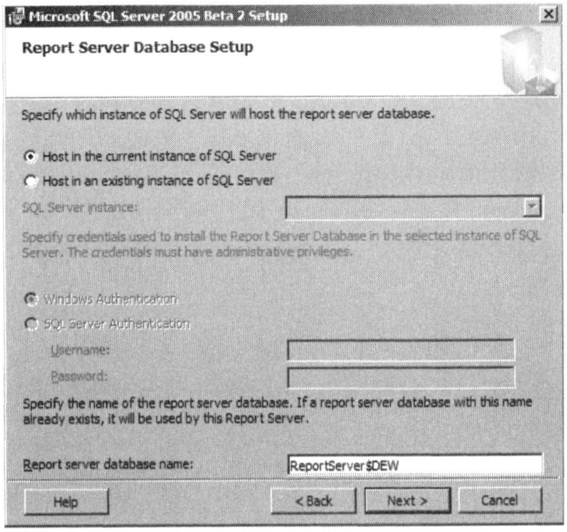

FIGURE 17.46   Configuring the report server.

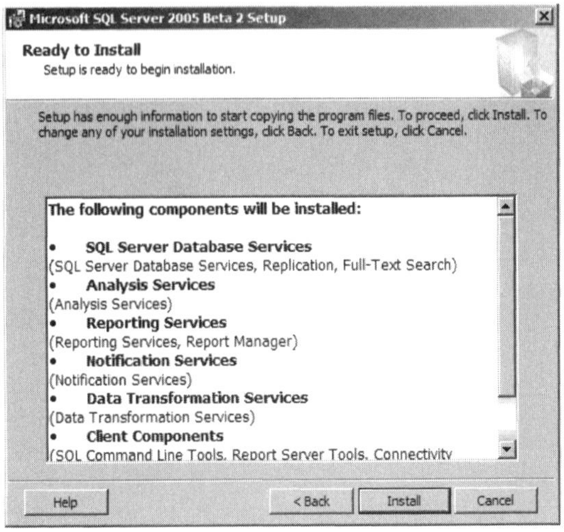

FIGURE 17.47   Installing SQL Server 2005 Beta 2.

INSTALLING SQL SERVER 2005 ON THE SECOND INSTANCE

Now that we have properly installed SQL Server 2005 on our first instance, let's move forward and install the second instance of SQL Server 2005. We will begin by moving all disks to NS2 in preparation for our installation and then we will run the setup on the NS2 node of our cluster. Next, we will repeat the same process but choose a different named instance and virtual server name in the wizard. We will also install the SQL Server database files to an empty disk. In this example, we have an R: and an S:. On the NS1 node, we installed the SQL Server database files to the R:. On the NS2 node, we will install the SQL Server database files to the S:. Once the installation is complete (see Figure 17.48) you will have successfully completed a virtual active/active clustered configuration of SQL Server 2005 and Windows 2003 Server on VMware Workstation 5.

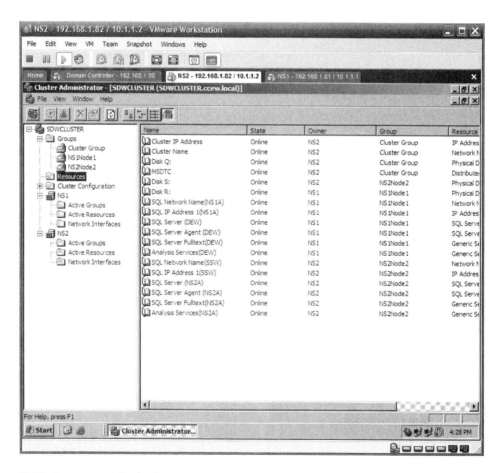

FIGURE 17.48 Active/Active SQL Server 2005 configuration.

In this chapter we gave you an overview of how to create and prepare your virtual environment for the installation of Microsoft clustering technologies. We also described in detail how to configure VMware Workstation to work with clustering and finally, how to install Microsoft Windows 2003 clustering in your virtual machines. Once we established the cluster, as a bonus we showed you how to install an active/active cluster of Microsoft's latest release of SQL Server: SQL Server 2005 Beta 2.

Congratulations on configuring a virtual cluster. Isn't it cool? Now it's time for you to play around and have fun. If you have any questions about virtual clustering, you can contact the author at *http://www.stevenscottwarren.com/contact.php.*

18 High Availability with GSX Server

In This Chapter

■ Creating a Shared Disk
■ Attaching the Shared Disks to an Additional Computer
■ Editing the .vmx File

GSX Server is VMware's enterprise-class virtual machine software for business-critical production/test environments. Currently in its third generation, it has gained momentum in the IT industry. With GSX Server, you can make high availability affordable and scalable. This chapter describes how to properly configure your virtual machine environment to work with Microsoft clustering on a Windows platform.

In order for clustering to work properly with GSX Server, you must create a SCSI disk via a SCSI reservation that has the ability to access and share a SCSI disk. By adding particular configuration paramaters to the .vmx file, you are able to successfully create a cluster. Let's start by creating a shared disk.

You can download an evaluation copy of GSX Server from http://www.vmware.com.

CREATING A SHARED DISK

Prior to creating your shared disks, you will need to successfully prepare the cluster with two virtual machines loaded with either Windows 2000 or 2003 Server and connected to a domain controller. For more information on creating your virtual environment, refer to Chapter 17.

Now that you have your environment configured, the first step is to **Edit** the virtual machine settings of the virtual machine you want to add to the cluster, as shown in Figure 18.1.

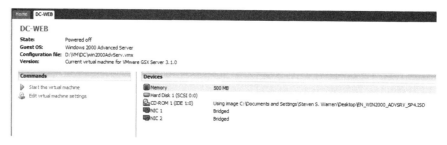

FIGURE 18.1   Editing the virtual machine settings.

Next, click **Add** (see Figure 18.2) to start the GSX Server Add Hardware Wizard. You are then prompted to choose the hardware type (see Figure 18.3). In this example, you will choose **Hard Disk**. On the Select a Disk window, choose **Create**

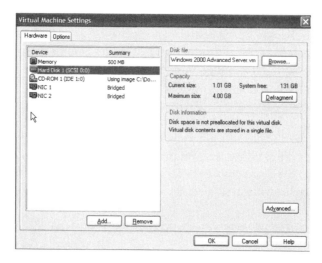

FIGURE 18.2   Choosing the hardware type.

a new virtual disk; this will ultimately become the SCSI shared disk for clustering. Figure 18.4 displays an example of the window.

FIGURE 18.3 Choosing hard disk as the hardware type.

FIGURE 18.4 Creating a new virtual disk.

On the Select Disk Type window, choose the default **SCSI** as shown in Figure 18.5. In order to configure a SCSI reservation, it is mandatory that you create a SCSI disk. The Specify Disk Capacity window (see Figure 18.6) allows you to choose the size of your shared SCSI disk. Remember to select **Allocate all disk space now**. If you do not, you will not be able to successfully create your cluster with GSX Server.

FIGURE 18.5 Choosing the disk type.

FIGURE 18.6 Selecting the size of the disk and allocating the space.

On the Specify Disk File window (see Figure 18.7), choose the location where the SCSI shared drive is located. For example, create a specific path for all of your shared disks. In this example, we use \vm\vmcluster\. Next, click the **Advanced** button to choose the **Virtual device node** and the **Independent** mode (see Figure 18.8). For clustering to work properly, you should add the shared disk to a separate SCSI bus channel in addition to the SCSI 0: bus.

FIGURE 18.7 Specify the shared disk location.

FIGURE 18.8 Specifying the advanced options.

For example, add the first shared disk to the SCSI 1:0 channel as shown in Figure 18.9. You must also choose **Independent:Persistent** (see Figure 18.9) for the shared SCSI disk to work properly. At this point, click **Finish** as shown in Figure

FIGURE 18.9 Choosing the SCSI bus channel.

18.10 to create the SCSI disk. Finally, repeat these steps for each shared disk you want to create, but remember to change the virtual device node or SCSI bus to the next appropriate number. For example, for each shared disk you create, choose SCSI 1:1, SCSI 1:2, SCSI 1:3, etc. Once all shared disks are created on the first machine that is in the cluster, the VMware Control Center will show a display as in Figure 18.11.

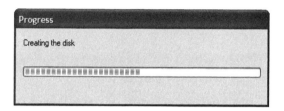

FIGURE 18.10   Creating the SCSI shared disk.

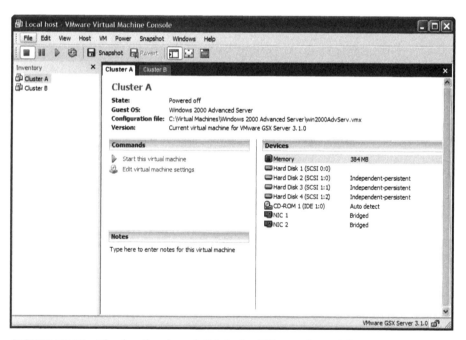

FIGURE 18.11   Viewing the shared disk in the VMware Control Center.

Viewing the Shared Disks

Now that our shared disks are created, we can browse to the directory to view the files. In our example, we created all of our shared disks in the following directory: \vm\vmcluster. Browsing to this directory or the directory where you created the shared disks will allow you to see a *.vmdk file and a flat.vmdk file. Figure 18.12 shows an example of three disks. These disks can be used to create an active/active cluster configuration.

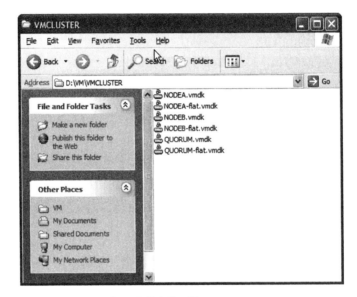

FIGURE 18.12   Shared disk flat files.

ATTACHING THE SHARED DISKS TO AN ADDITIONAL COMPUTER

In order to attach the shared disks to an additional server, simply choose the second server and edit the virtual machine settings. Click **Add** to go to the Welcome to the Add Hardware Wizard window and select **Hard Disk** for the hardware type. Select **Use an existing virtual disk** on the Select a Disk window, as shown in Figure 18.13.

On the Select an Existing Disk window, browse to the first shared disk that you created. Remember to browse to the .vmdk file instead of the –Flat file. In this

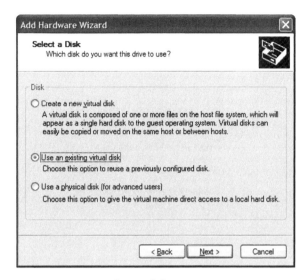

FIGURE 18.13   Select a disk.

example, we will browse to \vm\vmcluster Quorum.vmdk (see Figure 18.14). Next, click **Open** and the **Advanced** button and choose the corresponding SCSI bus channel (see Figure 18.15).

FIGURE 18.14   Choosing the appropriate .vmdk file.

FIGURE 18.15 Choosing the correct SCSI bus channel.

If you created the drive on the SCSI 1:0 channel on the first server, you must use the same SCSI bus channel on the second server that will become part of the cluster. For example, if you create a Quorum drive on Server A with a SCSI 1:0 then you must use SCSI 1:0 on the second server when you add the Quorum drive as well. Finally, do not forget to choose **Independent:Persistent** for each disk. The final result will be two servers sharing the same disks as shown in Figures 18.16 and 18.17.

FIGURE 18.16 Server 1 configuration.

Do not forget to add your second virtual NIC to each server as well. You can refer back to Chapter 17 for a detailed explanation on creating the virtual environment.

FIGURE 18.17 Server 2 configuration.

EDITING THE .VMX FILE

Once the shared disks are configured (refer to Chapter 17) and ready on each virtual machine, you must edit each *.vmx file in order to put the finishing touches on this configuration.

Make sure both nodes are powered off prior to making this change to the configuration file.

The first step is to browse to the location of the *.vmx file. This file is located where you originally installed the virtual machine. Once you have located the *.vmx file, open it in Notepad and add the following lines:

- Disk.locking= "false"
- Scsi1.sharedbus="virtual"

Figure 18.18 provides an example of the *.vmx file with the appropriate settings. These settings must be added to every *.vmx file in the cluster to properly share the disk. Once these steps are complete, you are ready to power on the first virtual machine and install Microsoft Clustering Services.

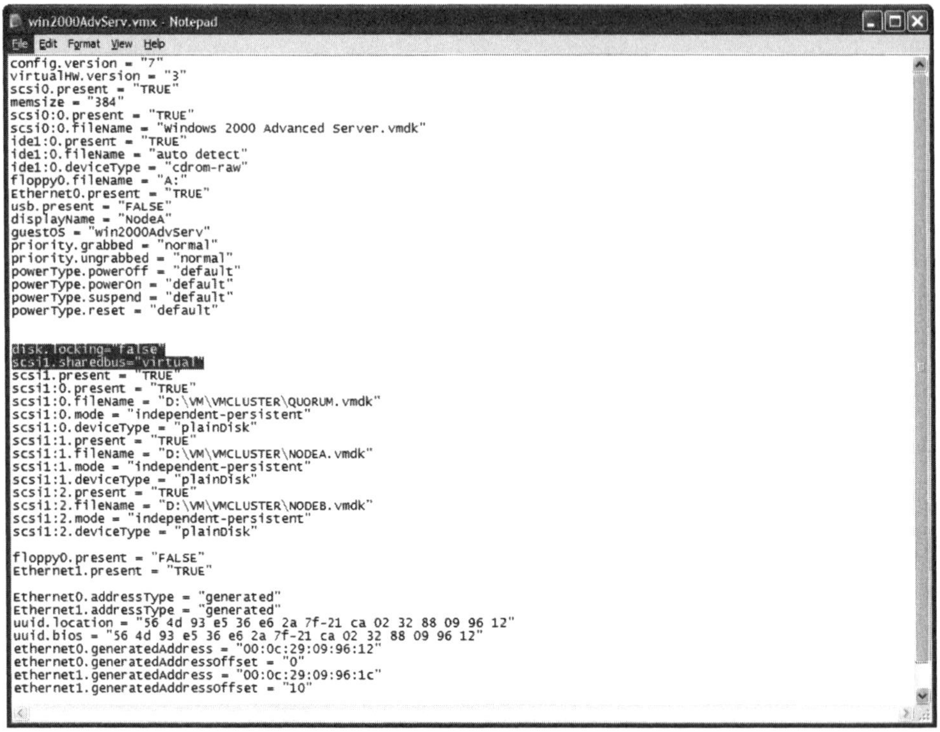

win2000AdvServ.vmx - Notepad

File Edit Format View Help

```
config.version = "7"
virtualHW.version = "3"
scsi0.present = "TRUE"
memsize = "384"
scsi0:0.present = "TRUE"
scsi0:0.fileName = "Windows 2000 Advanced Server.vmdk"
ide1:0.present = "TRUE"
ide1:0.fileName = "auto detect"
ide1:0.deviceType = "cdrom-raw"
floppy0.fileName = "A:"
Ethernet0.present = "TRUE"
usb.present = "FALSE"
displayName = "NodeA"
guestOS = "win2000AdvServ"
priority.grabbed = "normal"
priority.ungrabbed = "normal"
powerType.powerOff = "default"
powerType.powerOn = "default"
powerType.suspend = "default"
powerType.reset = "default"


disk.locking="false"
scsi1.sharedbus="virtual"
scsi1.present = "TRUE"
scsi1:0.present = "TRUE"
scsi1:0.fileName = "D:\VM\VMCLUSTER\QUORUM.vmdk"
scsi1:0.mode = "independent-persistent"
scsi1:0.deviceType = "plainDisk"
scsi1:1.present = "TRUE"
scsi1:1.fileName = "D:\VM\VMCLUSTER\NODEA.vmdk"
scsi1:1.mode = "independent-persistent"
scsi1:1.deviceType = "plainDisk"
scsi1:2.present = "TRUE"
scsi1:2.fileName = "D:\VM\VMCLUSTER\NODEB.vmdk"
scsi1:2.mode = "independent-persistent"
scsi1:2.deviceType = "plainDisk"

floppy0.present = "FALSE"
Ethernet1.present = "TRUE"

Ethernet0.addressType = "generated"
Ethernet1.addressType = "generated"
uuid.location = "56 4d 93 e5 36 e6 2a 7f-21 ca 02 32 88 09 96 12"
uuid.bios = "56 4d 93 e5 36 e6 2a 7f-21 ca 02 32 88 09 96 12"
ethernet0.generatedAddress = "00:0c:29:09:96:12"
ethernet0.generatedAddressOffset = "0"
ethernet1.generatedAddress = "00:0c:29:09:96:1c"
ethernet1.generatedAddressOffset = "10"
```

FIGURE 18.18 The .vmx file.

In this chapter we have gone over how to configure a Microsoft Windows cluster in a VMware GSX Server 3.1 environment. You now have the ability to create clusters in the VMware Workstation and enterprise-level platforms.

About the CD-ROM

The CD-ROM included with The VMware Workstation 5 handbook includes the trial installation/documentation of Workstation 5 on a Windows and Linux platform. It also includes the Leostream software to perform physical to virtual (P>V) and virtual to virtual (V>V) conversions using Workstation 5 as the platform.

SYSTEM REQUIREMENTS

The system requirements for this CD-ROM are:

- Windows or Linux platform
- CD-ROM drive

FOLDERS

The files on this disc are organized into folders as follows:

Demo: Part of the VMware demo package.

Docs: Contains the VMware documentation. See ReadMe.txt in the root directory of the CD-ROM for details.

Figures: Contains all the images in the book, in color, by chapter.

Leostream: Contains Leostream.

Linux: Contains VMware Workstation for Linux hosts. Please note that many of these files are support files and are not necessarily meant to be opened individually.

Windows: Contains VMware Workstation for Windows, which may be launched automatically when the CD-ROM is inserted.

SOFTWARE

The following software products have been included on the CD-ROM:

VMware Workstation 5® Demo

Provided by VMware, Inc.
3145 Porter Drive
Palo Alto, CA 94304
www.vmware.com
Please note that to use VMware Workstation, you will need to visit *www.vmware.com* to obtain the free 30-day evaluation license key. Alternatively you may contact Sales at VMware at the address above, by phone at 1-877-486-9273 (toll-free) or 650-475-5000, or by fax at 650-475-5005, or via email at *sales@vmware.com*.

System Requirements

■ Standard x86-compatible personal computer running Windows or Linux
■ 400 MHz or faster CPU; 500 MHz recommended; and enough memory to run both your host OS and your virtual machines
■ 128 MB RAM minimum; 256 recommended
■ Please see pages 15-16 or *http://www.vmware.com/support/ws5/doc/intro_hostreq_ws.html* for more detailed requirements

Leostream® Demo

Provided by Leostream Corp.
950 Winter Street, Suite 2400
Waltham, MA 02451
www.leostream.com

System Requirements

■ Windows NT 4.0 server and terminal server (Service Pack 6 and 6a); Windows 2000 Professional, Windows 2000 Server, Advanced Server, and Datacenter Server (all Service Packs); Windows XP (all service packs); or Windows 2003 Server.
■ Microsoft Virtual Server 2005, VMware GSX Server for Windows v3.1, VMware Workstation 4.5, or VMware ESX Server v2.5
■ For more information on compatibility, please see the Leostream manual on the CD-ROM (in the Leostream folder).

Index

A

ACPI S1 Sleep, 9
adapters
    determining manufacturer from MAC address, 182
    host virtual, 166
    I/O, 79
    network, assigning to LAN segment, 148–149
    VMware host (fig.), 165
Add Shared Folders wizard, 280–281
adding
    devices, 57
    Ethernet adapters, 186–189, 284–285
    host adapters, 174–175
    performance counters, 202–203
addresses
    MAC, and network adapters, 182–186
    static IP vs. DHCP, 179–180
administrative lockout, configuring, 156–158
Advanced tab, Virtual Machine Settings window, 61–62
AMC PCNET family network interface card, 243
AMD Operton, AMD Athlon 64, 8
analyzing network traffic, 181–182
archiving virtual machines, 270–272
assigning
    bridged network connection, 166–167
    network adapters to LAN segment, 148–149
    MAC addresses manually, 185–186
authentication options, SQL Server, 309
author, contacting, 313
Autofit tab, View menu, 44
automatic bridging, 167–168
automatic snapshot return, 160–162
.AVI files, 8–9

B

BgInfo tool, 257–258
BIOS, booting, 294
book, this
    CD-ROM. *See* CD-ROM
    contacting author of, 313
    contents of, 2
    conventions used in, 14

boot disks
    creating with Leostream, 235
    creating with Norton Ghost, 240–244
    VMware Workstation 5, obtaining, 261
booting new virtual machines from ISO image, 89–90
bridged networks, 57–58, 79, 165–166

C

CD-ROM
    about the, 325–326
    device, editing settings, 63
    drive polling, 199
    installing VMware Workstation on Windows platform,
        16–20
    mounting, 25–26
    vs. ISO images, virtual machine installations, 88
chip sets, Workstation, 13
Cisco-Linksys network adapter, 182
Clone Virtual Machine wizard, 125–126, 132–134
clones
    linked and full, 5
    making, 51
cloning
    P2V Assistant Wizard options, 222–225
    snapshots, 124–126
    VMware Workstation virtual machines, 131–137
Cluster Administrator, 300–301
clusters, Windows 2003 Server
    configuring cluster service, 296–304
    configuring shared disks in VMware Workstation,
        287–295
    configuring virtual environment, network cards,
        284–287
    configuring VMware Workstation to run, 283
command-line
    extracting VMware Workstation image, 23
    interface described, 8
    working with VMware Workstation with, 276–278
commands
    Ctrl-Alt-Del, 50
    VMrun, options (table), 278
community discussion forum, 14

components of virtual machines, 73–76
compression, file, 271
config.ini, lockout password in (fig.), 158
configuring
    administrative lockout, 156–158
    automatic snapshot return, 160–162
    bridged networks, 166–170
    cluster service on Windows 2003 Server, 296–304
    custom virtual networks, 186–189
    host-only networks, 171–175
    NAT (Network Address Translation), 176–177
    port forwarding, 178–180
    shared disks for clustering solution, 287–295
    shortcuts, 18
    snapshot options, 127–129
    virtual machine drives, 294–295
    virtual machine hardware, options, 51–52
    virtual networks, 39
    VMware Tools, 116–117
    VMware Workstation as service, 250
    Windows Host Agent, 227–230
connecting devices to virtual machines, 49
Connections tab, Control Center, 148
Control Center
    administrative lockout, configuring, 156–158
    described, 14
    displaying version of VMware Workstation, 68–69
    Linux (fig.), 85
    tabs, using, 47, 63, 148–151
    with updates ISO image path (fig.), 90
conventions used in this book, 14
converting
    Microsoft Virtual PC or Virtual Server into VMware
        Workstation, 9
    physical to vertical conversion. *See* P2V
    Virtual PCs to VMware Workstation 5, 209–215
copying
    cloning. *See* cloning
    VMware Workstation virtual machines, 132–134
counters, performance, 200–202
creating
    clones, 51
    screen shots or movies of virtual machines, 255–257
    shared disks, 316–320
    shared folders, 280–281
    snapshots, 124–127
    teams, 141–144
    virtual floppy disks, 262–263
    virtual floppy images, 97–99, 258–259
    virtual machine with Windows host computer, 37,
        76–86, 155–158
Ctrl-Alt-Del, sending command to virtual machines, 50

customizing
    NAT (Network Address Translation), 176–177
    Tip of the Day, 278–279
    virtual networks, 186–189

D
debugging
    kernel and user support, 10
    mode, using, 198
defragmenting virtual disks, 194–196
deleting
    See also removing
    snapshots, 124
    teams, 145
    virtual machines from disk, 51
devices
    See also specific device
    adding, removing, 57
    CD-ROM drive polling, 199
    connecting, disconnecting, 49
DHCP servers, 166, 171–172
DHCP tab, Virtual Network Editor, 171–174
disabling shutdown event tracker on Windows 2003
        Server, 254–255
disconnecting devices to virtual machines, 49
DiskMount utility, using, 267–270
disks
    mounting, 267–270
    SCSI, creating, 315–319
    virtual. *See* virtual floppy disks
Display tab, Edit menu, 42
displaying
    information about virtual computers, 257–258
    network traffic between virtual machines, 181–182
    version of VMware Workstation, 68–69
download sites
    BgInfo tool, 257
    DiskMount utility, 267
    GSX Server, 315
    Leostream P>V Wizard, 230
    Microsoft Sysprep utility, 245
    SCSI disk drivers, 93
    Virtual Floppy Driver (VFD), 260
    Windows 2003 Resources Kit tools, 250
    Windows 98 boot disk, 97
    Windows Installer 2.0, 22
    WinImage, 240
    winrar archiving tool, 270
    VMware Workstation knowledge base, online commu-
        nity, 14
dragging and dropping, VMware Workstation 4.x support,
    9

drivers, downloading SCSI device, 93–95
drives, partitioning, 272–274

E

Edit menu, menu bar, 38–43
editing
    CD-ROM device settings, 63
    DHCP settings, 171–174
    virtual machine settings, 89–90
    .vmx files, 159–160, 290–294, 315, 323–324
enabling network bridging, 167–170
encrypting information for P2V conversion, 228
ESX Server, 3
Ethernet adapters
    adding for Windows 2003 cluster, 284
    virtual networks, 186–189
Ethernet cards
    and bridged networks, 57–58
    virtual machine support, 13
exiting VMware Workstation, 38

F

Favorites window
    described, using, 46
    removing virtual machines from, 38
file compression, 271
File menu, menu bar, 37–38
files, file extensions, VMware (table), 74–76
floppy drives, 13
Floppy Image utility, 97
folders, shared, 10, 59, 280–281
forgotten passwords, 158
formatting virtual hard drives, 102
full clones, 5, 132–134
full screen mode, switching virtual machines to, 43–44

G

graphical user interface. *See* GUI
GSX Server
    creating high-availability solution with, 315–324
    described, 3
GSX Server Add Hardware Wizard, 316–319
guest operating systems
    book conventions and, 14
    fitting into windows, 45
    installing Linux, 107–112
    installing VMware Tools in, 113–120
    installing Windows and Linux generally, 87–88
    isolation options, 61
    selecting for optimum performance, 197
    shutting down, 49
    supported by VMware Workstation, 1

and virtual machines, 1
    VMware Workstation 5, new support, 7–8
GUI (graphical user interface), security option, 158–162

H

hardware
    P2V Assistant requirements, 218
    upgrading virtual, prior to VMware Workstation
        upgrade, 66–67
    virtual machine, overview, 13
Hardware tab, Virtual Machine Settings window, 57–58
heartbeats, configuring, 285–286
Help
    menu, menu bar, 53–56
    Tip of the Day, modifying, 278
high-availability solutions
    with GSX Server, 315–324
    with VMware Workstation, 283–313
Home tab, View menu, 45
host-only network, 164, 171–175
host virtual adapters, 166
Host Virtual Adapters tab, Virtual Network Editor,
    174–175
Host Virtual Network Mapping tab, Virtual Network
    Editor, 169–170
Hot Keys
    preferences (table), 41
    tab, Edit menu, 40–41

I

I/O Adapter, selecting types, 79
IDE drives, 13
images
    creating virtual floppy, 97–99, 258–259
    ISO. *See* ISO images
    P2V via, 247
Input tab, Edit menu, 39–40
installation system requirements, VMware Workstation,
    11–12
installer
    Tar, using, 70–71, 117–120
    VMware Workstation 5, 66–67
installing
    installation requirements, 15–16
    Leostream Host Agent Wizard, 226–227
    Leostream P>V Wizard, 230–231
    Linux guest operating systems, 107–112
    Longhorn (Windows operating system), 103–107
    Red Hat Linux 9.0, Mandrake Linux 10.0, 110
    SCSI drivers, 95–96
    SQL Server 2005, 304–313
    upgrading VMware Workstation 4.x to 5, 66–67

virtual machines, CD-ROM vs. ISO image, 88
VMware on multiple platforms, 2
VMware P2V Assistant 2.0, 218–219
VMware Tools, 50
VMware Tools for Windows guest systems, 113–115
VMware Tools in Linux, 117–120
VMware Virtual Machine Importer, 207–208
VMware Workstation as service, 249–254
VMware Workstation on Linux platform, 25–31
VMware Workstation on Windows platform, 16–20
VMware Workstation, unattended, 22–25
Windows 98/ME, 97–102
Windows XP Profession/Windows 2003 Server with
    SCSI drive, 93–94
Windows XP Professional/Windows 2003 Server,
    91–97
Intel EM64T, 8
Intel processor support, 16
ISO images
    booting new virtual machines from, 89–90
    creating with WinISO, 275–276
    downloading for P2V conversion, 219–220
    installing virtual machines via, 88
isochronous USB support, 6

K
kernel debugging, 10
kernel, Linux, support for guests, 10
keyboard
    Hot Key preferences (table), 41
    shortcuts (table), 282
    virtual machine hardware overview, 13

L
LAN Segments tab, Control Center, 150–151
legacy virtual machines, taking snapshots prior to upgrad-
    ing, 65
Leostream utility, 218, 226–239
licensing agreement
    Leostream P>V Wizard, 231–234
    SQL Server, 305
    VMware Workstation, 17, 21–22
linked clones, 5, 134–137
Linux
    configuring VMware Workstation on, 31–33
    Control Center (fig.), 85
    GUI, virtual machine settings editor, 10
    hosts. See Linux hosts
    installing guest operating systems, 107–112
    installing VMware Tools in, 117–120
    installing VMware Workstation on platform, 25–31
    uninstalling VMware Workstation from, 31–33
    VMware Workstation 5 user interface, 5–6

Linux hosts
    creating virtual machines with, 83–86
    upgrading VMware Workstation 4.x to 5, 70–71
locking out, administrative lockout, 155–158
Lockout tab, Edit menu, 43
log files, 75
logging, Leostream Host Agent options, 229
login, superuser, 26
Longhorn (Windows operating system), 10, 103–107
lost passwords, 158
LSI Logic Adapter, 284

M
MAC addresses and network adapters, 182–186
Mandrake Linux 10.x, 8, 110
memory
    guest operating system requirements, 16
    optimization, 192–194
    virtual machine size, requirements, 10, 13
    VMware P2V Assistant requirements, 218
    VMware Workstation 5's improved utilization of, 7
Memory tab, Edit menu, 42
menu bar
    Edit menu, 38–43
    File menu, 37–38
    Team menu, 52–53
    View menu, 43–47
    VM menu, 48–52
    Windows and Help menus, 53–54
    working with, 36
Microsoft Clustering Services, 323
Microsoft Sysprep utility, 245
Microsoft Virtual PC, Virtual Server, converting to
    VMware Workstation 5, 9
Microsoft Windows, Longhorn support, 10
monitoring
    virtual machines, 200–202
    VMware Workstation performance settings, 202–204
mounting virtual drives, operating systems, 267–270
movie record and playback, 8–9
movies, taking of virtual machines, 255–257
MSDTC resource, creating, 304
Msiexec syntax, 24–25
multiple virtual machines, VMware Workstation 5
    performance, 5

N
names, VMware file (table), 74–76
NAT (Network Address Translation)
    configuring, 176–180
    described, 171–172
    NIC hardware settings, 57–58
network adapters

assigning to LAN segment, 148–149
modifying available, 168–169
Network Address Translation (NAT), 171–172, 176–180
network monitors, 181–182
networking
host-only, configuring, 171–175
virtual machines. *See* networking virtual machines
VMware Workstation 5, enhanced performance, 5
networking virtual machines
configuring bridged networks, 166–170
configuring custom virtual networks, 186–189
configuring NAT, 176–180
generally, 163–166
MAC address assignment, 182–186
support for, 13–14
troubleshooting network traffic, 181–182
networks
bridged, 57–58, 79, 165–170
private, configuring for cluster, 285–286
New Server Cluster Wizard, 296–301
New Team Wizard, 37
New Virtual Machine Wizard, 37, 83–86, 103, 171, 273–274
NICs, managing through Virtual Machine Settings, 57–58
Norton Ghost
described, 218
using for P2V conversion of Windows platform, 239–247
Norton Ghost Boot Wizard, 242–244
Notepad, editing .vmx files, 159–160, 290–294
NTFS security, 155
NX bit support, 9

O

operating systems
See also Linux, Windows
choosing for virtual machine, 83–85
guests. *See* guest operating systems
VMware Workstation wizard configuration, 76–82
optimizing
guest operating systems, 197
memory, 192–194
performance tuning. *See* performance tuning
VMware Workstation settings, 191–200
Options tab, Control Center, 150–151
Options tab, Virtual Machine Settings window, 57–62

P

P2V Assistant 2.0 Boot CD Wizard, 219–220
P2V Assistant Wizard, 222–225
P2V (physical to virtual conversion) methods, tools, 217–218
packet sniffers, using, 181–182
passwords

administrative lockout, 156–157
NTFS permissions, 162
Pentium processors, 16
Performance Monitor, VMware Workstation, 200
performance tuning
See also optimizing
monitoring virtual machines, 200–202
virtual machines, 191
VMware Workstation performance settings, 202–204
permissions, NTFS, 162
physical to vertical conversion. *See* P2V
pipes (|), use of in this book, 14
playback, movie record and, 8–9
port forwarding, 178–180
ports, virtual machine hardware overview, 13
power
managing virtual machine teams, 52
options, configuring, 59, 160–162
resetting virtual machines, 49
turning on and off virtual machines, 48
turning on and off teams, 145–146
Preboot Execution Environment (PXE), 11
Priority tab, Edit menu, 42
private subnets, 32
processors
virtual machine requirements, 13
VMware Workstation requirements, 11
product updates, automatically checking for, 11

Q

Quick Switch window, 44–45

R

RAM (random access memory), optimizing, 192–194
Raw Disk partitions, using, 272–274
recording virtual machine activities, 8–9
Red Hat Enterprise Linux 4.0, 8
Red Hat Linux 9.0, installing, 110
removing
See also deleting
devices, 57–58
passwords, lost or forgotten, 158
unnecessary virtual hardware, 198–199
virtual machines from Favorites window, 38
VMware Workstation. *See* uninstalling
Report Server Database Setup, 310–311
resources
author contact, 313
VMware online documentation for upgrading, 71
VMware Workstation, 14
Windows 2003 Server cluster information, 301
restore points, using snapshots as, 122–123
restricting virtual machines' user interfaces, 159–162

Revert to Snapshot, VM menu, 50
routing, configuring between virtual machines, 163
RPM installer
    installing VMware Tools using, 120
    upgrading VMware Workstation 4.x to 5, 71
RPM version, installing VMware Workstation on Linux, 24–25, 30–31

S
SAMBA access for virtual machines, 32
screen shots
    capturing virtual machine's, 51
    taking of virtual machine, 255–256
SCSI devices, 13, 93
SCSI disks, creating, 315–319
security
    configuring NTFS, 155
    graphical user interface, 158–162
servers
    attaching shared disks to, 320–323
    DHCP, 166, 171–172
service, installing VMware Workstation as, 249–254
shared disks, creating, 316–320
shared folders, 10, 59, 280–281
shortcuts
    configuring, 18
    Hot Key preferences (table), 41
    keyboard (table), 282
    .vmx to run restricted virtual machines (fig.), 160
shrinking virtual disks, 194–196
shutdown event tracker, disabling on Windows 2003 Server, 254–255
Snapshot Manager
    described, 4, 50
    using snapshots in tree structure, 123
Snapshot menu, VM menu, 49–50
snapshots
    creating, 124–127
    managing VMware Workstation with, 121–129
    options, configuring, 59–60, 127–129, 159–160
    performance issues, 199
    restricting user control, 159–160
    settings, 127–129
    taking legacy, prior to upgrading, 65
    taking of virtual machine, 50
    taking with VMware Workstation 5, 4
    within teams, 148
    in VMware Workstation 4.x, 9–10
    VMware Workstation 5, improvements, 5–6
software, VMware Workstation installation system requirements, 11–12
sound
    device in VMware Workstation 5, 10

virtual machine support, 13
SQL Server 2005, installing, 304–313
SQL Server Installation Wizard, 305–311
SSL, enabling, 228
starting
    RedHat/Mandrake Linux virtual machines, 111
    SuSE Linux 9.1 virtual machines, 108
    VMware Workstation as service, 253
    Vnetsniffer, 181–182
    Windows 98 virtual machines, 100–102
    Windows XP Professional virtual machines, 91–92
static IP addresses vs. DHCP addresses, 179–180
Status bar
    described, using, 63–64
    removing, adding, 46
subnets, private, 32
Sun Java Desktop System 2, installing, 107–108
SuSE Linux 9.1, installing, 108
SuSE Linux Enterprise Server 9.0, 8
suspending
    power to virtual machines, 49–50
    teams, 146–148
SVGA driver, VMware, 225
switches
    virtual, described, 165
    VMnet, configuring, 186–187
    VMware Workstation command-line (table), 277
switching between virtual machines, 40, 53
Sysprep utility, 245
system requirements
    VMware Virtual Machine Importer, 206–207
    VMware Workstation installation, 11–12

T
tabs
    See also specific tab
    adding, removing from Control Center, 47
    workstation, Control Center, 63
Tar archive
    installation, 28–30
    installing VMware Tools via, 117–120
    uninstallation, 33–34
TCP/IP driver settings, Norton Ghost, 245
Team Console, 151–153
Team menu, menu bar, 52–53
teams
    Control Center (fig.), 153
    creating, 7, 141–144
    described, using, 7, 139–148
    tasks managed by Team menu, 52–53
    Team Console, using, 151–153
    working with settings, 148–151
templates, defining virtual machines using, 134

Terminal Service and Virtual Machine Importer
  installation, 207
testing
  connectivity between nodes in cluster, 286–287
  environments using virtual machines, 217
  high-availability solution, 283
  Windows 2003 Server cluster, 302–303
text, cutting, copying, pasting, 38–39
Tip of the Day, 11, 55, 278
toolbars
  Toolbars tab, View menu, 46
  VMware Workstation, 56
traffic, monitoring and troubleshooting network, 181–182
tree structures, using snapshots in, 123
troubleshooting
  network traffic, 181–182
  P2V Assistant installation, 219–220
tutorial, this book's, 2

U
unattended VMware Workstation installation, 22–25
Under Construction Web page, 179–180
undoing changes, Revert to Snapshot, 50
uninstalling
  current version prior to VMware Workstation upgrade,
    71
  VMware Virtual Machine Importer, 208
  VMware Workstation from Linux, 31–33
  VMware Workstation from Windows platform, 21–22
updates
  checking for automatically, 11
  checking for using menu, 56
  Software Updates tab, Edit menu, 39
upgrading
  virtual hardware, 50
  VMware Workstation 4.x to 5 on Linux host, 70–71
  VMware Workstation 4.x to 5 on Windows host, 65–70
USB input devices, 6, 11
user accounts, superuser, 26
User's Manual, viewing Help, 54–55
UUIDs, and virtual machines, 183–185, 253

V
version of VMware Workstation, displaying, 68–69
vertical bars (|), use in this book, 14
VFD (Virtual Floppy Driver), using, 260–263
View menu, menu bar, 43–47
virtual DHCP servers, 166
Virtual Disk Manager described, options, 264–267
virtual floppy disks, creating, 262–263, 288–290
Virtual Floppy Driver (VFD), using, 260–263
virtual floppy images, creating with WinImage, 240, 244,
  258–259

virtual hardware, provided on virtual machine created by
  VMware, 13
virtual MAC addresses, 182–186
Virtual Machine Settings window, using, 57–62
virtual machines
  anatomy of, 73–76
  archiving, 270–272
  capturing screenshot, 51
  configuring conversion to VMware Workstation 5,
    211–214
  creating screen shots, movies of, 255–257
  creating with Linux hosts, 83–86
  creating with Windows host computer, 76–82
  hardware overview, 13
  memory optimization, 192–196
  monitoring, 200–202
  networking. See networking virtual machines
  new, editing settings, 89–90
  opening, closing, 38
  physical to vertical conversion. See P2V
  recording and playback, 8–9
  restricting user interfaces of, 159–162
  running from network, 199
  snapshot options, configuring, 159–162
  starting, 91–92, 100–102
  switching between, 40
  teams. See teams
  toggling between views, 44–45
  upgrading to VMware Workstation 5, 66–70
  and UUIDs, 183–185
Virtual Machines tab, Control Center, 149
virtual network adapters, 166
Virtual Network Editor, 10, 167–170
virtual networks, configuring, 39, 186–189
Virtual PCs (VPCs), converting to VMware Workstation
  virtual machines, 205–215
virtual switches, 165
VM menu, menu bar, 48–52
.vmdk files, 320
VMrun
  command-line (fig.), 8
  commands, options, 278
VMware, history of, 3
VMware file extensions and names (table), 74–76
VMware GSX Server, VMware ESX Server, 3
VMware Hints, 254
VMware knowledge base, 14
VMware network adapters, 174–175
VMware on the Web tab, Help menu, 55–56
VMware P2V Assistant 2.0, described, using, 218–225
VMware Tools
  configuring, 116–117
  enhanced networking performance, 5

improvements to, 9
installing, 50, 105–107
shrinking virtual disks, 196
VMware Virtual Machine Importer, 205–208
VMware Workstation
    See also VMware Workstation 5
    command-line operation, 276–278
    Control Center described, using, 35–36
    exiting program, 38
    installation requirements, 15–16
    installing on Windows platform, 16–20
    introduction to, 1–3
    licensing agreement, 17
    managing, working with snapshots, 121–129
    menu bar. *See* menu bar
    networking, 164–166
    new to version 4.x, 9–11
    new to version 5, 3–9
    performance tuning and optimization, 191–204
    Raw Disk partitions, 272–274
    resources, 14
    securing, 155–162
    supported guest operating systems, 12
    teams. *See* teams
    tips and tricks, 249–282
    toolbar, working with, 56
    uninstalling on Windows platform, 21–22
    upgrading. *See* upgrading
    Virtual Machine Settings window, using, 57–62
    virtual machines. *See* virtual machines
    wizard, using, 76–82
VMware Workstation 4.52, 11
VMware Workstation 5
    converting Virtual PCs to, 209–215
    isochronous USB support, 6
.vmx files, 158, 185, 290–294, 315, 323–324
Vnetsniffer, using, 181–182

W
Web sites
    See also download sites
    VMware Workstation resources, 14

Windows 2003 Resources Kit tools, 250
Windows 2003 Server cluster
    configuring VMware Workstation to run, 283
    configuring cluster service on, 296–303
Windows 98/ME, installing, 97–102
Windows Host Agent, configuring, 227–230
Windows hosts
    creating virtual machines with, 76–82
    upgrading VMware Workstation 4.x to 5 on, 65–70
Windows Installer 2.0, 22
Windows menu, menu bar, 53
Windows platforms
    installing VMware Workstation on, 16–20
    using Leostream for P2V conversion, 226–239
    using Norton Ghost for P2V conversion, 239–247
Windows upgrade installs, 9
Windows XP
    removing effects, 200
    64-bit host support, 8
Windows XP Profession/Windows 2003 Server, installing, 91–97
WinImage, 240, 258–259
WinISO, creating ISO images with, 275–276
winrar archiving tool, 270
wizards
    Add Shared Folders, 280–281
    Clone Virtual Machine, 125–126, 132–134
    GSX Server Add Hardware, 316
    Leostream Host Agent, 226–227
    New Server Cluster, 296–301
    New Team, 37
    New Virtual Machine, 37, 83–86, 103, 171, 273–274
    Norton Ghost Boot, 242–244
    P2V Assistant, 222–225
    P2V Assistant 2.0 Boot CD, 219–220
    SQL Server Installation, 305–311
    VMware P2V Assistant Installation, 218–219
working directory, 192
Workspace tab, Edit menu, 39–40